Plants for Mediterranean Climate Gardens

Phormium x 'Sunset' is one of an increasing range of colourful New Zealand flaxes well equipped to strut their stuff in a Mediterranean garden. Watchword: be sure to 'rogue' (dig out) any growths that revert to plain colours. *Gladiolus tristis* flowers in the background, with *Artemisia* x 'Powis Castle' in the foreground.

Plants for Mediterranean Climate Gardens

Trevor Nottle

ROSENBERG

The ruined Castello di Ninfa with its crenellated tower lies on the Ninfa River, which runs into the sea on the western coast of central Italy and is today threatened by heavy water extraction in the hills behind. The spring in this wonderful place, where the Dukes of Sermoneta long ago made an astonishing garden for their enjoyment, has since pre-Roman times been considered the home of water nymphs.

First published in Australia in 2004
by Rosenberg Publishing Pty Ltd
PO Box 6125, Dural Delivery Centre NSW 2158
Phone: 02 9654 1502 Fax: 02 9654 1338
Email: rosenbergpub@smartchat.net.au
Web: www.rosenbergpub.com.au

National Library of Australia Cataloguing-in-Publication data:
Nottle, Trevor.
Plants for Mediterranean climate gardens.

Bibliography.
Includes index.
ISBN 1 877058 14 9.

1. Mediterranean-type plants. 2. Mediterranean climate. 3.
Gardens - Design. I. Title.

581.751

Cover design by Highway 51 Design Works using author's photograph: 'Wigandia' garden is made on an ancient cone of pure pumice stone called Mt Noorat in western Victoria. Despite, or because of perfect drainage, the garden is a wonderful expression of creativity on the part of William Martin – a landscape artist if ever there was one.

Set in 10 on 12 point Times New Roman
Printed in China by Everbest Printing Co Limited

10 9 8 7 6 5 4 3 2 1

Contents

Dedication

For my daughter Alex and my grandson Trewin

Acknowledgments

This book is one of a series about good plants for gardens in Mediterranean climates. My first thanks must go to David Rosenberg who reacted keenly to my proposal of the idea of a number of books written by different authors about the same general theme – Mediterranean gardening. The idea is not yet fully explored, with developments emerging from authors in New Zealand, California, Greece and France.

In Australia the idea has been enthusiastically supported by contributors such as Rodger and Gwen Elliott, Diana Morgan, Robyn and John Brader, David Glenn and Criss Canning, Peter Ormond, Don Barrett and Harvey Collins, Sophie Thompson and Richard Elston, and others. Behind the scenes other kind, interested supporters have offered garden ideas and bookish support – William Martin, Clive Blazey, Marie Leary, Bill Macoboy, Colin Olson, Judy Horton, Rudolf Schulz, Attila Capitany, Graham Cooke, Nynke van der Schaaf, Helen and Gary Woolford, Sandra Hutton, Penelope Curtin, Rob Cowell, Jeff Bowden, Michael and Pru Keelan, Jon Lamb, Chris and Nigel Steele-Scott, Danni Kaines and Andy Zdanowicz, Marie and Paul Collett, Michael and Sue Treloar, John at Back Pages, Jim Hincks, Mike Park, Phil Nesty, Pat and Steve Ronane, and Roy Motteram.

Support from overseas friends is gratefully acknowledged: Helene Pizzi, Joan Tesei, Charles Quest-Ritson, Martyn Rix and Lauro Marchetti in Italy; Derek and Megan Toms, Caroline Harbouri and Sally Razelou in Athens; Heidi and Enrique Gildemeister in Spain; Helene and Patrice Fustier, Odile and Georges Masquellier in France; Belinda and Nick Legge, and Jennifer Hewitt in the UK. In the New World I have to thank Mercedes and German Drever de Villar, Rosemarie Symonds de Chilibroste, Janet Gruy-Winter, Rosario Algorta de Carrau and Cornelis and Frederike Vreedenberg in Uruguay; Christina Raffo and the generous members of the Garden Club Argentino in Argentina; Dick Turner, Katherine Greenberg, Sean O'Hara and Bill Grant in California.

Peter Moorhouse and Alexander Cullen kept my garden in good order while I tapped away indoors on good gardening weekends so my thanks are due to them.

Margaret, my wife, tolerated the ups and downs of a partner preoccupied with writing and organising a new book – lost references, forgotten details, blockages, stoppages, moments of elation and hours of silent concentration, messy piles of books and journals, phone calls at all hours and all the other necessary disruptions to family life.

Prostrate rosemary spreads between variegated New Zealand flaxes and a juvenile *Furcraea gigantea*, which will eventually dominate the scene with a massive crown of glaucous, sword-shaped leaves.

Introduction

The intention of this book, and the series that follows, is to introduce to readers a wider range of plants suited to gardening in Mediterranean climate areas of the world than is commonly used. Since the 1970s appreciation of the challenges and pleasures of gardening in Mediterranean climates has grown rapidly, sufficiently so for a thriving society to operate on an international scale and to support a number of books that explore the plants, style, history and personalities of the genre. Yet there remains ample room to write more, especially concerning the enormous variety of plants as yet scarcely known that can adorn our gardens.

It is significant then to introduce and give recognition to a body of works that pushes the traditional boundaries by introducing the Mediterranean climate as one that can equal the opportunities for creative design and plantsmanship familiar to us from the gardening pantheons of Europe, Japan and China, and the temperate climate regions of the USA. Acknowledging that equivalence is important in developing a confident approach to new directions in design and planting; a confidence that is needed for more gardeners in Mediterranean climates to move in exciting new directions.

It is now widely accepted that the Mediterranean climate regions are those found around the shores of the Mediterranean Sea itself, much of coastal, central and southern California, the Cape region of South Africa, the south-west corner of Western Australia, coastal and southern South Australia and the east coast of the North Island of New Zealand. Many other parts of the world also offer climates that fall within the broadest boundaries of the concept – cool, wet winters and long, hot, dry summers.

To better understand the climatography of these regions there must be some appreciation of just what is meant by the Mediterranean climatic homotype. A colloquial translation from *Flore des Arbres, Arbustes et Arbrisseaux: Région Méditerranéenne* by R. Rol and M. Jacamon (La Maison Rustique, Paris, 1968) provides a very useful insight:

The Mediterranean region is above all defined by its climate: heavy rain in autumn and winter, summer rain rare, irregular and violent and poorly absorbed by the vegetation. Summers hot and dry, winters mild and frosts rare along the coast. Bright light is important. Although less marked in other regions of the Mediterranean these characteristics are well defined in France. The physical characteristics although secondary are also important. High altitudes exist near the coast and because of this there are two different sorts of vegetation in the strictest definition of the Mediterranean area, and a third type of vegetation due to the Mediterranean influence:

1. The semi-arid Mediterranean *inferieur* zone, such as is found along the coast of North Africa and the Middle East.
2. The sub-humid Mediterranean *superieur* zone, with slightly cooler summers, and wetter winters.
3. The humid zone, less hot and with more rain, but the Mediterranean influence still very strongly felt and reflected in the patterns of weather and plant growth.

The strictly defined limits for the Mediterranean used to be the culture of olives (*Olea europaea*) but we prefer the association with the evergreen oak (*Quercus ilex*).

For those resident in areas outside the Mediterranean basin there must be a certain degree of interpretation of the situation as described in France, so that the three climatic subtypes within the concept are included in our understanding of the places where we live. With this understanding it is possible to include significant parts of Uruguay, Northern Argentina and coastal Chile, and microclimates in many places including the Scilly Isles and the coasts of Devon and Cornwall.

That done, the task of garden making in Mediterranean climate zones becomes one of happy exploration and discovery among the floras of those countries and climates. To make that adventure more pleasurable and leisurely is the purpose of this book.

Observant readers will notice that some entries have no accompanying illustration but are, instead, published with illustrations of companion plants described in the sub-text. The reasons are simple enough; in cases where the plant in the main entry is very well known a less well-known companion plant may be illustrated so as to make the text as wide-ranging as possible. In other cases I have taken advantage of an old editorial saw that the captions can tell another story alongside the main text – a chance for authors to make maximum use of the space allowed by the publisher. I have taken that opportunity and trust that my *readers* will forgive my wish to convey as much information as possible.

I find the subject matter is so compelling that I cannot help but let my imagination and ideas range as far as possible to illustrate the rapidly expanding horizons for creativity in Mediterranean gardens.

Trevor Nottle

1 Shade makers

This selection of ten trees, but a small sample of the trees that will thrive in the warm, dry climates of the Mediterranean regions of the world, is by no means exclusive. It represents a personal selection based on experience gained in the arboreta, private estates and botanic gardens around Adelaide in South Australia, and on observations made further afield in south-eastern Australia, California and southern Europe. There are no large trees such as pines, eucalypts, *Ficus* or planes; nor are there any large palms such as the Canary Island palm, the date palm, blue palms or washingtonias – all familiar in 'dry' gardens and landscapes. Old favourites such as the strawberry tree are not included. There are no large flowering trees such as jacaranda or *Brachychiton*. All these are well suited to inclusion in Mediterranean gardens, however, some make more visual impact than shade. And there are no trees of questionable garden value such as the Itchy Cow Tree or Norfolk Island Hibiscus (*Lagunaria patersonii*), nor trees with weed potential away from their natural habitats and controls, such as acacias and mimosas.

What follows is a selection made in part on suitability for smaller gardens, and in part on extending the list of possibilities with a few trees that might not otherwise attract attention.

Elaeagnus angustifolia
Russian Olive

In more ancient terminology sometimes referred to as Oleaster, this is a small tree with a good canopy if trained with thought from the outset by maintaining a whipstick until the desired branching height is reached. Juvenile growth carries hard, long and sharp thorns, presumably developed for protection from grazing animals, but the tree eventually ceases to produce these as it ages. Very useful planted in a small group, under which a pleasant shady bower can be created.

Elaeagnus angustifolia has silvery deciduous foliage along much the same lines as a willow, perhaps somewhat broader. Once the new leaves have made their appearance in mid-spring there follows a flowering of many small pale greenish yellow blooms borne in small clusters. Each flower is a short tubular affair with the open end appearing starry. While the flowers are almost inconspicuous they carry a very fine perfume which scents the air under and around the trees, especially noticeable in confined spaces such as courtyards or where high walls reflect warmth from the sun. This feature alone is what sets Russian Olive apart from other silver-leaved trees that might appeal, particularly the Silver-leaved Weeping Pear, *Pyrus salicifolia* 'Pendula', or a sterile form of the common olive. An attractive companion tree, also with silver leaves, is the deciduous *Crataegus tanacetifolia*, the Tansy-leaved Hawthorn from Turkey, which has the added advantages of producing a froth of white flowers in spring, and a heavy crop of handsome orange haws in autumn.

Overall, a mature Russian Olive will stand above 10 m (35 ft) tall and slightly less across, and be broadly pyramidal in shape, though this can change according to growing conditions. A native of southern Europe and western Asia, its widespread distribution means it is adaptable to a wide range of conditions, as long as winters are not severe. A smaller, shrubby version is to be had in *Elaeagnus argenteus* from the south-central United States. Using the two together can form the backbone of a silver garden.

Although these plants have been in cultivation since the mid-nineteenth century they have infrequently been effectively put together with other silver-leaved plants to compose a complete garden design. The possible combinations become quite exciting when the South African Silver Tree, *Leucodendron argenteum*, and a number of silver-leaved Australian gum trees are brought into play, for example, *Eucalyptus gunnii*, the Cider Gum, or *E. perriniana*, the Spinning Gum or Silver Dollar Gum. Both these would require pollarding every four or five years to keep their interesting silver juvenile foliage, which is almost circular, and prevent development to the mature foliage stage. This would shorten the lives of the trees and alter their shape, but maybe it's worth thinking of using plants in this old-fashioned way? Treated this way they can still attain 4–5 m (14–17 ft) of growth, forming a dense backing group for smaller silver-leaved plants such as *Agave americana* or *A. attenuata*, along with variously named silver groundcovering gazanias, many of which seem to be derivatives of *Gazania rigens* subsp. *leucoleana*. Just be certain to get a good solid silver.

Russian Olive is a hardy and adaptable tree that tolerates a variety of , as long as they are well drained and not saline. Young trees need some training to achieve a single trunk clear of growth to a height that will allow easy passage for adults. This is easy to do. Simply train one main growth up a tall pole, removing all side-growths, which have a tendency to be rather pendulous, until the desired height is reached. This will look very gawky for the first few years but is worth the effort of tying up and rubbing off unwanted growths. Soon the young tree will look quite respectable and grow into a graceful shape.

Vitex agnus-castus
Chaste Tree

The seeds of this true native of the Mediterranean were utilised by the ancients as a homoeopathic

Growing gum trees for their foliage may seem odd to some Australian gardeners but it cannot be denied that the Cider Gum, *Eucalyptus gunnii*, and the Silver Dollar Gum (or Spinning Gum), *Eucalyptus perriniana*, are two winners.

treatment for venereal disease. That is not the reason it is grown today. *Vitex agnus-castus* is a delightful small tree with palmate foliage – usually 5–7 leaflets, silvery underneath – and bearing small spikes of lilac-blue flowers. There are also white and pinkish forms in cultivation that are worth consideration though neither, any more than the species, could be said to be colour blockbusters. But who needs eyestrain from the glare when the tree flowers in summer?

This tree is fairly long-lived in comparison with some other blue-flowered trees and shrubs that might otherwise be given first preference, particularly some

The Chaste Tree, *Vitex agnus-castus*, is such a useful small tree that it should be planted far more frequently than it is. Especially attractive for small gardens and confined courtyards where it can be featured as a single trunked specimen or a multi-trunked mini-forest depending on how it is pruned from the outset. Easy, unfussy, hardy with delightful flowers and scented foliage. Courtesy Clive Blazey.

of the larger *Ceanothus* cultivars such as 'Blue Pacific' that have a life span of roughly 20 years. The Chaste Tree is not widely planted, despite being known for so long a time, but recently it has enjoyed a strong surge of interest in Australia and California, being viewed as a 'new' introduction to the nursery trade. Perhaps a case of 'everything old is new again' – at least in the New World. It is botanically related to *Caryopteris*, an east Asian group with which it associates well in gardens, particularly *C.* x *clandonensis*, which exists in several named forms.

Although rather shrub-like if allowed to grow untrained, the Chaste Tree can easily be encouraged to attain more tree-like dignity by limbing up, that is, cutting off the lower branches to reveal the tree structure within the growth. It naturally forms a strong framework that needs neither support nor repeated pruning to retain a good shape. Too frequently this

tree is planted as a single specimen where it could be shown to greater advantage by being treated in a more lavish manner. In situations where it is desirable to create an allée, or hedge on stilts, a grove or bower, the Chaste Tree can be an excellent choice. Imagine the possibilities of just four trees planted at the corners of a 5 m (17 ft) square. Whether specimens of all one colour are chosen, or combinations of blue and white or pink and white, the potentials for creative companion planting are there. As the pink and blue forms are not especially pure in tone, planting them together may give a rather too indefinite overall effect. Bearing that in mind, it should still be possible to devise numerous combinations of lavenders, cistus, rosemaries, geraniums, artemisias, erodiums, saturejas, oreganos and other hardy plants to build some refined colour schemes.

A selection of terracotta pots could be added,

Hardy companion plants for low water use areas are attractively combined with small trees. Blue and pink forms of rosemary help create a tough understorey that can be planted to approximate the garrigue of Provence.

Creating the Mediterranean image is half the fun of gardening in warm, dry climates. A few well-chosen pieces of terracotta, placed with an eye to picture making and planted simply or not at all, will do the trick every time.

particularly where the area under the trees is paved with fine gravel or sand in the southern European manner. With the wide range of terracotta now available from all points of the globe it should not be too difficult to find pieces in the soft rose-pink range rather than the more strident orange-red shades. Recently some excellent 'European' forms have been supplied from Chinese potteries working in collaboration with designers from California, Australia and Europe. The brick-pink shades of these copies readily associate with the muted shades of *Vitex* and many other Mediterranean plants.

The mature trees may reach over 10 m (35 ft) in height, with approximately the same spread, after 20 years or so, but can easily be kept smaller by sensitive pruning and shaping. Tolerant of a wide range of soils and conditions, except for strong onshore salt-laden winds, the Chaste Tree in all its forms should be much more widely deployed as a contributor to foundation planting than at present. As a bonus, the leaves are sweetly scented when crushed.

Historically minded readers wishing to discover more details of this tree's usefulness and cultural attachments should consult John Gerard's *The Herball, or Generall Historie of Plantes* (1597) which is still available in fairly recent editions, and still good fun to read. Those who seek detailed information concerning ancient Greek and Roman religious and cultural links to particular plants will find a vast literature to fill idle hours, ranging from books like *The Garden Lore of Ancient Athens* and *Ancient Roman Gardens* to hefty tomes such as *The Gardens of Pompeii* (see Recommended Reading, p. 136).

Rothmannia globosa

A South African native, *Rothmannia globosa* (syn. *Gardenia rothmannia*) is relatively uncommon in Europe except as a large greenhouse shrub in the grand conservatories, but is now being introduced as a garden plant. In situations where plants are 'new', you as consumers have two choices about deciding whether or not to try one: check it out, if possible, in a botanic garden (or on the Web), or place your trust in the advice of the nursery selling it. Where do you stand with the nurseries you deal with? Are you a discerning consumer? Do you expect good service and trustworthy advice? And what do you do if you don't get it? Gardeners are a notoriously soft touch for hard-pressed sales assistants. A good relationship with suppliers is important to successful gardening and landscaping, so it is time to develop reasonable expectations of those businesses that supply you. You can be demanding and particular without being aggressive, mean-minded, superior or abusive.

So what about *Rothmannia globosa*? It is one of those shrub-like trees, or tree-like shrubs, depending more than anything on how well it grows in any particular location and how it is managed. In general terms it can reach around 7 m (25 ft) or so in favourable conditions, much less in the grand conservatories – but there have to be some compensations for not living in the Old World. Pretty much the same comments apply to the Tree Gardenia, *Gardenia thunbergii*, another South African generally regarded as a conservatory plant that actually does very well outdoors in warmer, drier climates. In southern Australia it has been grown since colonial times, being

Rothmannia globosa makes a small evergreen tree with masses of creamy white scented flowers in summer and is hardy once well established. Think of it as the centrepiece of a shady patio or the creator of a microclimate for special pot plants. Photo courtesy Clive Blazey.

found in older gardens as a huge sprawling shrub of tree-like stature that with sensitive pruning can be turned into an attractive small tree. Expectations are that *Rothmannia globosa* will respond in pretty similar patterns. This makes it potentially very useful, and so it should be treated by those searching for plants that will add to the Mediterranean gardener's palette.

Of small tree proportions, and tolerant of alkaline soils and hard water, how may *Rothmannia globosa* be used in garden design? According to those familiar with its habits and patterns of growth it makes an excellent tall, informal hedge. Slow growing, evergreen and well-clothed in foliage, blessed with perfumed flowers and a hardy constitution, it is plainly a good choice for a boundary planting, either solo or in a mixture with other hedging plants such as *Carissa* spp. Given its stature it has potential as a hedge on stilts too, though such a plantation would possibly not be

cut as crisp and smart as those of linden, beech and hornbeam so loved in colder climate gardens. It remains for a plucky warm climate gardener to make the experiment. Other formal treatments would be well worth trying. For those so minded, the shrubby plants could be trimmed into huge domes and other similar, simple geometric shapes in the way that yew is often treated. Or standards could be raised up to make allées, avenues and more stylised formal arrangements.

Without tying development of these ideas too closely to old European models, there are charming ideas to be played around with when small trees are treated formally. Imagine a simple quartet of rothmannias planted on the points of a square, surrounded by a pea-gravel pavement and each tree encased in a circlet or square of some plant trimmed low – *Artemisia* x 'Powys Castle' or *A.* x 'Poquerolle', or slightly taller and thicker *Westringia fruticosa*, *Teucrium fruticans*

Incidental displays such as this, provided by garden antiques, can add great interest to any garden, and can easily be moved or changed. In Mediterranean gardens such things can act as eye-catchers when the garden is resting over summer.

A large green-glazed *vase d'Anduze* holds a dwarf form of Bull Bay Magnolia, *Magnolia grandiflora*, that establishes an instant Mediterranean ambience, especially when teamed up with a hardy trailing geranium (*Pelargonium* x *peltatum*).

15

or even one of the newer dwarf Indian hawthorns, *Rhaphiolepis* hybrids such as 'Ballerina' or 'Dancer'. A simple circlet of prostrate rosemary would equally serve in a less rigid composition. The central opening could be set with a table, chairs or garden lounge as a place of quiet relaxation. The glorious perfume of the flowers of the rothmannia would be the icing on the cake. For those so inclined this could be the setting for a collection of garden antiques – old watering cans, a wheelbarrow, a well-worn trug, old gardening implements or a show of *vases d'Anduze*, *pithoi* and *amphorae*. Others might choose to set up a small charcoal grill, rattan chairs and a wrought iron table, yet others might circulate a changing display of flowering succulents, epiphytic cacti, glassy haworthias or colourful bromeliads. The opportunities are really only limited by the imagination – and the purse!

Rothmannia globosa is also one of those adaptable plants that can serve in those awkward narrow side gardens that are the curse of many city gardens. Airless, dry, dusty, alternating between blazing heat and gloomy shadow, they provide a real challenge to any gardener's ingenuity. In warm, dry climates, rothmannia and the tree gardenia can make an evergreen screen capable of being trimmed quite tightly, though at the expense of flowers. Where many other plants would fail this tough performer can give coverage and stature.

Retama monosperma
Bridal Veil Broom

Retama monosperma (syn. *Genista monosperma*), introduced long ago from southern Spain, Portugal or north-west Africa, is a hardy garden stayer frequently found in old and derelict gardens in nineteenth-century gold mining areas around the world, where it was treasured as the one decent-sized tree-like shrub or shrub-like tree that would flourish in the harsh conditions common to these places, producing shade and scented flowers, and resisting the advances of the house cow too. Discarded as too old-fashioned since the 1950s, and even before that relegated to the outermost reaches of fashionable gardens, it has made something of a comeback in the cottage garden revival, and more recently in the gardens of old mining town cottages now taken up as weekenders by city folk.

For all the rough treatment it has had at the hands of the fashionistas it remains a lovely, elegant plant that shines through in its season with a curtain of small white flowers.

Intolerant of wet situations but otherwise unfussy this broom, like most others, is successful on hard alkaline soils, even those that comprise a thin, lean sandy loam over hardpan or a limestone cap. Often employed originally as a barrier hedge, roughly trimmed and laced with fencing wire, it kept children in and grazing animals out. Today it is more likely to block out unsightly views and prying eyes.

Treating Bridal Veil Broom as a hedge in the trim and crisp sense may reduce its life span, but given an occasional haircut it seems to last and last. Even so, like most members of the Leguminosae it is relatively short-lived alongside pines, olives or evergreen oaks. Around 30 years might be reasonable. Certainly once

The weeping form and charming white flowers of *Retama monosperma*, Bridal Veil Broom, have long endeared it to gardeners. Tolerant of a wide range of conditions, it is a very useful addition to the Mediterranean garden in late winter.

this age has been reached it would be a question not of calling for a tree surgeon but of planning for what comes next. Another Bridal Veil Broom is one choice but other options could be Spanish Broom, *Genista hispanica* – but beware its weedy potential – or Mt Etna Broom, *G. aethnensis*. The former is dumpy, hard-edged, tough as old boots, strident, well scented and long-lived; the latter is graceful, lithe, fine, ethereal and short-lived. Both would be most accurately described as big shrubs that can be trained as small trees. Another replacement could be the South African Blue Pea Bush, *Psoralea pinnata*, with blue pea-shaped flowers and deep green needle-like foliage. Any of these three could be expected to reach 4 m (14 ft) or so in height, and depending on the training they receive to develop as multi-trunked tall shrubs or single-trunked small trees. As trees for small city gardens and courtyard gardens they can serve well, particularly the Mt Etna Broom and the psoralea. However, these two are best avoided in rural settings, or any place where self-sown seedlings could naturalise.

Clearly, comparatively short-lived trees such as the brooms have no place in a long-term garden. Any development plan on a bare-field site, however, will call for quick-growing shelter belts, privacy screens and nurse plants to give protection to slower growing long-term trees and shrubs. For purposes such as these the brooms, and other leguminous plants, are ideal. The nitrogen-fixing ability of their root systems is a beneficial extra, especially on the rather poor soils found in many Mediterranean climate zones. For this reason compressed lucerne hay, such as is found in pelletised feeds for rabbits, goats, guinea pigs and poultry, is often recommended as a garden mulch: it is high in available nitrogen.

There is one other use for which brooms, especially the Bridal Veil Broom, are very useful – and that is as components in a wild garden, or in those parts of a garden that are not required to present as a crisp, smart, defined area. That could sound like a wild garden, but that term implies a planned 'wilderness', whereas the other is simply a kind of fill, or stuffing, to utilise the available land and maybe build some sort of compatible background. The Bridal Veil Broom grows well in rocky places where it can get its roots down between the cracks and boulders. In these circumstances young seedlings, or even seeds, will succeed where conventional potted youngsters would fail.

Gleditsia triacanthos 'Sunburst'

This broad-spreading deciduous tree has a rather pendulous branch structure that is graceful and most attractive. It is a good shade tree, casting a light but even shade that enables many plants to flourish underneath. It is one of those trees that has a wonderful embracing feel about it; from outside the canopy looks solid but once inside it is revealed as a coverlet of leaves held aloft by arching branches – perhaps not quite cathedral-like, but nonetheless a very serene and calming atmosphere. This particular form exhibits yellow new foliage that turns green as it matures through summer. Each leaf has a ferny appearance, being made up of around 32 small leaflets. The species name commemorates Gottlieb Gleditsch, a mid-eighteenth century director of the Berlin Botanic Garden. *Gleditsia triacanthos* has been known to gardeners and horticulturalists since 1700 and has produced several forms, including a dwarf form and a thornless one from which 'Sunburst' and 'Burgundy Glow' are derived.

As a family gleditsias are characterised by a fierce armature of strong thorns, which can be simple straight spines or a crown of branched spines. Fortunately *Gleditsia triacanthos*, sometimes known as the Honey Locust, has no spines in the selected forms grown in gardens. In other situations the thorns can be a decided advantage, especially for keeping cattle and other grazing animals in or out of fields, or where security and privacy are primary considerations. The fresh, soft, new growth, even the thorns, as well as the seed pods, can be used as supplementary fodder for cattle when seasons are hard, and in the nineteenth century trees were often pollarded to produce strong new succulent shoots. In many farming areas today the roadsides and uncultivated fields are thick with the high stubble of remnant plantations.

A mature gleditsia grown under ideal conditions may reach 40 m (130 ft), but as a general observation the long periods of summer dryness in Mediterranean climatic conditions restrict the vigour found in its North American habitat. More commonly the tree reaches about 21 m (70 ft) in height with a similar spread, making a dome-shaped tree of a good size for small to medium gardens. As the tree becomes established the inconspicuous white flowers of late spring give rise to long scimitar-like pods. In cool areas few flowers will be pollinated and there may be no display of these highly visible fruits. There are those who enjoy the sounds of the pods as they clack and clatter in the breeze; a sound of summer just as familiar as the drone of cicadas.

One tree this size is probably enough for most gardens, though they also make very handsome plantings along drives and avenues on larger properties – especially where that long cool tunnel of shade is sought as a distinguished entrance. The sheltered space beneath the canopy can easily be made into a place of welcome shade for sitting, reading, eating, having drinks. The roots do not make problems by lifting paving, nor do they sucker as do those of the somewhat similar *Robinia pseudo-acacia* 'Frisia', with which *Gleditsia triacanthos* 'Sunburst' is sometimes equated by unscrupulous sales assistants.

Juvenile growth tends to be rather haphazard, with strong side-branching and no definite leader developing. The result can be a tree with low, broad, spreading growth that has a tendency to be all over the place, perhaps a not very satisfactory result for small places, and really only suited to farms and estates. However, this wayward habit can easily be rectified by simple training from the time of planting using the technique described for *Elaeagnus angustifolia*.

Besides making a shady adjunct to outdoor living, *Gleditsia triacanthos* is amenable to underplanting with many other plants tolerant of dry shade. A particularly effective combination can be made using a mass planting of *Euphorbia characias* subsp. *wulfenii* or any of its forms such as 'Green Velvet' or 'Ascot Gnome'. The variegated forms sometimes found in the stocks of rarities at specialist nurseries would also appeal, bringing light to a shady situation, but as they require careful attention to watering they are not a savvy choice for sustainable garden making in Mediterranean climates. Consider instead lifting the glaucous green of the solid forms through background and foreground plantings that could include *Agapanthus orientalis* 'Aureo-vittatus' (variegated gold), *Yucca gloriosa* 'Variegata', *Yucca* 'Garland's Gold' or *Agapanthus* x 'Jehan' (variegated cream).

Bold foliage effects and reliability are great assets in any garden. *Yucca* 'Garland's Gold' is a beauty and a wonderful basis for creative design and planting.

Punica granatum 'Madame Legrelle'
Pomegranate

Known since ancient times as a source of refreshing juice and a potent symbol of fertility, the pomegranate very early spread from its habitat south of the Caspian and in north-east Turkey to Greece, southern Italy and Egypt and eventually as far afield as China and southern Japan. Westward it was carried to Spain, Portugal, southern France and northern Africa while these places were still trading posts of the Greek city states or outposts of the Roman Empire. Any plant with such a lengthy provenance would have to be regarded as a survivor, and it is, so much so that the common fruiting form (discussed in chapter 4, Useful too …) is often thought too common for inclusion in modern gardens. While its fruits, ripening in late summer, might be considered messy and not worth eating, there are at least two non-fruiting forms that have attractive flowers and the same hardy constitutions as the species.

The most attractive commemorates one Madame Legrelle who, while she must have been significant to have such a conspicuous flower named after her, remains a mystery. A request for information sent to the French equivalent of the Garden History Society has produced no reply; maybe they don't know who she was either. This cultivar is a fine-flowering small tree, evergreen in warm situations and briefly deciduous where winters are cool or cold. The glory of this tree, quite apart from its solid dome of neat,

Pomegranates are too often overlooked by new gardeners yet several forms, such as 'Madame Legrelle' and the double white variant, are highly attractive and just as hardy as the plain fruiting kinds.

glossy foliage and smooth brown bark, is its flowers. Their lively scarlet-orange is given an added sparkle by a creamy white margin that creates an impression reminiscent of a carnation. The flowers are carried in profusion in spring, the display lasting for several months unless halted by a burst of hot weather or a late frost. The infantile fruits noticeable behind the flowers never develop.

To promote good floral displays these trees should be allowed to achieve their full natural dimensions. They respond well to being clipped into hedges up to 4 m (17 ft) tall, but this treatment effectively prevents the formation of flowering shoots and is best reserved for the common red variety.

The pomegranate is easy and adaptable. It is equally amenable to being grown as a single-trunked specimen or as a multi-trunked tree. By nature its canopy and branches reach to the ground, but in farming areas grazing goats or sheep will often nibble and trim it clear of growth for the full reach of their height, goats even climbing into the branches, to produce an umbrella-shaped tree. While this can be a problem for gardeners on Mallorca, Sicily and Sardinia, and in Greece, the end result suggests a potential treatment to imaginative gardeners elsewhere.

'Madame Legrelle' casts a relatively dark, solid shade, as the leaves hang close together and the branch structure holds them in such a way that the canopy is pretty much impenetrable. Unless subtle branch removal is undertaken this situation will remain, to either torment the gardener or be utilised as an asset. Cool, dark shade like this provides an ideal place for lounging and daydreaming – but also offers mosquitos

respite from daytime heat. Take heart, however, for it can be rendered safe for human habitation by the judicious use of mosquito coils, incense sticks, citronella candles and the like. Such inviting nooks also provide good homes for potted plants that prefer shade. Ferns are prime contenders here, especially if a sandy or fine gravel floor can be contrived. The overflow from watering the ferns will soak into the porous paving and maintain the humidity they love.

With such a bold colour combination in the flowers, with a bright orange-red base colour to boot, it could be a challenge to think how best to utilise 'Madame Legrelle' in a garden. The old China rose 'Comtesse du Cayla' has similar shades that could be effectively paired with it. This, with a selection of tough foliage plants, tubbed or in the ground, would create a striking composition. Try adding cycads – *Cycas revoluta, Zamia furfuraceae, Dioon edule, Macrozamia riedlei* or *M. lucida* – with hardy dwarf palms such as *Rhapis excelsa, Phoenix roebelenii, Trachycarpus fortunei* or *Chamaerops humilis.*

Aesculus californica
California Buckeye

This is one of those special trees that attract attention yet remain for some indefinable reason largely unknown away from their habitat, which in this case is the foothills of the coastal ranges of California, and the San Joaquin Valley. Although not mentioned by all authorities, *Aesculus californica* is poisonous in all its parts and thus requires thought before being planted where grazing animals or adventurous vegetarians might come to harm. Otherwise it is a striking tree and worthy of a garden in any Mediterranean climate region.

Typical of the genus, the leaves are palmate with broad leaflets, slightly toothed along the margins and a mid-green in colour, slightly glossy, bold and handsome. Mature specimens carry masses of white 'candles' comprised of dozens of small fragrant flowers, each with long, protruding anthers. These are followed by smooth pear-shaped fruits that split open to release the chestnuts contained within. These may not be formed in areas outside the natural habitat but it must be remembered that they are poisonous to humans and animals.

A feature of this buckeye is the white bark, evident when the tree is bare in winter. The tree can also be deciduous following a period of extended dryness, as is a natural feature of the climate of southern California. This phenomenon will occur in other dry summer areas and hence the plant can be striking garden feature from late summer onwards as a sort of white skeletal sculpture.

The California Buckeye's natural habit of growth is a sprawling, ground-hugging dome of branches and foliage. In parklands and mixed plantations it may be appropriate to allow the tree to develop naturally but clearly this would severely restrict its use in smaller gardens.

Without the benefit of irrigation during summer the plant grows slowly and forms a compact dome. Mature specimens attain 12 m (40 ft) or so and can spread to twice that without pruning. Limited to one main trunk and limbed up to make a more tree-like shape, the California Buckeye may still reach the indicated height but its spread will be considerably reduced.

A tree such as this with singular characteristics can be made much of in a garden setting, especially where its ghostly branch structure can be contrasted against a dark evergreen background such as would be created by ceanothus, evergreen oaks such as *Quercus coccifera, Q. suber, Q. douglasii, Q. ilex* or *Q. rotundifolia*, low-growing pines, coprosma or the strawberry tree, *Arbutus unedo*. Grown in the rougher parts of a garden with trees such as these, an underplanting of simple, hardy bulbs would be an added attraction in winter and spring. Appropriate Mediterranean-type companion bulbs would be grape hyacinth, paper-white narcissus, dragon lily (*Dracunculus vulgaris*), *Arum italicum* 'Pictum', musk hyacinth (*Muscari macrocarpum*), *Nectaroscordum siculum*, sea daffodil (*Pancratium maritimum*) or any number of alliums. Interspersed with a few clumps of Butcher's Broom, *Ruscus aculeatus*, the effect could be likened to a dry climate meadow. Equally it associates well with traditional Mediterranean plants such as cistus, lavenders and rosemaries. Other good companion plants are *Rosa glauca* and once-flowering, low-growing old-fashioned roses the likes of 'Raubritter' and the Rugosa roses 'Frau Dagmar Hastrupp', 'Roserie de l'Hay' and 'Alba'. An underplanting could be as simple as a carpet of *Vinca minor* 'Alba' with groups of the lovely Cape bulb

Veltheimia capensis, or *Tulbaghia fragrans* (Society Garlic) and *Iris unguicularis* (Algerian Iris).

In the wild the California Buckeye is reported as growing taller and broader, and staying in leaf longer, in canyon bottoms and creek beds, and on hillsides facing away from the setting sun – no hot afternoons, you see. It grows happily in more exposed conditions, including hillsides facing west, but its habit is altered by the harsher environment. It becomes more like a shrub, less like a tree, losing its leaves as soon as the heat and drought send it into late summer dormancy. This shows just how adaptable and hardy the California Buckeye can be. Despite its poisonous properties it can, with care, be planted far more widely than it is. And it will join the ranks of those other very useful plants with degrees of risk attached – oleander, brugmansias, narcissus and crinums.

Calodendron capensis
Cape Chestnut

A fine medium-sized tree, evergreen and prolific in flower, the Cape Chestnut has oval leaves of a very dark, rich and glossy green that make a dense canopy and cast a deep shade. In spring and early summer masses of five-petalled, rather starry flowers appear in great numbers and cover the tree in a mass of pale pink blossom. And that makes it quite a star performer.

It makes a tree shape naturally and may only need light trimming of the lowest branches to enable people to comfortably get under its skirt. It seems to have no pests to spoil its leaves. It requires a soil where it can get its roots down into a deep watertable, thus sustaining it over long, dry summers. While not suited to really difficult soils it is well adapted to life on river flats, inland valleys and coastal plains where soils are generally better. It is somewhat frost tender but after a few years youngsters are usually tall enough to hold their leaves above the frost line and thus will be just fine. However, this should not be misunderstood: the tree is not hardy where frosts are frequent and frost pockets deep.

The best use of the tree? Its habits of growth and characteristics suggest that the best use for *Calodendron capensis* is as a shade tree, for its shade is deep and dark and cool and seems to embrace and shelter those who enter under the leaf canopy. No better uses can be made of the tree than to daydream

Where opportunity exists the Cape Chestnut, *Calodendron capensis*, is an excellent large tree suitable for avenues, treescapes and solitary planting.

under it after breakfast on a day that promises to be scorching, snack under it at lunchtime, nap under it on a hot afternoon, take drinks under it at sundown. With the branches hung with tea-lights or Moroccan tin lanterns the inner space can be transformed into a haven from evening heat – just remember to deal with any mosquitos.

Calodendron finds infrequent use as a street tree, probably because the canopy would be virtually impenetrable by street lighting. As an avenue the trees would make a mysterious dark tunnel that could have some appeal to estate designers, although so much evergreen darkness in the grey days of winter might make the approach to a house rather depressing. One way of lightening the impact would be to whitewash the trunks in the manner that citrus tree trunks are painted in parts of southern Europe, an idea that was taken up with great effect by landscape designer Roderick Cameron when he developed the gardens at

'La Fiorentina' on Cap St Hospice for his mother.*

Companion planting under such a dense canopy would be a challenge because of the low light conditions and the canopy's impermeability to rain. Plants would have to be rotated frequently and watered attentively to ensure growth remained even and attractive. Plants tolerant of shade and winter dryness are not all that common, but the huge begonia family revels in these conditions and offers a wide choice to interested gardeners set on making a collection for display.** Among the best choices for this particular situation are those begonias classified broadly as 'cane-stemmed begonias', 'hirsute begonias' and 'large rhizomatous begonias' which are blessed with fairly stout constitutions. While all these begonias will grow perfectly well in sheltered positions outdoors they are intolerant of frost, and thus are most frequently found in the catalogues of greenhouse specialists and growers of exotic specialties.

The Cape Chestnut is regarded as a fairly fast-growing tree, at least where conditions suit it, and will mature to a height of approximately 15 m (50 ft) and a spread of about 10 m (35 ft). The overall habit is a rounded dome with the canopy free about 2 m (7 ft) above ground level. Trees known to be over a hundred years old are common in nineteenth-century parks and botanic gardens, so there need be little concern about longevity and general hardiness. As a rule the Cape Chestnut is propagated from seeds or semi-ripe cuttings but it is not always easy to locate a supplier. The most likely sources are those nurseries that specialise in plants for Mediterranean climate gardens; even then it may be necessary to order well ahead.

*Shirley Johnson and Roberto Schezen, *The Villas of the Riviera*, Thames & Hudson, London, 1998. ISBN 0-500-34167-2
**Roger Phillips and Martyn Rix, *Conservatory and Indoor Plants* (Vol. 2), Macmillan, London, 1997. ISBN 0-333-67738-2

Banksia marginata
Coastal Banksia

A very variable plant from site to site within its habitat along the coast of southern Australia, *Banksia marginata* is in some places prostrate, in others shrub-like and in yet others a small tree to 7.5 m (18 ft) or so. This diversity of habit can taken as an advantage for gardeners on sites exposed to salt-laden winds, with sandy and calcareous soils, low rainfall and saline watertables. The added advantage is that this banksia is native to climates with long, hot and dry summers. In other words – a good hardy plant well suited to gardens in exposed places, where soils are difficult and the climate harsh, a natural choice for seaside windbreaks and holiday house gardens.

Over time, seedlings from the taller growing forms will develop into small trees that present a characteristic appearance of open branchwork supporting an open canopy of bluntly rounded, long grey-green leaves slightly toothed along the margins. From the apex of the growing points bottlebrush-style flowers appear in late spring – not particularly colourful, being a greenish-yellowish cream. Like the tree the flowers also vary in form, from small and comparatively insignificant to quite large and noticeable. Growing seedlings from known sources with the desired characteristics gives a more than reasonable chance of getting a good form.

Harsh critics might label *Banksia marginata* lacklustre or even dull but hey, it grows in very difficult spots, and grows well too, besides which it attracts many honey-eating birds in its season. The flowers are lightly but sweetly perfumed. If I were pushed to say why it appears here other than for its overall thriftiness, it has curiously attractive bark. Rather spongy and soft-looking, the warm brown bark encases the trunk and branches in a manner reminiscent of the skinfolds of the Michelin man. This effect is even more pronounced in some of the other tree banksias, especially *Banksia grandis* and *B. robur*, but these species would need summer irrigation to be successful in Mediterranean situations.

In nature the tree grows in mixed stands, though often the predominant species, in association with hardy sedges, saltbush (*Rhagodia* and *Atriplex* spp.), coastal wattles (*Acacia pycnantha* and *A. spinosa*) and Coastal Tea-tree, *Leptospermum laevigatum*. In some southerly locales it is also found with the Bracelet Honey-myrtle, *Melaleuca armillaris*, and the paperbark *Melaleuca linariifolia*. Since the plant dislikes root disturbance it is preferable to locate it in some part of the garden designed to be pretty well self-sustaining, where no digging or supplementary watering is done,

and no fertiliser given. It will benefit from mulching; in such a setting a leaf-litter cover will amass naturally over the course of a few years. This may represent a degree of risk if bushfires are likely to occur, which can be lessened by an annual clean-up, rake-off and carry-away exercise, or managed by installing a low-level sprinkler system that can be turned on to dampen things down on high risk days. Wherever native plants are grown in a natural manner the risk of wildfires taking hold in accumulated mulch can be a concern, a concern that is best handled by working with local fire authorities to set up a garden plan that minimises the danger with a regular schedule of maintenance and active management.

In areas where Coastal Banksia is endemic, mature specimens in the garden can be treated as features with strong sculptural qualities. Thoughtful professional tree surgery will reveal the peculiar characteristics of any given tree, exposing the branch and trunk structure to create strong visual patterns in silhouette, or through which views to other parts of the landscape can be seen. Amateur slashing and hacking is not advisable. Similar treatment can be carried out with equal effectiveness on ancient olives and carobs and has been used with great effect on Coast Live Oak, *Quercus agrifolia*, in areas around Carmel in California where real estate developments have intruded on still-forested valleys.

Quercus douglasii
Blue Oak

At home in the dry foothills of the inner coast ranges of California, *Quercus douglasii* is widespread and very resilient to hard conditions. It is admired by many for its ability to survive in extreme circumstances, particularly those associated with very low rainfall, scorching summer winds and barren situations. Endurance, above all else, is the characteristic of this tree; a characteristic that should recommend it to many Mediterranean climate gardeners.

A cast-iron constitution is not the only asset this tree bears. It has fine grey-blue foliage that has, among oaks, the unique capacity to be shed during extended rainless hot periods in summer. This summer dormancy is but one of the tree's survival techniques. From the moment an acorn falls from the branch it has specialised mechanisms to support survival. The seeds germinate more rapidly than those of other oaks, the roots grow faster and longer, the proportion of root to top growth is greater, the leaves are adapted to minimise transpiration. Even when a tree sheds its leaves in mid-summer the acorns continue to develop, thus ensuring the next generation.

The principal challenge for gardeners outside California will be to obtain viable acorns, for like those of all oaks they have a fairly short period of viability. However, it can be done. There are several well-established blue oaks in the Waite Arboretum at Adelaide in South Australia that were raised from seed 40 years ago. Acorns that drop to the ground here germinate freely, especially around the skirts of the ground-sweeping canopy. Incidentally, the trees in this arboretum exist on natural rainfall. The only supplementary watering is given to get young trees established within the groves of mature trees. The arboretum also holds significant collections of other Mediterranean climate oaks, some from California and others from Turkey, Spain and Greece, which makes it a great reference collection for gardeners, garden designers, landscapers and urban planners.

Urban development becomes a significant problem for already-established trees in that it can radically alter the watertable due to run-off from roads and pavements, flooding from downpipes and gutters, and altered drainage patterns created by cut-and-fill techniques, road making and so on. The oaks of California come under this pressure, especially the Coast Live Oak, *Quercus integrifolia*, because so much of its range has been taken up by housing developments. Planting young specimens can sometimes bypass the problem, but of course the tree takes a generation or two to develop the majesty of maturity. Careful landscaping can also ensure that the impacts of altered watertables and drainage patterns are minimal. But even where young trees will answer

the needs of the garden maker and designer, excessive watering to promote faster growth should be avoided. There is a rule of thumb for gardeners that says things that grow quickly generally tend to die quickly too. It is especially apt when applied to trees. In the case of English oaks grown in warmer climates, their life span is reduced from 400–500 years to less than 150 years. In the case of Mediterranean climate oaks the loss is more likely to lie in the alteration of their usual shapes, so that the venerable characteristics for which the trees are known and valued are lost.

Techniques for saving and moving mature California oaks have been developed to a high degree. For an astonishing story, read up on the removals and relocations undertaken at 'La Cuesta Encantada' (San Simeon Castle) by Julia Morgan and Nigel Keep (and around 150 workmen) at the behest of William Randolf Hearst. Some of the mighty oaks moved from the mountaintop site of the yet-to-be-built castle were encased where they grew in concrete 'boxes' weighing up to 600 tons so they could be safely moved and replanted. The survival rate appears to have been excellent but, as has been discovered more recently, the repair of damaged roots can easily take many decades, during which time the trees are especially vulnerable to fatal fungal infections. Solving these challenges is the subject of ongoing research by California arborists and horticulturalists.

Offering any information on the final dimensions of the Blue Oak seems a matter of academic interest to those who live outside their natural range. Published information is that a medium to large tree could be around 21 m (70 ft) high and slightly less in diameter. A typical growth rate would see young trees beginning to achieve these dimensions after at least 50 years.

Bruce Pavlik, Paula Muik, Sharon Johnson and Marjorie Popper, *Oaks of California*, Cahuma Press, Los Olivos, California, 1992, ISBN 0-9628505-2-7, is an excellent all-round reference for the Blue Oak and other California oaks.

2 Statement makers

These ten plants with pizzazz are but a tiny selection from the numerous xerophytes so well suited to low water use gardening; all will survive quite well in Mediterranean climates without summer irrigation. In general they are disease free and pest free, though mealy bug and scale insect can sometimes mar their beauty when viewed up close. Several of the plants included here need particular care in placement, being highly succulent and thus liable to damage by frost and especially liable to damage by hail. If they would need protection by way of bagging, wrapping, sheeting and so on, I suggest you choose something else better adapted to your locality. While most are best as solitary specimens that will draw attention, even bring you to a full stop, others will happily grow into sizeable clumps that draw attention for reasons other than individual form. Foliage colour and density can be just as arresting as plant shape, as can flower colour – though it must always be borne in mind that flower displays rarely last more than three weeks in succession and so make a relatively short-lived contribution to any part of a garden's design.

Plants that have the capacity to perform as statement makers are the sorts of plants that call out across the garden, 'Come over here and look at me.' And when the garden visitors get there, there needs to be some new direction in which to move, some new attraction beckoning them down the path, further into the garden's depths. Such plants can also bring finality to the scene, stating boldly, 'That's all. This is the end.' Any plant used this way needs to be maintained to a high degree so that it always stands out. Dead leaves and flowers must be removed. Surrounding plants must be kept trimmed of wayward overgrowth so the significance of the attention-grabber is never obscured. The plant chosen to fill this role must itself be managed so that the growth of new side-shoots or top growth never blurs its image. Keep attention focused by paying heed to the housekeeping.

When attention to such key plants becomes a chore, why not switch attention elsewhere by replacing them with something new? Renewing plants can seem to be a bother, especially for new gardeners who think gardening is all about 'plant and forget', but it has a remarkable refresher effect on the creativity of the garden maker and on the imagination of garden visitors. Once plants outgrow their allotted parameters they need to be renewed to maintain the effect for which they were first chosen.

Romneya coulteri
Matilija Poppy

In the semi-arid wasteland and wonderland that is Baja California, that long skinny finger running on from the south California coast, the Matilija Poppy finds a home in the gravel screes and washaways that are transformed by occasional storms into impermanent creeks. It spreads north too, into southern California, where it is found in equally hard circumstances. With stringy succulent roots it runs about, suckering shallowly and making great thickets of silver stems and leaves. Not only is it tough and tolerant of harsh environments, it is also prolific of growth and lavish in its production of its pure white flowers. Crumpled and crimped as a poppy should be, crystalline white and with a huge boss of golden stamens, it is perhaps the king of all poppies.

Classed as a softwooded shrub or shrubby perennial, *Romneya coulteri* is difficult to propagate and very slow to establish, but then so dogged it is almost impossible to kill. Its tenacious roots occupy the most barren of soils – bare clay and shale, sands and gravels, rock-filled substrates. Even if burned to a crisp by summer heat and drought, it will come back once autumn rains soak the soil and the wide-ranging roots absorb every available drop of moisture. Growing vigorously and soaring to 2 m (7 ft) or so high, it is in flower by early summer. Leaves and stems are all silver-blue in colour, a feature which has made the plant desirable to English and European gardeners since the late nineteenth century, when its beauty was extolled by William Robinson, publisher and gardener. The large white flowers are said to be fragrant, though not everyone seems aware of it. Even with no perfume the flowers would be sufficient to recommend the plant to most gardeners.

Difficulties experienced in trying to grow the Matilija Poppy are easily comprehended when its natural habitat is understood. It is not a plant to be fussed over, watered, weeded and dug around. It likes to be left pretty much alone. Given initial care at planting to ensure excellent drainage and an open, sunny situation, the only after-care required should be an occasional drop of water during the first year. After that the only attention necessary should be the removal of dead flower stalks and branches from time to time. If these few simple requirements are met, *Romneya coulteri* should be easy as pie to grow in Mediterranean climate gardens.

The plant's suckering habit may prove annoying to obsessively tidy-minded gardeners but others will see its abundance and willingness to grow as a blessing. Suckers can be dealt with either by pulling them out, or by chopping back extraneous growth with a spade. Digging around the plant will break the thick surface roots and suckers will proliferate at these points. Great if you want more plants. Not so great if the plant has outgrown its allotted space. A word of advice – transplants taken from freely growing plants are notoriously difficult to re-establish, even when given every care. Root cuttings are the way to go. This is not difficult but takes time and a bit of common

sense. First the roots have to be dug from around the parent plant. Pieces of about pencil thickness are about right. These must be cut into sections about 10 cm (4 in) long – less if you are well practised, or a surgeon – and care must be taken to keep them in the right top-to-tail order – that is, remember that the end nearest the plant stem is the bottom end of the cutting. Dipped into root-promoting hormone and dibbled deep individually into a very free-draining potting mix, they can be set aside in some lightly shaded position where you won't forget to water them. If the weather is cold put them somewhere warm. Within a few weeks the cuttings will have formed callus at the root end and should show signs of growth within another few weeks.

Having secured plants there remains the question of how to include them in a garden scheme. It is almost impossible to confine romneyas in a formal garden or border. Perversely, they will almost certainly occupy any gravelled or dry-paved path, drive or court near where they have been planted, having a tendency to move from where you want them to be to the places that best suit them. Counting on this certainty, it is best to think of these poppies as nomadic and almost ephemeral, so put them where their wayward habits won't distress you, say in a wilder patch inhabited by tough shrubs, cistus, rosemaries and such like. Here they can wander at will and look great among these other dry-growing plants.

Nolina recurvata
Pony-tail Palm

One of the most popular indoor plant curios in the world, *Nolina recurvata* (syn. *Beaucarnea recurvata*) is widely mass-produced by nurseries to fill a demand for vegetable novelties. The Pony-tail Palm can be grown indoors in strong light situations for many years but will eventually outgrow most windowsills and porches. In relatively frost-free areas it can be planted outdoors, where it will grow into quite a sizeable tree to 15 m (50 ft) tall, with many side-branches and a crown equally wide. Mind you, this will take 50 years or so, so it can be planted with every confidence it won't grow large before its time (or yours). The mid-green, strongly recurved leaves are 1–1.5 m

Pigface is colourful, easy to propagate and well adapted to exposed, hot situations. Dozens of forms, species and genera offer a wide range of colourful carpeting and groundcover plants.

(3–5 ft) long, strap-shaped and sandpaper smooth. In due course tall, much-branched flower spikes will develop atop the leaf clusters, bearing hundreds of tiny cream flowers.

The most interesting feature of the plant is the way in which the trunk forms a swollen base up to 3 m (10 ft) across as it grows. From the very earliest stages of growth this is visible, which explains why it makes such a fascinating indoor plant: it looks unlike most other plants. The trunk and swollen base develop grey-brown bark that shows a squared pattern of splits, especially towards the bottom, adding to its curious charm.

From a garden point of view the Pony-tail Palm is of value because of its hardiness and interesting shape, but it is also a challenge to locate so unique an appearance. It looks out of place underplanted with petunias or other bedding plants and its chief attraction is hidden if it is surrounded by other growth. It really demands a space all its own and is frequently displayed in desert gardens as a solo specimen. Where there is plenty of room, or a special feature is to be made of it, *Nolina recurvata* can be planted in larger groupings. A grove of such distinguished trees forms the foundation planting for a section of the desert garden at the Huntington Botanic Gardens in Pasadena. Here the tree takes on a new dimension, carpeted underneath with mats of pigface (*Drosanthemum* spp., *Lampranthus* spp.) and other succulents.

The root system is also worthy of note (not that it can be seen), an unusual characteristic making itself useful to gardeners. The roots emerge from the base of the swollen trunk and while not ephemeral are neither particularly substantial nor in the short term necessary. This observation was made when need arose to move a semi-mature specimen from one garden to another. The plant was dug up and left standing with a small root-ball for two years in a holding area. It was not potted, heeled-in or planted. It did get an occasional watering from a sprinkler system but otherwise got by with natural rainfall, surviving two summers exposed full-on to sun and wind. Growth slowed and some foliage was shed but it was very much alive when it was eventually moved into its new position. By this time the ball of soil and root system had pretty much disappeared; all that remained were a few wiry broken roots emerging from the rounded bottom of the swollen trunk. Settled carefully in its new spot, a large courtyard where it did not need to be staked against the wind, within weeks the whole thing plumped out noticeably and in a month or so there were signs of new leaves emerging. Soon new growth points developed along the trunk. Just how tough is this plant?

The small root system explains why the pony-tail palm can be kept as an indoor plant for many years, and why it is such a good pot plant for a terrace or patio. Just take care it cannot be upset by passing traffic and gusty winds. As the plant itself has such an exceptional appearance, it is probably as well to keep the pot as simple as possible so as not to distract attention. Then again, it would look fabulous in a mosaic-covered pot decorated with broken crockery, mirror shards and shells. Or, come to think of it, in one of those large foundry crucibles that look like raku pottery.

An inhabitant of the summer-deciduous tropical forests of Mexico, *Nolina recurvata* has proven well adapted to Mediterranean type climates. It can tolerate short periods of frosty weather. In really hot desert and semi-desert regions young plants will need some protection from sun scorch and wind blast, but once established will tolerate extremely hard conditions, prolonged drought and merciless sunshine.

Slow growing and of ancient lineage, the Japanese Sago Palm, *Cycas revoluta*, is but one of a large number of cycads now being introduced to gardens through the efforts of specialist growers and collectors. It is eminently suited to pot culture, as in this terrace display – this terrace display with bougainvillea and plumbago under date palms at the promenade café, Parc Güell, in Barcelona.

Cycas revoluta
Japanese Sago Palm

Sometimes seen in old Japanese prints cloaked with straw matting and a thatched roof to keep out rain and cold, this common 'palm' is widely planted in climates far removed from the chill of central Japan. It is really a semi-tropical cycad and its appearance in classical Japanese gardens was due to its rarity and difficulty of care as much as to its distinctive appearance and aesthetic qualities. Today it is a red-hot favourite with landscapers and garden maintenance crews because it is very slow growing, makes almost no mess, needs no annual schedule of care, has very few pests and will grow almost anywhere, particularly in hotel lobbies, forecourts and around swimming pools. And it is evergreen, stylish and glossy too. As if that were not enough, home gardeners also like it.

As plants go *Cycas revoluta* is ancient. The fossil record shows its ancestors to have been about in the age of dinosaurs – the Jurassic Period, 250 million years ago.* If you have children or grandchildren, growing 'dinosaur food' might be sufficient to justify buying a small potted specimen. Yet others will marvel at the manner in which the older plants produce generous quantities of offsets by the formation of 'bulbils' on the trunk. With care these can be propagated by gently prising them out and planting in a free-draining potting mix. Given a protected warm location they will make roots and grow into independent juvenile plants. A neat trick, and a very handy means of propagating a plant that is very slow to produce seed, especially as a male and female plant 'in season' at the same time are needed to achieve pollination. Others will find its strong palm-like form, stiff, bold, dark green foliage and stocky, clump-forming trunk much more garden worthy than pot worthy.

Originating in the southernmost subtropical islands of the Japanese archipelago, this species has been spread around the world since its introduction to European horticulture in 1782. It is a venerable plant not only in terms of earth history, but also in terms of garden history. Without doubt it is the most widely grown cycad in the world, at home in the greenhouses of Europe and North America and equally at home in gardens in all the temperate and Mediterranean climate zones of the world.

Though as tough as they come, *Cycas revoluta* grows best in areas where it is not exposed to full sun all day, when the leaves take on a yellowed appearance rather than their characteristic deep, glossy green. Plants will survive quite well in dark parts of a garden, generally with almost no etiolation or bending towards the light. This capacity enables the plant to grow in such spots as the bottoms of exterior stairwells and other poorly-lit corners of large buildings, making it a boon to landscapers. But gardeners have found them of much greater use than simply populating pokey architectural dead-ends.

In superior private gardens and on the terraces of exclusive hotels, tubbed specimens of *Cycas revoluta* have been given pride of place since the tourism boom on the Riviera and around the Italian lakes of the mid-1800s. Surrounded by bedding petunias, scarlet salvia, lobelias and geraniums, they have dominated such settings and still do. Each winter the annuals and bedding plants are tossed away and the cycads wheeled in their tubs into the safety of orangeries and greenhouses to keep them warm until winter is done. Then out they go to star in a new bedding scheme for the following tourist season.

A more relaxed idea, also dating from the mid-1800s, is to create lush semi-tropical displays of foliage plants to fill shady spots. One of the most lavish and still extant examples is found under the portico of the Huntington mansion in Pasadena. Here sago palms thrive in the company of kentia palms, other cycad species, philodendrons, begonias and tree ferns to make a wonderful display that can be enjoyed by anyone who uses the covered portico; a table setting and lounges encourage to escape the afternoon heat and enjoy the cooling breezes and the view.

On a grander scale is the cycad garden at Lotusland in Montecito, California.** Here hundreds of cycads of varying genera and species are planted en masse in a display that is claimed to have cost its maker, Madame Ganna Walska, millions of dollars. Getting on in years, she had to buy mature specimens to fulfil her vision! The rest of us may have to opt for a more affordable approach but even quite small plants have immense character and within a few years have made enough leaves to establish such a garden. Worth doing though.

*David L. Jones, *Cycads of the World*, Reed, Sydney, 1993. ISBN 0-7031-0338-2

**Theodore R. Gardner, *Lotusland: A Photographic Odyssey*, Allan Knoll, Santa Barbara, 1995. ISBN 0-9627297-5-2

Agave vilmoriniana
Vilmorin's Agave

A grand plant of rare distinction whose popularity will grow as news of its striking appearance spreads among gardeners and landscapers. If you think *Agave americana* has the typical appearance of *all* agaves, think again. Vilmorin's Agave has a telling character all its own. First described in 1913, it was named in honour of a member of the Vilmorin family of great French nurserymen — and women. At first limited almost exclusively to the great gardens of the south of France along the Riviera, to which the family supplied numerous novelties, it has slowly spread in commerce in California and Australia. Being fairly large

Graceful, large and different, Vilmorin's Agave, *Agave vilmoriniana*, offers swirling grey foliage and magnificent stature to Mediterranean gardeners looking for drought tolerance and a rare touch of distinction.

at maturity, and needing to attain that size to show its characteristic 'octopussy' form, it hasn't featured much in greenhouse succulent collections in colder climes. Since the 1990s its popularity has burgeoned in the United States as it has been taken up by landscape designers as a feature xeriscape plant, particularly in southern California and the dry south-west states of Arizona, New Mexico and Nevada. More recently still it has been distributed in significant numbers by at least two specialist nurseries in Australia.

Vilmorin's Agave is large, with a characteristic spider-like swirl of slender silver-grey leaves. It has none of the more rigid form and thicker leaves of its everyday counterpart, *Agave americana*, and is altogether a more open and gracious plant. When well grown, in a fairly open setting, the intensity of the silver 'bloom' on the leaf surfaces is also greater. The foliage can yellow somewhat when exposed all day to a blazing summer sun, but this can easily be avoided by ensuring it gets some light afternoon shade and perhaps a little extra water from time to time; otherwise, the plant will recover its colour with the return of cooler seasons. Unlike *Agave americana*, *A. vilmoriniana* seems to produce few offsets by basal suckers, instead generating masses of young plants by 'bulblets' that form along the flower stems after the plant has flowered – usually when the rosette of leaves reaches about twelve years of age.

Besides being impressive as an architectural plant, Vilmorin's Agave has another great attraction for home landscapers: it has virtually no spines and so is safe to plant even where children pass nearby. The leaf edges are described as smooth, but in fact are slightly rough, rather like sandpaper, with very small, soft teeth along the margins. There is a spine at the tip but it is soft and flexible and so presents no potential danger to youngsters.

Most specimens of this agave will be acquired as small seedlings, since few growers are able to supply mature, landscape-ready sizes and large plants would be almost impossible to transport without damage to the sprawling rosettes of leaves. While baby plants can be set directly where they are to grow to maturity they may struggle to establish themselves adequately in the open. In my experience it is preferable to grow seedlings on for a year or two in pots where they can benefit from the more attentive care of a daily round.

Even so, out of a batch of 50 or so one or two will fail to thrive, lingering on for several years hardly moving. In the end these can be planted out and left to fare as they will. Be ready to try again if necessary. One cause for failure is over-watering, always a problem with succulent plants in their young stages. This is best dealt with by veering on the side of caution, under-watering and making absolutely certain that the potting soil is open, gravelly and free draining. Contrary to popular belief, agaves and other succulent plants are not able to thrive in barren soils bereft of nutrients. Slow feeding with controlled-release fertiliser granules is effective in warm weather, while in cooler seasons half-strength liquid fertiliser can keep plants moving along without forcing an unnatural rate of growth.

A plant with the stature of *Agave vilmoriniana* has a presence that needs to be acknowledged and respected. It is not the sort of plant that can be jammed into cramped quarters, nor should its dramatic shape be subjected to the ignominy of having lesser beings crowded about it. It can look great at the end of a vista where a punctuation point is called for. Set against a wall or a background of dark greenery, its elegant lines and silver leaves are shown to advantage. However, its best use by far is where it can be set on the edge of a wall and seen from below, such as on a terrace or atop a retaining wall. Here its silhouette of spidery leaves will be magical, the more so when a towering flower spike emerges and looms high against the sky.

The overall dimensions of a mature plant are approximately 2 m (7 ft) across and 1.2 m (4 ft) high. The flower stem will attain about 5 m (17 ft), marking the end of the growth cycle of any one rosette. After flowering the rosette slowly dies, usually taking two or three years to dry and fall during which time numerous baby plants will grow where the flowers once were.

Aloe plicatilis
Book-leaf Aloe

Confession time; this is my favourite aloe and one of my favourite structural plants. In my estimation the Book-leaf Aloe is an outstanding example of a plant with presence, dignity, strength and unique style. It is like no other. And it flowers too.

Truly unique in appearance is the Book-leaf Aloe, *Aloe plicatilis*. Eventually making a substantial shrub-sized bush, it can take the form of a large bonsai or a striking tubbed specimen.

Aloe plicatilis is a fairly common succulent shrub-like aloe. It rarely reaches more than 2 m (7 ft) high in cultivation, and spreads somewhat wider, although habitat reports record specimens up to 5 m tall (17 ft). It stands upon a very stout trunk covered in dun-brown papery skin. The branches hold up a solid canopy of greyish green leaves, each one folded with the next like a fan, or like the pages of a book splayed open. In winter short spikes of tubular orange-red flowers appear between the leaves. Honey-eating birds love them. Occasionally stubby oval seed pods form here and there along the flower stalks. The habit of growth of the branches is peculiar in that each growing point divides and keeps on subdividing, eventually creating a broad domed crown of leaf fans. Its appearance is that of a rather pudgy, oversized bonsai.

And that's the way I like to grow it – in a large squat pot placed where its knockout silhouette can be appreciated from a distance and its complex branch structures enjoyed close up. The plant is top-heavy

because of the heavy succulent leaves and its spreading manner of growth so care is always needed to ensure it cannot be tipped over, knocked over or blown over and damaged. It gets very heavy as it ages so extra care will be needed in shifting it; maybe a tub with wheels on a supporting base, or a strong sack truck, will be needed to keep backs safe from strain.

Growing a mature plant from a seedling or single stem cutting would be a lifetime's work but by good fortune larger cuttings, sometimes known as truncheons, can easily be rooted in barely damp, coarse sand. This may take several months but accept this as the way to go; attempts to hasten root growth by watering or feeding will almost certainly lead to the whole branch rotting. How large is large? It is entirely possible to root a trunk-like cutting 1 m (3 ft) high and with 20 to 30 leaf clusters. It just takes patience. And there it is, an almost instant mature plant. The trick is to find an even larger plant from which to take a large cutting, and an owner willing to part with it!

While *Aloe plicatilis* definitely makes a garden statement it lacks the sophistication and elegance of some of the other plants I've listed. It has a more homey quality about it that calls for a rethink of its possible range of uses. Yes, it can be eye-catching as a focal point. Yes, it can look wonderful in a large tub or pot at the end of a vista, or in an archway. As a solo act it is a front-row performer. But it can also act as anchor to a cluster of pots. Its umbrella of leaf fans spreading wide suggests a mother-hen quality, and in this role it becomes the centre of a cluster of smaller pots and seed pans that add richness and diversity to the scene. Other succulents could form the permanent foundation of the group, while occasional displays of flowering bulbs or annuals could move on and off stage with the passing seasons. Not being particularly fond of fussing over potted annuals, I would focus my efforts on building up a discerning collection of low-growing echeverias, sedums, crassulas and other weatherproof succulents with subtly colourful leaves.

Be aware that the Book-leaf Aloe is a plant of the open grassy hills of western Cape province, and as such needs all-round exposure to the sun to maintain an even pattern of growth, an important watch point where it (or any other plant requiring high levels of sunlight) is grown in a pot. It is also critical to ensure there is no risk of the potting soil becoming waterlogged. True, it does come from a relatively high rainfall area but it is always found growing on rocky slopes and hillsides where drainage is excellent and rapid.

Set to show to advantage in the garden, the Book-leaf Aloe benefits from a surrounding low groundcover. The colour of the winter flowers could be picked up by hardy South African bulbs such as orange sparaxis and hardy yellow or red lachenalias, or contrasted with the blues of babianas and geissorhizas. No need to bother about rare varieties here. What is called for is mass planting, so go for the more common sorts. Exotics such as California poppies, nasturtiums and even Flanders poppies could also work. Just choose winter-flowering plants. A simple underlay of small gravel would suffice to cover the ground after the bulbs have disappeared in early summer. For complementary adornment a small grouping of dwarf aloes such as *Aloe aristata*, *A. brevifolia*, *A. humilis* or *A. longistyla* would make a handsome association.

See Ben-Erik van Wyk and Gideon Smith, *Guide to the Aloes of South Africa*, Briza Publications, Cape Town, 1996. ISBN 1-875093-04-4

Yucca whipplei
Our Lord's Candle, Chaparral Yucca

Travellers in California are often struck by the impressive sight of tall spires of creamy white flowers rising from this widespread stemless yucca among dry grasses on hillsides and road cuttings. The semi-arid landscape is enlivened for months by these 3.5 m (12 ft) spears of blossom standing sentinel in their hundreds alongside freeways and byways. Down at ground level a basal rosette, usually solitary, nestles, the blue-grey, narrow leaves hidden among a thatch of grasses and wildflowers. Each rosette is about 1 m (3 ft) wide and comprises hundreds of narrow leaves, hard edged and equipped with a sharp terminal spine. Within each rosette the rigid leaves are arranged in regular, almost formal patterns which add to the architectural qualities of the plant. It's not the sort of thing you'd want near a swimming pool or play equipment but nonetheless is a truly worthy plant for dry landscapes.

Stripped free of the scurf of dry grasses and

highway trash, the plant stands out as one of bold stature with a well-defined shape. Individual plants convey a sinewy strength capable of withstanding the longest dry season, only the prodigious quantity of flowers suggesting luxury and lushness.

Like many others of the genus, *Yucca whipplei* has useful features. In some yuccas the leaf fibres are long and tough; in this case the flowers are edible. In Mexico and for Native Americans in the dry south-west states the flowers in their season add to the wild foods that supplement foods produced by cultivation. They are baked and toasted, or used fresh as a salad ingredient, and the flower buds fried in a manner similar to potatoes. Interesting though this quality may be, it is hardly likely to lead to a major rush to grow the plant as a food crop. But as a crop grown by specialist growers to the landscape trade it has been available on the Mediterranean coasts of France and Italy, and in Australia, since the mid-nineteenth century. Like most succulent and xerophytic plants it has gone in and out of favour, but now that sustainable water use is high on community agendas it is being planted more widely.

Where gardens are being constructed on steep rocky hillsides in new subdivisions, and where cut-and-fill construction techniques have destroyed natural soil profiles, all attempts at landscaping are bound to be a challenge, particularly in discovering a range of plants that will grown happily in soils that are all too often crude mixes of subsurface clays and shales, a little topsoil, builder's rubble and bedrock. What could look more natural than *Yucca whipplei* grown in a setting that so closely approximates its natural preference for rocky hillsides, especially when planted at well-spaced intervals and underplanted with sprawling sheets of pigface (*Aptenia* spp. and *Drosanthemum floribundum*), gazanias, *Arctotis stoechadifolia* and its hybrids, and *Osteospermum* cultivars?*

By reputation this yucca can be grown satisfactorily in a large pot, and may even flower after 50 years or so. While growing it in the open garden may not make it bloom any faster, it will at least help eliminate the spiky problems of handling it for repotting, working around it or moving it. Where the situation calls for *Yucca whipplei* to be grown as a potted display specimen to occupy some pivotal role in a design, serious consideration must be given to how the plant will be managed and handled. The tip spines are hard and sharp, and there are lots of them, so the potential for damage to tender skin and body parts exists, especially where close work like weeding needs to be done. On the flip side, the plant needs protection too. It will have little value as an eye-catcher if its symmetry is ruined by broken leaves here and there caused by careless handling. In many cases moving it will be a two-person job involving old blankets, sacks, old newspapers, cardboard or pieces of discarded carpet, and even then both parties will have to work carefully and keep alert for protruding terminal spines. Before attempting any relocation, or planting out of mature specimens, it is crucial to have a clear plan of action – and this applies to all manner of succulents and cacti: prepare the planting hole, wrap the plant in its protective covering, dig out or de-pot carefully, shift gently onto a strong carry-blanket, pack around with newspapers or whatever so it is stable, take to the planting site and carefully lower to the ground, move into position, unwrap and settle into place using shovel handles or long poles, backfill with free-draining soil and leave for a week or so! Then water. This way broken roots will have time to form a protective callus that will prevent rots getting established.

* See Peter Goldblatt and John Manning, *Wildflowers of the Fairest Cape*, National Botanical Institute, Cape Town, 2000. ISBN 0-620-24787-8

Purple-brown foliage makes a great foil for other dark-coloured leaves and for silver-leaved plants. *Cordyline australis* 'Purpurea' combines here with the richer purple of *Tradescantia pallida* to great effect.

Cordyline australis 'Purpurea'
Cabbage Palm, Giant Dracaena

A most distinguished plant from New Zealand, and not really a palm or a dracaena – but common name confusion is often met with in the world of plants. To be sure you get what you want, check the label for the botanical name before you buy. This is a very adaptable plant that tolerates heat and drought well despite its habitat being generally wetter than most Mediterranean climate regions. It is also cold tolerant, though it may come through a cold spell looking very ratty. If the growing point is damaged by frost or any other means it is not necessarily the end; the chances are good that new shoots will develop lower down on the trunk and grow into a multi-trunked plant. This effect can also be induced by pruning. Otherwise the plant can develop as a single trunk with one growing tip for many years. The dimensions of a mature plant vary according to how the plant has developed and at what time it produced side-growths. At maturity *Cordyline australis* can reach 10 m (35 ft) or so with a canopy somewhat smaller in diameter.

A growing crown is made up of a cluster of narrow leaves about 1 m (3 ft) long. In the different forms available commercially these can be a rather dull green, purplish, red-brown, or variegated cream and green. For the purposes of garden making I suggest the purple-leaved form 'Purpurea' as it offers something extra to work with in developing colour themes. This form may also be found as 'Atro-purpurea' – a minor difference that appears to arise between suppliers in the USA and elsewhere. As the plant matures flower spikes will appear at the terminal points of leaf clusters, large panicles of creamy white that are pleasantly, if sweetly, scented.

Be aware, if seeking other colour forms, that the variegated cordyline is much less vigorous than the green or purple-leaved forms. It will make a very attractive potted specimen but is not so well adapted to the competitive state of the open garden. It is also harder to locate, and costs more: two more reasons to keep it in a pot.

Being an unashamedly tidy person (well, at least in the garden), I like to see the skirt of dead leaves that accumulates on each trunk removed from time to time. Native rats and other creatures may choose to make

Aeonium arboretum 'Zwartkopf' is such a great addition to the Mediterranean gardener's palette of colourful, hardy plants that it is worth any effort to deploy it in any variety of planting schemes – even if that means replanting the rosettes annually.

their homes in this dense thatch, and it may be the natural growth habit of the plant, but I still prefer to see the dead foliage removed. Spent leaves will come away easily if they are pulled downward with a quick jerk. Finished flower spikes will have to be cut down; not an easy task if the plant is old and multi-crowned.

Searching for a solution to the challenge of highlighting a silver garden with some other colour, I settled on a combination of silver and 'black'. To allow room to move creatively I took a broad view of 'black' plants and included *Cordyline australis* 'Purpurea', *Aeonium arboretum* 'Zwartkopf' (syns 'Blackhead', 'Tete Noire', 'Zwartkop', 'Schwarzkopf') together with *Sedum* x 'Bertram Anderson' and *Tradescantia pallida*. For extra oomph I added one or two New Zealand Wire-netting Plants (*Corokia buddlejoides*) and a broad clump of *Echeveria* x 'Black Prince'. The cordylines

Sedum x 'Bertram Anderson' is a willing coloniser capable of providing solid blocks of colour and foliage. The plummy silver leaf colours are emphasised by silver or purple toned neighbours such as artemisias and *Tradescantia pallida*.

were planted in clusters of three of varying sizes to add to the visual interest. Such formality as was planned came from saltbush clipped in wave-like forms. Where the degree of formalism required is of a higher order, purple cordylines fit perfectly as their general habit is to grow at a reasonably uniform rate and until they begin branching they present an appearance of soldier-like regularity. Once this stage has been passed you might need to consider other options. Still, once an idea has outgrown its conception it is a stimulating exercise to come up with fresh ideas and implement them. Gardens are not static and gardening need not be dull. Plan for changes.

As *Cordyline australis* 'Purpurea' is such a dark colour, and the leaf surface dull, exercise a degree of caution when planning a design around its strong

Contrasting form and stature are dramatically provided by *Echeveria* x 'Black Prince'. It looks well solo but even better when combined with rusty red pansies and violas in winter, or with purple basil in summer.

33

vertical form. Too much of the dark dull colour range will present a very gloomy prospect, lacking vivacity and appeal. Plenty of leavening is required to bring out the purple foliage as a highlight. Bold garden colourists would superimpose even stronger, redder tones, as are found in the leaves of some cannas and dahlias; scarlet and orange flowers would be introduced, as well as the bold foliage of Castor-oil Plant (*Ricinus communis* 'Purpurea') and New Zealand Flax (*Phormium tenax* 'Purpureum'). Those seeking to create an atmosphere of greater calm might opt to set off the purple-red of the cordyline and its cohort with a heavy counterbalance of silver-leaved plants.

Yucca guatemalensis 'Silver Star'

Introduced to the world by the Dutch greenhouse industry, 'Silver Star' is a much-maltreated beauty that deserves to be liberated from its role as a dusty, drawn, half-dead house plant and given a chance to shine outside. In frost-free Mediterranean climates it will make a large tree-like plant, and even in mild frost areas will survive without disfiguring damage, just growing more slowly and taking longer to flower.

Also known as *Yucca elephantipes*, a reference to its natural habit of growth with massive trunk and multi-headed crown, *Y. guatemalensis* inhabits the edges of jungle clearings and open grasslands across a range of subtropical highlands in Central America. Several forms exist apart from the plain green species, distinguished by less or more variegated silver or pale yellow stripes running the length of each leaf. Flower stalks are formed at the centre of each rosette of leaves, bearing numerous creamy white bell-shaped flowers arranged on a short spire: it would be unkind to say they were 'stumpy' for they have a certain modest grace. After flowering seed pods may be set, and eventually the rosette will branch into a least two new growths. Mature plants will reach 5–6 m (17–20 ft) but are easily controlled by simple pruning and lopping. The fibrous trunk and branches yield to a pruning saw or loppers and the plant is quickly reduced to appropriate proportions. New plants can be started from large stem cuttings rooted in dry sand, and may also be made from individual rosettes and the new shoots that appear from the base of the plant. Taken

off clean with a sharp knife or secateurs, offsets will quickly form a callus and then roots. A large section of trunk laid lengthwise and half-buried in a sandy, free-draining compost will form many small shoots which can be detached and rooted. Kept in a warm well-lit area and watered from time to time, such a trunk will produce offsets for several years before becoming exhausted.

'Silver Star' is distinguished by a broad silver-grey stripe running the length of each leaf, the overall effect being a stately grey plant with a strong outline and bold appearance. It is not hard to see why it proved so popular with owners of post-Modern apartments and lofts, and to understand why it was promoted so heavily as an architectural plant to be grown in a large pot by a swimming pool. The foliage is certainly splash-proof, and the leaves, though held erect, are soft and have no spiny tip. But the plant is much more versatile than that.

Planted with other silver-leaved plants, 'Silver Star' is capable of holding a scene together, so strong is its form and mass. Try it with a background and underplanting of artemisia, santolina and helichrysum clipped into low mounds and domes. Place a tall single-stemmed specimen at the end of a vista, or where it is framed by a garden doorway or opening, or set a potted series to mark the edge of a terrace.

This yucca can easily be cut down and re-started when it gets too big for its purpose. It is very hardy and generally free from diseases and pests. Maintenance is simple – remove dead leaves periodically by tugging each one gently downwards; take care not to grab the leaves roughly because the edges are quite sharp and can cut tender skin. Cut off spent flower stalks and feed every six months with slow-release fertiliser granules.

For information on additional yucca species and varieties see:
Mary and Gary Irish, *Agaves, Yuccas and Related Plants*, Timber Press, Portland, Oregon, 2000
Fritz Hochstätter, *Yucca I: In the Southwest and Midwest of the USA and Canada*, self published, Mannheim, 2000
John Milton Webber, *Yuccas of the Southwest*, US Dept of Agriculture, Monograph No.17, Washington DC, 1953

Looking for something with stature, presence and that 'hey-look-at-me' quality? *Crassula argentea* 'Hummel's Sunset' is a stunner with striking form, stately appearance and bold yellow, red and green leaf colours. Easy to grow and sun hardy too.

Crassula argentea 'Hummel's Sunset'
Jade Plant

The jade plant. *Which* jade plant? What a confusion of common names. There are at least three that I know of – *Crassula arborescens*, *Portulacaria afra* and this one. Fortunately for the botanically challenged *Crassula argentea* is easily identified, even without the dubious benefit of a colloquial name.

Crassula argentea is a shrubby succulent with smooth bark and rather elephantine-looking trunk and branches. The thick, succulent leaves are elliptical to rounded, edged with a fine red margin and closely packed on compact stems and branches. The almost

The pure golden yellow tones of *Portulacaria afra* 'Aurea' are set off by red stems. At a distance the overall effect is that of a clear yellow block of colour. Grown in full sun the colour will be well developed year round.

sure-fire ID for this particular jade plant is the way in which the leaves change from green when young to yellowish with age. This is most noticeable around the leaf edges, especially when the plant is grown in full sun – as it prefers. Mature plants also develop heavy flower clusters in the leaf axils in winter. The flowers are pale pink, almost white.

'Hummel's Sunset' is a selected form that adds to the above colouration with an overlay of red on the leaf surface, thus creating a striking tricolour effect. Since the bush grows around 3 m (10 ft) tall, and much the same across, the total impact is both bright and cheery, writ on a satisfyingly large scale.

Like *Aloe plicatilis*, 'Hummel's Sunset' and the species from which it derives have appeal as a kind of giant bonsai, in this instance a sort of elephantine bonsai. And like *Aloe plicatilis*, when treated this way the crassula needs a broad low pot to safely hold it against being upset. Not that it requires a large root-run; it does not, and can be kept in the same pot for a long time without repotting or potting on to a larger size.

Picking up on the colouring of 'Hummel's Sunset' with companion plantings at first seems a challenge to the imagination. What would partner with something that is yellowish-greenish-reddish? And rather muted hues at that. Narrowing the choices down a bit, my first thought would be to scout through the increasing range of hybrid echeverias, succulent cabbages if you like.* 'Succulent cabbage' is really too crude a term for these fine hardy plants but it does convey some suggestion of what they look like. Each grows as a rosette of thick succulent leaves that may be wavy, crimped or plain along the edges. Some varieties also have tubercles – a nice term for warts – at the centre and base of each leaf, and as breeding becomes more complex forms with spoon-shaped and almost tubular leaves are being introduced. Since hundreds of these plants are now available, it is necessary to exercise some discrimination in making choices, otherwise you will fall into that class of person called 'collector' – a polite term for plant nut. That can be great fun, but for the purposes of selecting a cluster of companion plants for 'Hummel's Sunset' a more focused approach may be best. Taking up the colours of the crassula are *Echeveria* x 'Ballerina', 'Mary Butterfield', 'Fireball', 'Ruby Lips', 'Mauna Loa' and 'Bittersweet', to which could be added species such as *Echeveria agavoides* 'Corderoyi'.

In the open garden 'Hummel's Sunset' also finds a place, being well able to hold its own even in quite difficult, hot, dry locations. It can be a strong vertical feature among a planting of succulent groundcovers, or in a more mixed cottage display where colour schemes are less a concern than achieving a rich variety of leaf colours, shapes and patterns. Where such things are allowable, kerbside plantings can also feature 'Hummel's Sunset', though care must be taken not to disrupt pedestrian traffic or vision from the driveway onto the street by poor siting.

Propagation of 'Hummel's Sunset' is easy once it is understood that highly succulent cuttings are very susceptible to rot. It can be propagated by simple leaf cuttings. Pull a leaf gently downward and away from the stem – it should break off clean and entire – and lay it on, or shallowly insert it into, barely moist, coarse sand. Within weeks it will have put out roots and a tiny growing bud will appear at the point where the leaf joined the plant. From then on it's just a matter of time. Stem and trunk cuttings can be very successful too. This is where the extra care is needed. The cutting must be dried off before it is planted, so leave it in a cool, dry place for a week or more before planting it in barely damp, sandy potting mix. It will slowly make a root system over a number of months. During this time water must be given sparingly or the stem may rot and the whole thing collapse in a slushy, smelly mess. This process of propagating highly succulent plants can't be rushed by watering. It can be helped if you can keep the cuttings in a brightly lit, warm situation, but even then patience is the key to success.

*See Attila Kapitany and Rudolf Schulz, *Succulent Success in the Garden*, Schulz Publications, Teesdale, Australia, 2002. ISBN 0-9585167-4-X

Dasylirion wheelerii
Desert Spoon, Sotol

Sotol is a pretty crude form of rot-gut liquor which is made in Mexico from the hearts of this widespread, abundant plant. Apparently it bears some resemblance to mescal and tequila though they are each more refined in taste and production. No more needs to be said. This is just by way of an explanation of the curious for the curious.

Dasylirion wheelerii is a very attractive plant that represents a small family of a dozen or so similar species. They are stemless or have short trunks, usually erect but sometimes reclining, solitary but occasionally branched, green-leaved but tending more or less greyish in some species and forms. So there you have it; botanically speaking all bases are pretty well covered more or less! The characteristics are variable within a range of features that are pretty much very similar. Try reading Hermann Jacobsen's *Das Sukku-lentenlexikon* (1970) for a full serving of the 'more or less' approach to botanical description. For gardeners the differences between dasylirions are slight and all are attractive. From a design point of view their shapes are the same, though dimensions at maturity vary, and leaf colour, as already noted, varies between green and grey. Some of the green-leaved species have attractive tufts of fibres at the leaf ends – *Dasylirion acrotiche*, in particular – but I have opted for the grey-blue tuftless-leaved *D. wheelerii* as the species with most appeal for Mediterranean climate gardeners. Indeed, it has been known to gardeners in these climatic regions since the late nineteenth century.

Noted for its fine leaf colouration and cold hardiness, *Dasylirion wheelerii* has proven a popular exotic akin to agaves, cycads and the Mexican Lily, *Beschorneria yuccoides*, a desirable inhabitant of subtropical bedding schemes and lush foliage displays of the kind favoured in the Victorian and Edwardian eras. Ancient specimens can be found lingering on in a mass of dead flower stalks and tangles of dried leaves amidst the wreck of many a park rockery.

A huge plant with a rare capacity to draw the eye and hold attention, the Desert Spoon, *Dasylirion wheelerii*, is worthy of a place where space is not a problem. It should never be cramped as it cannot be pruned or held in suspended animation by trimming.

Fortunately for its reputation the plant has been assigned new roles in modern desert and south-west gardens, numerous examples being found in books on the Tex-Mex, Santa Fe style of architecture and landscaping. These places are at the drier end of Mediterranean gardening but such an adaptable plant can confidently be deployed by those who garden in other parts of the spectrum. If proof of the plant's structural drawing power is needed, readers are advised to confront the pictorial evidence* or to scout around in the old-fashioned parts of local parks and public gardens.

Each plant is made up of a large number of very narrow, fine-spined, grey-blue leaves arranged in a stiff rosette about 1.8 m (6 ft) across. In advanced age it produces a short trunk about 1 m (3 ft) tall holding the rosette aloft. From this a flower stalk up to 6 m (20 ft) high will eventually develop. Quite an impressive sight, even though the individual flowers are very small and rather nondescript in colour. Since the plant is grown for its leaf colour and strength of character the flowers are a moot point; a tidy and colour-conscious gardener might even be led by a set sense of style to cut the stalk down before the flowers open. It probably wouldn't matter all that much, especially outside its habitat range.

Given its splendid dimensions this is not a plant for pot culture, so where does it fit into the scheme of things? As a general rule the Desert Spoon works well in company with other bold and statuesque plants of the kind designated 'architectural' by post-Modernists. It really needs to be contrasted alongside broad-leaved agaves, tall cereus cacti, flat-padded opuntias, barrel cacti, tree aloes and twiggy see-through small trees such as Palo Verde (*Cercidium* sp.) or Ocotillo (*Fouquieria splendens*) if the situation is really dry. In desert gardens it forms one component of a collection of 'plants as statuary'.

Aside from desert gardens *Dasylirion wheelerii* is adaptable to somewhat better watered locations where it finds a more conventional role as a strong focal point by virtue of its distinct blue colour and its shape and size.

*See Paula Panich and Nora Burba Trulsson, *Desert Southwest Gardens*, Bantam, New York, 1990. ISBN 0-553-05735-9

3 Structure makers

One of the outstanding features of traditional Mediterranean garden design is the manner in which native plants have, from Roman times, been the backbone of garden making. Although this limited flora has been vastly enriched over the ages the ethos of these gardens hasn't altered much: the plants survive on the rain that falls with minimal, or no, supplementary irrigation. Thus olive, bay, laurel, box, myrtle, *Phillyrea* and Bird Cherry (*Prunus padus*) entered early into the Western garden tradition. Before the Romans the Greeks took a similar range of plants into cultivation but their 'gardens' were more about religious affinities and civic obligations that found horticultural expression in sacred groves, temple precincts, sacred sites and public spaces rather than gardens for personal relaxation and enjoyment. The Romans, however, developed private gardens to a high degree, creating intimate inner spaces and larger complex formal designs that linked villas and their gardens with the rural landscape. They also developed the concept of taking the wild landscape into a garden to be enjoyed as a prospect, and built maritime villas to enjoy the drama of the Italian coastline. What is clear from the surviving literature is the Romans' love and expertise in training the evergreens listed above in formal hedges and topiary. Following that example today would be too difficult for many and too confining for others, but perhaps we can take from it something that offers modern garden makers a chance to develop the structure of their designs without making great demands on their topiary skills. I have seen the idea expressed both in colloquial gardens and in more sophisticated ways by Dutch garden designer Piet Oudolf.*

The notion is a very simple one: to extend the idea of a hedge by merging it with the idea of a living sculpture, not to make a topiary but to make a 'plat' – a sort of vegetative plateau. The top surface can be billiard-table flat, cut on a bevel, or made undulating and wavy like water. The height can be as high or low as you wish. The shape can be any form that you like, though bear in mind that the centre must be able to be reached somehow. Keeping things simple is always a good rule, at least as a starting point.

The simplest form is that of a table-top, and it was this plain form that first attracted my attention when it appeared near my home in a few commercial landscapes maintained by old southern European men. Varying in height from 10 cm (4 in) or less to almost 1 m (3 ft), sheets of common saltbush, *Rhagodia spinescens*, were turned into miniature plateaux spreading out around boulders and conifers in low maintenance gardens. Perhaps the low level of maintenance required was too boring for those who tended them and, seeking diversion and engagement, they began to snip, clip and trim in a very simple way. The plat works well, serving as a groundcover, anchoring rocks and free-form shrubs, carpeting beneath trees and occupying sun-scorched areas that would otherwise be barren, or jarringly blanketed with red pebbles of volcanic scoria.

Plants such as saltbush, and the others listed below, have a habit of low, spreading growth that works out from a central rootstock to cover quite a large area. This means that though the density of growth is high the density of roots is sufficiently well spaced for the plants to survive in difficult, dry situations. This is a survival strategy for many plants in arid, coastal and Mediterranean environments, one that we can adopt with considerable benefit to our efforts at water saving and sustainable gardening generally.

Building on the basic idea, an imaginative gardener or designer could make a tableau of clusters of different plants clipped at different heights and cut square at the points of convergence. An added layer of visual interest can be injected by allowing small working tracks between the different groups. This creates easy access for maintenance but, more importantly, the dark shadows cast in the tracks intensify the contrast between the adjacent blocks of foliage, and the tracery created emphasises the relationship to abstract tapestry. This association was not lost on seventeenth-century French garden makers, who termed such layouts *tapis verts*. It is unlikely that anyone today would wish to attempt the creation of a green tapestry equal to the complexity of those elaborate horticultural weavings, or even to limit themselves to green. But taken at its simplest level the idea can be developed as an alternative to the endless swathes of gravel and bark mulches deployed in dry gardens, or the equally repetitive sweeps of gazanias or osteospermums planted willy-nilly with little thought and no imagination. Give the idea a go.

*Piet Oudolf with Noël Kingsbury, *Designing with Plants*, Conran Octopus, London, 1999. ISBN 1-84091-055-0

Rhagodia spinescens
Coastal Saltbush

A very tough groundcovering plant with close-knit twiggy growth, *Rhagodia spinescens* sprawls over a large area. Native to sand dunes along limestone coasts in southern Australia, this unlikely plant is capable of making a significant impact in a dry landscape. It has the attractive capacity to respond well to clipping and can easily be turned into a rolling, lumpy, bumpy groundcover or a surface as flat as a billiard table, depending on the gardener's whim. Quite large areas of otherwise desolate ground can be transformed in this way, creating, in effect, a carpet of groundcover. Treated this way *Rhagodia spinescens* always looks neat and presentable and provides a

Australian native plants are not often thought to be adaptable to garden techniques such as regular trimming and shaping. *Rhagodia spinescens*, the Coastal Saltbush, proves the exception; here it is combined with *Helichrysum petiolare* to create a series of flat trimmed plats.

degree of formality in conditions where one would usually be grateful to see a cactus survive. Eagerly grazed by sheep and producing the far-famed saltbush lamb, the plants are endowed with the ability to regenerate from both their lowest branches and their twiggy superstructure. They seem to need neither fertiliser nor water, even in harsh coastal conditions. They withstand light frosts but their rather fleshy foliage would be susceptible to moderate frosts and probably turn to blackened mush.

The small, trowel-shaped leaves are greenish when new but as the foliage matures with the advance of hot summer weather it assumes the silver tones common to all the tribes of saltbush. The flowers have no significance whatever, being very small and colourless. Propagation by simple side-cuttings taken with a small heel of older wood is relatively easy; plant 6–8 cuttings around the edge of a pot filled with free-draining potting mix, place in a shady but well-lit place, water and wait. Taken in late spring, over summer and in early autumn, the strike rate should be sufficient to keep any gardener happy. The plants can also be propagated by layering a low branch or twig shallowly into the soil and separating it from the mother plant after six months or so, by which time it should have formed roots of its own.

For variety and simplicity try it grown as a carpet with taller silver plants behind treated in a similar manner. *Helichrysum petiolare* is a good companion and takes this treatment well. Drawing on the Provencal tradition so cleverly adapted by Nicole de Vesian, the carpet could be varied by gradually turning it into a series of clipped balls, it could be pierced by sentinel specimens of other plants, or the scene could be punctuated by clipped upright cones or even corkscrew shapes of dwarf myrtle. Grown naturally, *Rhagodia spinescens* looks neither here nor there and has few qualities to recommend it other than its considerable capacity to cover bare, stony ground and sand dunes. But even that is an asset for gardeners working on difficult sites. American equivalents are found in several members of the *Atriplex* family: *A. semibaccata* (Creeping Saltbush) and *A. lentiformis* (Quail Bush).

Taller and leafier is the Silver Saltbush, *Atriplex rhagodioides*, which comes from a wide area of southern Australia. This plant can add a further dimension to a plat garden by virtue of its more intense silver colour and greater height. It has insignificant flowers that don't intrude on any plans a designer-gardener may have for it.

To any scheme that involves *Rhagodia*, *Helichrysum* and *Atriplex* it is possible to add a further dimension of colour that the varied silvers will set off to great advantage. This can easily be achieved by interplanting the taller saltbush varieties with a relatively unobtrusive plant with silvery leaves and bright flowers. Ideal for this purpose is the California Fuchsia, *Epilobium californica* (syn. *Zauschneria californica*). It will interweave inconspicuously with its companions, stand clipping well and in autumn make a terrific display of small tubular orange-red flowers – a bold contrast but one that works well and really perks up the scene. If its suckering habit invades the lower plat it won't really matter. It can easily stand cutting down to that lower level and if a few flowers are produced their appearance will be of no consequence to the big picture.

Propagation of these plants is easy: all will make roots wherever branches or stems touch the ground; they are easy from cuttings taken in autumn and rooted over winter, and they can be raised from seed. And, as reported by European gardeners about many Mediterranean plants, they will self-sow very successfully in gravel paths and paving cracks.

See John Wrigley & Murray Fagg, *Australian Native Plants*, 5th edn, New Holland, Sydney, 2003.

Clivea miniata

Although not the first choice for gardeners working in the drier Mediterranean climate types *Clivea miniata* does excellent service defining areas under deep shade in those regions where some summer rains can reasonably be expected, or where it can receive some summer irrigation. It will survive in quite good condition until autumn rains arrive to spur it into fresh growth and eventually into flower. For making a solid block of dark foliage it can scarcely be bettered. Out of flower it has a mass that is weighty and reassuring. Its simple strap leaves remain green and unchanged for month after month in the shade while elsewhere the sun blazes unremittingly down, scorching grasses brown or bleaching them pale yellow, cracking the earth and roasting the skin. Clivea's dark green actually deepens the shadows and makes them look cooler and more restful. The coverage it creates is even and dense. No weeds will break through a well-established planting. Its height, at 75 cm (30 in), is sufficient to define an area as not one to be traversed. It sets a boundary, establishes a form, directs the flow of plants and foot traffic, and creates a pool of colour and shadows as deep and mysterious as a pond.

Am I too enthusiastic? No. When in winter the flower stalks appear, a moment of rare magic is about to burst through the grey rainy days like a ray of light. Commonly found in a shade of soft orange apricot with a yellow throat, the open trumpet-shaped blooms are held up in a large cluster. The head may contain 20–60 flower buds which develop and open over a period of a month or so. It is quite a stunning performance, the more so because these exotic, tropical-looking flowers come in the depths of winter. A whole bed of cliveas in bloom will give your soul (and your garden) a lift.

Just recently a number of cream-coloured variants have been made available at a cost quite out of proportion to their garden value. That said, cream cultivars such as 'Vico Yellow' are a valuable addition to the colour palette. Within a few years Dutch and Japanese breeders, and some others in Africa, Europe and the USA, have brought out a range of more expensive and more complex hybrids that are variously described as creamy white, apricot, peach pink, burnt orange and red; some are even greenish. In time these may well find uses similar to those assigned to the more common forms but for now they remain pretty much in the hands of serious collectors and plant breeders. The Japanese also admire cliveas with variegated leaves and are breeding to achieve new 'breaks' in that direction too. Miniature cliveas are also getting about. These originated in Japan but have been taken up enthusiastically in Europe as having great potential as indoor pot plants, since they can be grown in conditions that are similar to those in which bonsai are produced. But apart from the common form and some of the cream forms, the above are all too scarce even to be considered for mass planting.

In some public parks cliveas are used to make broad bands under large trees, quite often the large evergreen subtropical figs. Beneath these towering canopies gardens of exotic foliage can be created using a range of hardy plants such as aspidistras, philodendrons, rhoeos and tradescantias, evergreen hardy ferns, cliveas, bromeliads, cycads, bamboos and small palms. This diversity can be reproduced on a much smaller scale and still be effective. Occasionally found under lath-covered patios and decks, this garden form could add a degree of distinction to far more outdoor living spaces with overhead protection. In these situations the main emphasis should be on developing a feeling of richness, of luxuriance, an almost jungle-like quality. This would be fine in summer, easy on the eyes and suitably tropical. In winter a ground-level coverage of cliveas with their apricot orange flowers would really spark up the grey days.

The structure provided by the cliveas is defined by their natural form – uniform dark green colouring, uniform leaf shape, uniform plant height and, apart from the flowering season, no appreciable variation in seasons of growth. The form can be free-flowing over any given area, or moulded to comply with more regular, formal shapes. Planting individual leaf crowns on a grid pattern, in concentric circles or staggered rows can introduce subtle patterns that reinforce larger, overall design shapes. The plants proliferate only slowly so such conceits remain visible for many seasons before they disappear in a mass of leaf cover and demand dividing and replanting.

See Harold Koopowitz, *Clivias*, Timber Press, Portland, Oregon, 2002. ISBN 0-88192-546-2

Artemisia x 'Powis Castle' and 'Poquerolle'

Trying to separate these two artemisias is as difficult when seeing them side by side as it is when I try to think through which one could be preferred over the other. 'Powis Castle' has been available for a good many years, and is well established in catalogues and nursery stocks. But in that time it has been much confused, in Australia at least, with the much larger growing *Artemisia* x 'Lambrook Silver', even though their habits of growth are very different. 'Powis Castle' is low, squat, with long, almost lateral flower stalks whereas 'Lambrook Silver' is bushy, upright, rounded and has stubby flowering stems. How can this confusion have arisen? Laziness, I suspect, is the key element, care not being taken to keep cuttings of the two well separated during the propagation phase of production, or maybe outright sleight of hand replacing one variety with another to meet demand. Being very compact and close jointed, 'Powis Castle' is relatively shy in producing material suitable for taking cuttings. In contrast 'Lambrook Silver' produces masses of side-shoots along its branches from which masses of new plants are grown. 'Poquerolle' is a later introduction that bears a strong resemblance to 'Powis Castle'. These two are so similar to my eye that I keep them well separated in the garden so there can be no risk of confusion.

Whether 'Powis Castle' or 'Poquerolle' is chosen, the effect and habit of growth will be pretty much the same. Planted at 60 cm (24 in) centres, they will prove accommodating in forming a solid mat of divided silver foliage that hugs the ground closely. They could be planted at the front of a garden bed, or plantings extended to make a complete margin along a border if a formal concept was being developed. Both are equally useful in less structured settings and can be associated with plants of similar stature such as *Nepeta* x 'Walker's Low', bushy thymes and *Sedum* x 'Bertram Anderson'. By trimming off the developing flower stems in early summer the dull creamy grey flowers can be eliminated and at the same time the plant will be encouraged to send forth a burst of fresh new leaves. The dense cover of leaves keeps the soil cool and damp when the garden gets a baking. This makes it a useful host over which to grow *Clematis texensis* or *C.*

viorna – both with pearly pale mauve pitcher-shaped flowers – or one of the dark red texensis hybrids such as 'Ladybird Johnson' or 'Sir Trevor Lawrence'. The viticella clematis hybrids like 'Etoile Violette' and 'Sodertalje' are too vigorous for this type of planting and would completely smother the diminutive artemisias. The growth of these artemisias is sufficiently open to permit some bulbs to grow through. I like the combination of their silver leaves with the rosy purple drumsticks of *Allium sphaerocephalum*. These grow through with no difficulty, as do those of *Allium cernuum*, and they enjoy the shade and dampness created by their plant companions.

If a low foundation planting at the base of a wall was called for, either 'Powis Castle' or 'Poquerolle' would be excellent choices, easy to maintain, hardy, tolerant of reflected heat, compact, neat and tidy. In some situations alongside a path they would be a better choice than the frequently nominated catmints – the artemisias don't attract bees.

Don't overlook their potential for creating a distinctively Mediterranean look in the form of a garden of clipped, dome-shaped subshrubs and bushy herbs. The idea is well worn by now but still an attractive alternative to more precarious notions such as meadow gardening that are not well suited to long, dry summers – when the whole area given over to such an idea would be dead and brown. Better to plan for some visual interest, even if it cannot be of the floral kind that consumes too much water during the hottest months. This notion developed first in Provence under the discriminating eye of couture designer Nicole de Vesian.* Like all good design, the idea is timeless and can be relocated, re-interpreted, enlarged, reduced and enriched. Playing around with an idea can be great fun and the end result can be something all your own. How might it work, I wonder, with trimmed plants of Cushion Bush (*Calocephalus brownii*) and Curry Plant, *Helichrysum italicum* (syn. *H. angustifolium*)? How might the silver domes of these artemisias look growing out of a carpet of misty *Artemisia canescens* or a sweep of blue fescue, *Festuca ovina* 'Glauca'?

*Nicole de Vesian – see entries in Louisa Jones, *The French Country Garden*, Thames & Hudson, London, 2000, ISBN 0-500-51005-9; and *Gardens of Provence and the Côte d'Azur*, Taschen, Cologne, 1998, ISBN 3-8228-7229-6

Myrtis communis
Myrtle

One of the plants beloved of the ancients, myrtle is still highly valued. Where boxwood fails myrtle is often a superior substitute, especially its compact form. It is found in the wild in coastal and inland woodlands and mixed scrub, especially in valley bottoms where there are natural collection points for any soil moisture that may be available. This said, *Myrtis communis* is a hardy and adaptable shrub or small tree that manages well in most situations though in arid areas it will probably need a modicum of supplementary irrigation mid to late summer.

Myrtle was often included in wedding bouquets in the mid-nineteenth century, and as often as not a slip was made from a piece of the bouquet to be grown in the newlyweds' garden. Many of these plants, now in advanced old age, are still to be found in older suburbs and country towns. A similar practice was sometimes associated with the end of life, sprigs of myrtle included in funeral wreaths being rooted and grown on the grave of the deceased. If nothing else this shows just how tough the plant is: it can survive for a century or longer in country graveyards where there may be no rain for five months of the year.

From a gardener's perspective appearance is at least as important as durability, and in this the myrtle completely satisfies. It has a dense cover of small, dark green leaves, among which masses of small white flowers are produced in early summer – and they are sweetly perfumed.

Traditionally myrtles have been used for hedging. They have a habit if growth that is almost hedge-like in nature and responds well to training and trimming. The usual form is too large and vigorous to be a suitable alternative to box in Mediterranean climates but the compact form 'Nana' is admirable for the purpose. Myrtle's advantages over box are that the foliage won't burn in strong sunlight, nor will it yellow or turn bronze when conditions are less than it likes. For those blessed with discriminating noses I imagine the spicy aroma of the myrtle's foliage would be preferable to the foxy aroma attributed to box. Myrtle is also very adaptable as to soils and very drought tolerant, which makes it the only real choice for low to medium hedges in climates where summers are warm, dry and long.

A roadside *bricolagerie* in rural France? Not a bit of it. At Black Springs Bakery outside Beechworth in north-eastern Victoria Rob Cowell created this simple image of Provence with trimmed myrtle balls, an ancient wirework pot stand and open-weave baskets.

The variegated form 'Variegatus' is widely planted and though equally as vigorous as the other kinds seems to offer no particular advantage. At a distance it looks pallid rather than silvery, an insipid, indistinct colour that is neither one thing nor the other in terms of garden value. Where the plain dark-leaved forms perform beautifully when clipped as columns, cubes, plinths or plats, the variegated kind can make no equal contribution despite being sturdy, hardy and easily managed. It just doesn't have the strength of character or visual clout of the plain sorts.

Travellers may recall the Patio do los Arrayianes (Court of the Myrtles) at the Alhambra in Granada where, in partnership with a simple long rectangle of water and two small fountains, a pair of straight myrtle hedges makes a most refreshing garden under the blazing Andalusian sun. Common myrtle is also found in several recreated gardens in Pompeii and Herculaneum. If it has lasted all this time, not that the living plants are original to either period, then it can

be safely assumed that this is one hardy plant. The only word of caution must be that myrtle is not cold hardy and soon suffers if frosts or snows are deep or frequent, which is why you will find it written about by northern European gardeners as a 'choice green', that is, needing to be taken into a greenhouse during winter. This should not be necessary in Mediterranean climate regions.

Propagation is easy; just use short side-slips with a small heel attached, pulling them gently down and away from the parent plant. Dipped in rooting hormone and dibbled individually round the rim of a pot filled with free-draining potting mix, placed in a well-lit situation sheltered from full sun, and watered weekly, the cuttings will root in a matter of a month or so. The best time is just after new growth has hardened up, when the tip growth is no longer sappy and soft. An even easier method is to let the fruit-eating birds do it for you. Self-sown seedlings will appear here and there and can be dug and planted where they are wanted.

To raise new plants from seed, soak the fruits and mash the pulp, allow to ferment, rinse and strain through a fine sieve. Sow the seeds in a conventional potting mix, administer the usual attentions and wait. Seedlings will appear between two and six months depending on when they were sown.

Where fungal diseases are killing off box hedging, myrtle may well provide a suitable replacement, as long as winters are not too cold, wet and frosty.

Olea europaea
Olive

In the true Mediterranean I was amazed to see the size of ancient olive trees being rescued from old groves and derelict sites by nurserymen who make a fortune from retailing these venerable beauties to landscapers on superior new real estate developments. Such is the intensity of competition for these living sculptures that suppliers pay scouts to keep an eye open for suitable trees and to keep sources to themselves – yet I was equally amazed at the general lack of imagination shown by Mediterranean garden makers where olive trees are concerned.

An olive tree is an olive tree is an olive tree, to paraphrase a well-known circular poem by Gertrude Stein. It is used as a metaphor for almost everything – peace, victory, healing, productivity, utility, hope, renewal, longevity, heroism, betrayal, resignation, acceptance – and yet to Greek, Italian and Spanish gardeners it remains just what it always has been – a tree. An olive tree, a thing that produces table fruits and oil. A thing that is grown in a set way. A thing with a set image. A thing that does not change from one generation to the next. It is, in fact, a concept that has been developed over millennia. To speak in terms outside this comprehension of this most Mediterranean of Mediterranean things is almost heresy.

Since the 1840s, however, olives have been planted in the environs of the Adelaide Plains not far from where I live. They have been planted as groves to be harvested for oil production and to a lesser extent for table fruit but, more significantly, they have always had another purpose, being used for making tall, thick boundary hedges. In all the oldest suburbs of

Olive hedges were a common feature of colonial-period gardens in Australia but are under-utilised today as an effective and drought-hardy barrier. That's a fact that needs revisiting by creative Mediterranean gardeners everywhere.

Adelaide, those developed from the original colonial estates around the first site of settlement, ancient olive hedges remain as relics. They are treasured, well tended and afforded the care of tree surgeons, arborists and expert hedgers. From serving a utilitarian purpose they are now highly sought-after landscape features and the subject of conservation orders. Speaking of this way of using olives in gardens to European audiences was scarcely credited as a real possibility. Surely it was my fantasy? Jobbing gardeners in southern Europe would never, ever take such a planting seriously. It just couldn't work. Such a waste of a productive tree!

A different but equally frivolous or scandalous use for an olive tree would be to turn it into a giant topiary cylinder, as has been done with a tall pair on the 'Filoli' estate at Woodside in California. This would seem inconceivable to European minds and eyes. Yet it has been done and looks stunning; an idea that could be transposed to other monumental shapes, or to make an ever-grey hedge on stilts.

If there is a problem with olives as garden plants it must surely be their numerous black fruits, which when they fall stain paving and clothes alike, not to mention the several weeks taken up sweeping, raking and carrying them away. Less messy but perhaps more troublesome is the hayfever-inducing pollen which is generously broadcast in late winter when the trees flower. In California at least these problems have been partly overcome by clones selected because they do not produce fruit, or produce very little pollen. 'Swan Hill' is often cited as a cultivar that produces very little pollen and is therefore desirable where the risk of allergenic reactions is a challenge to the designer. Three non-fruiting olives are listed by Bob Perry – 'Fruitless', 'Little Ollie' and 'Majestic Beauty'* – but how widespread their distribution may be is unknown to me. Given the advantages these, or any other non-fruiting sorts, would have for landscapers it would be surprising if they were not slowly making their way into global distribution. Otherwise spraying the trees at fruit-set with an inhibitor may be possible where commercial-industrial agricultural sprays are available to home gardeners.

*Bob Perry, *Landscape Plants for Western Regions*, Land Design Publishers, Claremont, California, 1992. ISBN 0-9605988-3-9

Carissa grandiflora
Natal Plum

Here is a plant to scare the living daylights out of some folks. It has large strong thorns; double trouble since they are usually forked. But why would anyone focus on just that feature? After all roses have pretty nasty thorns and no-one worries too much about that. It certainly hasn't made any serious impact on the popularity of roses as garden plants. But it seems as well to get the bothersome bit out of the way before getting down to the attractions of this hardy shrub from northern India.

Confusing commercial names aside, *Carissa grandiflora* makes a splendid evergreen barrier and compact hedge. 'Green Carpet' is but one selection well suited to hedging or making into a broad groundcover to 1 m (3 ft) high.

Its biggest attraction by far is that it is tough and tolerant of a wide range of conditions. As far as Mediterranean climates are concerned it will grow almost anywhere. The better the conditions the better shape the plant will be in but even in the usual summer regime it will stay fresh and green without additional watering. That's a big plus when we are trying to set up gardens based on drought-tolerant plants into which we may insert a few areas where plants dependent on supplementary irrigation can be cultivated. As background greenery *Carissa grandiflora* is reliable, a pleasant shade of rich green and adaptable. Just what is needed.

Besides, to its generally useful characteristics can be added delightful white flowers of a good size that are carried almost year round, especially in warm and protected locations. These are pleasantly scented and the perfume carries well. The flowers are followed by fruits: red, succulent, plum-like and recorded as edible – if your fancy runs to relatively tasteless, wet flesh. No doubt a handy thing to come across in the dry gullies of northern India while on frontier patrol but not the sort of thing you'd serve up after a polo match. No doubt those so determined will be able to make them into jam or chutney!

For the purpose of giving structure to a garden the Natal Plum is very obliging. It grows almost anywhere, responds well to trimming and pruning, comes back strongly when cut hard and stays fresh even after months of summer heat and drought. So where structure that has height, bulk and mass is called for, *Carissa grandiflora* is a good candidate. No unsightly brown patches, no die-back, no sudden collapses – it just goes on and on for a century and longer. Recorded in habitat as a tree to 5 m (17 ft) or so, it can be relied on to achieve that height under cultivation – even without extra water during summer. So where cypress hedges need replacing this may be a better choice, and where new high hedges are called for it can be considered before the usual coniferous offerings. It is not as fine textured as the conifers but it doesn't die back embarrassingly either. It has rounded to elliptical leaves, plain and of a solid dark green. It bears no resemblance to yew but for its dark colouration, which if the plants are not starved will be maintained year round. In very cold weather the leaves can turn yellow and may be very briefly deciduous. The comparatively coarse foliage and free-breaking new growth mean that unlike coniferous hedges it can be maintained with basic equipment and a low level of expertise. There's no risk of it being cut back beyond the hope of recovery. And any damage will be quickly repaired by strong new growth. As a general rule *Carissa grandiflora* needs shearing once a year after the flush of early summer growth. Pruning more frequently will keep the lines sharper but where a little allowance can be made for a degree of shagginess the extra effort can be avoided without harm.

Even more useful in today's smaller gardens are the dwarf forms. These get around under a variety of rather dubious cultivar names that seem to change every time the plants appear on the market, but it is my suspicion that they are all the same thing: *Carissa grandiflora* 'Nana'. Names like 'Green Carpet', 'Emerald Carpet', 'Green Dwarf' and so on seem to denote no significant difference other than the creative source that named them for the marketplace. All are low growing with branches that tend to be prostrate and spreading. Growth is dense and coverage is excellent so a few plants will cover quite a good-sized space. These forms really recommend themselves for creating low hedges and plats. Their solidity shows up strongly and the dark foliage makes a terrific foil for terracotta sculptures or flower displays.

Acokanthera oblongifolia
Wintersweet

An African tree often found lurking in the background of old gardens as a massive, bushy small tree with many trunks. Tell-tale characteristics are plain, lance-shaped, tough leathery leaves, dull on the surface and coloured in muted shades of purple-red-brown, and small fig-like fruits coloured pretty much the same. In the warm months a succession of sweetly scented white flowers is produced, spread evenly over the canopy.

All parts of the tree are inedible, exuding a sticky white sap. The poisonous qualities of the plant should not be ignored but neither should they be overstated; there is a risk, however. Animals seem instinctively to know not to eat it, and none of it is in the least attractive in the sense of saying 'Eat me' to passing humans.

With a degree of hardiness that would have to rate equally with oleander, *Acokanthera oblongifolia* once found much use as a tall hedging plant for garden perimeters and as a screening plant suited to shrubberies. These old-fashioned uses are worth revisiting now that water-wise gardening is a major concern. Where only five years ago such a plant was considered so outdated as to be beyond the pale, it is now finding employment in areas that receive minimal or no watering. In car-parking areas and around service yards at shopping centres where screening and greening are required, and where virtually no maintenance programme is allowed for in the budget, *Acokanthera oblongifolia* and other care-free plants have been revived as supporting stars to the inevitable Canary Island palms, Cocos palms, cycads, lantanas and gazanias.

A companion plant just as durable and versatile is *Duranta repens*, another small tree from Africa that appears virtually insignificant alongside more fashionable, water-dependent plants, and yet has fine qualities – not the least of which is its toughness and adaptability. Like the akocanthera, durantas can be cut as a hedge, allowed to grow freely as a small tree with many trunks and ground-sweeping canopy, trained as a large standard, or limbed up to reveal the structure of the supporting trunks and larger branches. *Duranta repens* is available in a least three colour forms – plain pale blue flowers, the usual sort; deep blue with a paler edge that creates a starry appearance, and pure white. These are carried in long drooping panicles and later develop into small, round, orange berries. All three forms have small, light green leaves, and no record of being the least bit harmful in any of their parts.

Finding a use for the acokanthera is not so hard given that it has coloured foliage and sweetly scented flowers. Clearly the coloured foliage is something to build on as a support to a more adventurous kind of garden design featuring one or some of the strong colours now available for painted outdoor surfaces, particularly walls. Its deep-toned foliage would assort well with bold Tuscan reds and faded brick colours, or set off nicely the burnt oranges and rusty reds found in some new Mexican architecture. The purple-red-brown of the acokanthera would be a good foil to any colours in this range, even the purple-reds, pinks, lilacs and beetroot colours favoured by new wave designers from Montecito (Jack Lionel Warner) to Morocco (Lippani et Naldi). Bold colours such as these will swamp delicate touches and gentle features so, if

you've an eye for the fantastic make the most of them with equally bold plants and garden furnishings such as pots.

Acokanthera is best cut simply into solid shapes based on squares, ovals or circles. Its foliage is too large to be convincingly snipped into anything complex or detailed. Imagine, if you will, a simple large block of deep purple-brown foliage standing behind a sculptural cactus such as *Opuntia robusta*, with its huge circular silver-grey leaf pads, the uppermost pads rimmed with bright purple-red fruits the size of hens' eggs. Well on the way to a piece of living conceptual art! Add what you will, in a minimalist sort of way, to complete the picture. With a plant so versatile the picture could be completely reworked from time to time, giving opportunities to explore the joys of collectivism, the jollity of naivety, the sophistication of Classicism – all depending on what items are assembled with the acokanthera to give a brand new take.

In bringing *Acokanthera oblongifolia* to attention

There's no need to be afraid of Modernism in Mediterranean style gardens – it just needs to be done with panache and carried through. No half measures allowed. Bright colours, clean shapes, hardy plants and bingo: planting pizzazz.

I mean to acknowledge the value that truly tough plants have for Mediterranean gardeners everywhere. Its value, along with others like it, has been downplayed for too long.

Juniperus horizontalis

From a large tribe of very variable conifers *Juniperus horizontalis* is selected as a representative of the numerous prostrate forms available and adaptable, more or less, to difficult situations including exposed coastlines. Most are slow to get going but eventually make excellent dense groundcovering mats of glaucous leaves that range in colour from greyish green to intense shades of silver-blue. In climates cooler and wetter than Mediterranean regions the junipers are generally extremely accommodating as to soils and rainfall, but in Mediterranean settings they may need some supplementary watering to stimulate growth at a satisfactory rate and to maintain them in acceptable condition, especially where they are being relied on for some important front-row role. This is especially so in situations where soils are shallow and rocky, where their roots cannot penetrate deep into moisture-bearing sands or substrata.

Juniperus horizontalis is a North American species that has proliferated into dozens of named cultivars over the years. A good many of them tend to be grey-blue selections such as 'Bar Harbor', 'Douglasii', 'Glauca', 'Lividus' and 'Wiltonii' – all pretty enough and reasonably hardy. There are almost as many silver-blues from other countries – *Juniperus squamata* 'Meyerii', *J. virginiana* 'Silver Spreader', *J. sabina* 'Blue Danube', *J. procumbens*, *J.* x *media* 'Pfitzeriana Glauca', to name but a few long-established cultivars. The main attractions of all of them are their low growth habit, silvery blue foliage and reasonable degree of hardiness and drought tolerance. Although often touted as great plants for the seashore, care must be taken in their placement as they are not well adapted to strong, continuous onshore winds bringing salt spray.

Selection might be restricted to what can be found locally, the number of cultivars being so large that even the most dedicated specialist would be hard-pressed to justify listing all of them in a catalogue. That being so, choose just one and plant in bulk to achieve a dense

groundcover. Conifers such as junipers, some *Chamaecyparis* and a few prostrate dwarf pines form virtually weedproof mats once they are well established. The pines and junipers are the most hardy kinds, especially in relation to drought.

Siting these prostrate plants is not so much a problem as choosing the best form for the particular situation. Heights vary from 15 cm (6 in) or less to more than 1 m (3 ft). Typically, prostrate conifers are selected for duty on low banks and cuttings, especially alongside driveways, or in excavated areas not immediately obvious as prime garden locations but nonetheless sufficiently important to warrant careful plant selection and placement, or to highlight ground contours or emphasise sudden small changes of level. More formal treatments, of course, are possible, where conifers other than true pines (*Pinus* spp.) will adapt quite well. The trick is to trim regularly so that it is never necessary to cut hard back into older wood where there are no evident growth points. Conifers cannot be relied on to come back from such savage treatment; some will shoot away happily, others may shoot away and then dwindle, others won't do it at all. So don't risk it.

Earlier in this chapter I described how saltbush (*Atriplex* and *Rhagodia* spp.) and artemisias of various kinds could be utilised to make a plat garden with flat or sloping or wavy planes against which other garden features could be displayed, or to complement an overall design idea. In conditions colder but less

Early settlers in South Africa and Australia utilised the Carob, *Ceratonia siliqua*, as a stockfeed-cum-ornamental. It found use as hedges, shelter and street trees, examples of which still survive – models to be copied by modern garden designers and makers.

Ceratonia siliqua is an adaptable plant. Colonial examples demonstrate its effective use as a hedge. It remains to use it to create stilt hedges so beloved in English gardens.

Ceratonia siliqua
Carob, St John's Bread

About 50 kilometres (30 miles) inland from where I live, in the rainshadow of the Mt Lofty Ranges, is a small town whose main street runs gently downhill following the gradient from the ranges behind to the gorge cut by the Murray River some 30 kilometres (18 miles) or so further distant. Settled by colonists from Germany, the town is neat as a new pin and laid out along either side of the single main street – a tradition carried here from the Old Country. At the best of times the town is surrounded by rolling fields of wheat but for eight months or so of the year the entire landscape is dry and sere, pale yellow and sandy red. From ploughing to harvest and harrowing the town is coated with a fine layer of dust. Through all this the main street is lined with deep green trees; trees that are impervious to dust and heat, unfazed by the annual six-month 'dry' and equally undaunted by the ungiving limestone soil; trees that have stood sentinel for almost a hundred years and give no sign of not going on for at least another hundred, although at the outskirts of town a grove of olives looks as though it might give up the ghost one of these summers. The street trees are the glory of the town; a source of civic identity and the key element in the communal landscape, anchoring the town to a sense of place by shared history, shared hardship and shared celebration. They are *Ceratonia siliqua*, the Carob.

In other German towns in the Barossa Valley the Carob finds a strong role as a street tree, and also as a hedging plant and a subject for Teutonic topiary, trimmed in forms that are simple and pragmatic, leavened with simple spirals or chunky geometric shapes, the very essence of solidity.

And yet, where modern home owners struggle to grow weeping cherries, magnolias, Japanese maples and other ephemera, these hardy doers are eschewed to the point where the only regular supplier of carob trees plies his trade over 800 kilometres (500 miles) away, south of Melbourne! To reverse the cultural cringe against the carob would be a marvellous thing. If it were once again taken up, the form and colour of the tree would be a strong visual and unifying link in the region, joining the endless panorama of vineyards and the ancient River Red Gum, *Eucalyptus camaldulensis*, as the signature plants of the region.

harsh than those tolerated by saltbush and the like, conifers could be used for much the same purpose, being perhaps be a better choice away from the coast, or in places where frost is a known regular factor. The conifers also lend themselves by association to garden designs that want to suggest a link to Oriental themes. Without slavishly making an outright copy of some Japanese or Chinese garden, conifers can pick up and enrich the connection without pretending the garden is something it isn't. It could be something as simple as a single item like a stone garden lantern or a dipping stone that sets the idea. Imagination doesn't really need all the paraphernalia of bronze cranes, koi carp, clacking watersources, millwheel stepping stones, red lacquer bridges and bamboo fencing to make a garden a strike zone for the association of ideas and feelings.

Carob is found distributed over a wide range in southern Europe and the Middle East. It thrives in relatively warm and dry climates, though it can withstand some frost and periods of cold. Its other common name, St John's Bread, is a reference to its supposed role feeding John the Baptist when he was lost in the wilderness. The beans of the tree are held to be valuable as cattle fodder in hard times but they are also edible for humans, being used to make a chocolate substitute for chocophobes and health nuts.

In all the grand landscapes now being laid out in the Barossa Valley and other wine-growing areas as wineries endeavour to Frenchify their appearance – featuring rose gardens, allées of plane trees, terrace bistros and the like – I find it a great shame that little thought is given by owners and designers to the traditions of the region. Do they go around with their eyes shut? Old-established properties have magnificent carob hedges that funnel tourist traffic from roadways to cellar door areas while maintaining the strictest privacy for the owner's family in the adjacent homestead. There is no need for signage, no need for high walls, no need for security personnel – the immaculate hedges block each sector of the property from the other. It is curious that designers seem not to observe patterns of human behaviour either. At any winery blessed with high carob hedges, or even a plantation of standard carobs, guess where all the cars will be parked? In their deep, deep shade of course. So why persist with flimsy, water-hungry trees?

A very long-lived tree, *Ceratonia siliqua* will attain 10–15 m (35–50 ft) in height after about 50 years, depending on the hardships it may have to endure. It is broad domed, evergreen, rather greyish overall, with reddish stems and smooth dark bark. It produces sickly sweet, tiny yellowish flowers in spring which in turn produce long, slightly twisted pods that contain a dozen or so beans.

Attractive companion trees are *Dais cotinifolia*, *Bauhinia variegata* and *Cercis siliqua* (Judas Tree), though only the Judas Tree comes near the carob for extreme drought tolerance.

Coprosma 'Black Cloud' is a mat-forming kind of Mirror Plant that makes an excellent and colourful groundcover that may also serve to retard wildfire, so long as it is maintained weed free and cleared of blown-in garden debris before the fire season starts.

Coprosma x 'Black Cloud'

This relatively new introduction is a prostrate hybrid form of New Zealand's Mirror Bush, *Coprosma repens*. As tough in hard conditions as its larger kin, 'Black Cloud' is a dark-leaved beauty that merits wider attention. Described, obviously, as having black foliage, this mat-forming plant makes a solid contribution to bold colour schemes that integrate brown, bronze, orange, apricot, cream, silver and clear reds. Clearly not an idea to be considered by the faint-hearted but one that wears well under a blazing summer sun. This kind of exoticism is only at home away from cloudy skies and cool weather.

'Black Cloud' is more accurately described as dark

Like all this clan, *Coprosma* 'Walter Brockie' comes from New Zealand where it has been selected for its upright habit and marvellous colour, particularly in winter. The reflective leaves are best displayed where they can catch the sunlight and add sparkle from the play of light.

brown with some greenish hints, especially when light levels are low during winter or in shaded situations. To keep the colour strong, plant it where it will receive direct, bright sunlight. As to soil it is not particular, as long as it is not waterlogged and drainage is good. While tolerant of dry conditions, achieving a good balance between rate of growth and strength of colour is a matter of how much water the plant receives during the year. In areas where winter rains are the norm 'Black Cloud' should produce good results without additional irrigation. Newly set young plants may need some extra water to get established over the first summer. Lush, soft growth is not an objective here so go with minimal fertilising. Indeed, plants should get sufficient

nutrients for adequate growth from decomposing mulch; nothing further should be needed. Growth rates will be relatively slow but the plants will be sturdier, better coloured and better able to withstand drought and summer heat.

Treating 'Black Cloud' as a plat is a simple matter of trimming its naturally low spreading growth. Most often this needs to be done only once a year, after the flush of growth in late spring. Fastidious gardeners can snip and nip more frequently to maintain the sharpness of the image. Taller than 'Black Cloud' and brown rather than black is *Coprosma* x 'Walter Brockie'. This has been around for quite a while now and is well distributed through nurseries and garden shops. It will grow 2 m (7 ft) or taller if left unpruned, but does get rather leggy. Since it responds well to cutting back it can be kept much lower than that – 50 cm (20 in) would be fine. Between these two coprosmas a stage on two levels could be grown, offering a terrific opportunity for some easy theatrical effects. Imagine a checkerboard made up from the two forms, perhaps all on one level, or the two colours set at different levels. Pretty ordinary stuff? See what happens when this idea is taken as the foundation for a show of large terracotta pots, plinths hidden by the plats, overflowing with succulents – or left empty. Or try highly decorated pots, embossed with swags of leaves and fruit, coats of arms or masks. The selection of succulents could be wide-ranging and folksy, or single-minded and restrained. Consider the likes of *Crassula coccinea* 'Flame', *Echeveria multicaulis*, *Kalanchoe longiflora* subsp. *coccinea*, *K. thyrsifolia* 'Bronze Sculpture', *Sedum* x *rubrotinctum*, *S. nussbaumeranum* and *Pachyphytum kinmachi.** To turn the idea into something altogether more formal, limit the planting to single rosettes of one of the more stately solitary agaves such as *Agave victoriae-reginae*, *A. stricta* or *A. guadalajarana*.

As a broad groundcover *Coprosma* x 'Black Cloud' is perhaps less demanding than some of the flowering groundcovers often chosen on impulse when in bloom. These things are, of course, meant to sell themselves on the basis of their pretty colours. The downside of this is that flowers die and shrivel and turn brown and stay there. Their scrappy remains admonish the harried gardener every time they are passed. Calling out to be dead-headed and cut down, they join the ranks of spent agapanthus, finished red-hot pokers, dead

51

daisies until they can't be left any longer. If beginning or completing that task is not a high priority then maybe it is better to go for something that doesn't require that level of maintenance. This is where the coprosma comes into its own; it doesn't produce flowers. (In truth it does but they are stemless, insignificant and well hidden in the leaf axils.)

*For these and others see Yvonne Cave, *Succulents for the Contemporary Garden*, Florilegium, Sydney, 2002. ISBN 1876314176

Agave guardalajarana is a relative newcomer to gardens. Its strong form and rich green leaf colour set off by dark brown spines immediately mark it as an excellent accent plant well suited to being grown in tubs, or in the open garden.

Agave guardalajarana is a relative newcomer to gardens. Its strong form and rich green leaf colour set off by dark brown spines immediately mark it as an excellent accent plant well suited to being grown in tubs, or in the open garden.

4 Useful too ...

In this chapter I include a selection of trees both productive and interesting, some traditional and some novel, that may find a place in Mediterranean climate gardens and orchards. By and large these trees require minimal supplementary irrigation through dry seasons. This should not be taken as indicating that they can be neglected; good mulching practices, careful feeding and basic tree care are necessary to keep these large plants healthy, vigorous and fruitful.

Sharp minded readers will notice that there are entries here for some plants already mentioned in other chapters. Is this repetitious? Have I lost the plot? No. I have included the olive, carob, pomegranate and Natal plum in the previous chapters where their decorative qualities and hardiness make them useful plants for flower gardens and landscapes. Here the same plants are included for their usefulness. In some cases different cultivars are recommended, as is the case with olives; here the cultivars listed are included because of the various qualities of their fruits; previously they were listed for their decorative charms, however simple.

Those fortunate enough to be travelling through southern Europe for the first time will no doubt recognise these useful plants as familiar migrants to other Mediterranean climate areas on the other side of the world; what does not become immediately apparent is that in Europe these plants are seen strictly as utilitarian agricultural crops. Gardening friends in Athens were taken aback when I suggested that hedged wild olive would be as effective as yew in creating a garden division along the lines of those favoured in cooler, wetter England and northern France. Relating to them how carob is trained as a standard street tree produced looks of astonishment and disbelief. The lesson to be learned from this is that traditional uses and attitudes towards familiar plants should not blind us from realising how they may also find other uses as decorative plants in Mediterranean gardens.

By no means an exotic collection, this list could be extended to include a good many that are, however, marginal without due care and the utilisation of microclimates. Where the production of a variety of fruits is a prime consideration for the gardener, thought will need to be given to how the remaining garden areas can be developed without recourse to additional watering in summer. It is a matter of swings and roundabouts: the amount of extra water that is spent on the orchard, rose garden or vegie patch has to be saved elsewhere in the garden.

Unusual varieties will most often be found in the lists and stocks of specialist fruit tree growers and it is to these worthy folk that gardeners should turn to make sure they get the kinds they want. Order early to ensure timely delivery, and seek advice from experienced growers so that you meet all possible requirements for ultimate success.

Olea europaea
Olive

The Olive is the definitive plant of the Mediterranean region; the limits to its cultivation, the deserts on the southern shores and the mountains of the northern shores, in effect define the limits of the climate type.

The good qualities of the tree are numerous, ranging from its wonderful oil, delicious fruit and fine, hard, close-grained timber to the usefulness of its waste products as fuel, animal food, fertiliser and soil improver. Over the last 3000 years or so a huge variety of types has been selected that produce fruits (drupes in fact) with high oil content, or have good pickling and preserving qualities, as well as types that are cold tolerant, heat tolerant, early and late croppers, heavy croppers and just good all-round plants. Most horticultural and agricultural research and teaching institutions maintain sizeable collections of these varieties as a gene pool for future study and breeding. Many varieties have fascinating names and histories, but especially in post-colonial places such as Australia, Argentina and California the majority of olives grown are restricted to a very few comparatively modern varieties.

Feral trees and old colonial survivors will find their enthusiasts – who could resist 'Petite de Nicoise', 'Buckland Park Estate', 'California Mission' or 'Old Adelaide Gaol'? Most home gardeners, however, will be looking for something more than a charming name and will turn to commercial growers and commonplace cultivars.

Recommending named varieties is a bit risky as the recent boom in developing commercial olive groves has resulted in a great deal of inaccurately named material being propagated and sold. Buying from a grower who guarantees his stock true to name, and is a member of a professional olive producers' organisation, should ensure that you get what you pay for. So what would you buy? With new varieties being introduced every year it may be best to leave the latest registered and patent-protected kinds to commercial growers and concentrate on more reasonably priced and time-tested sorts. Two trees would be adequate for gardeners wanting to grow olives for the table while four or six would produce enough fruit for a modest amount of oil once they mature. Multi-purpose varieties would serve well enough but there seems little point in them when special purpose varieties can so easily provide exactly the right qualities.

Table varieties are those that produce large, fleshy fruits – at least according to current marketers – so the likes of 'Nychatiof Kalamata', 'Hardy's Mammoth', 'Jumbo Kalamata' and 'Colossus' are probably appropriate. For oil production choice can be more varied and emphasis laid on early, mid-season or late croppers, especially where modern mobile presses can be called on to process small harvests on site. 'Frantoio', 'Verdale' and some of the newer Israeli-bred varieties such as 'Barnea' may be better as oil varieties but it pays to ask around and take the benefit of local experience. 'Swan Hill' is a new sterile variety.

Like all fruit trees olives need some shaping and pruning. Too tall a tree makes harvesting risky and hard work; too much old wood reduces productivity and the free admission of light and breezes to the heart of the tree. Observation of commercial groves gives few clues to successful home garden cultivation as groves are managed to accommodate harvesting machinery. Best look to local immigrant gardens to see how trees can be managed. As a general rule the trees are kept fairly low, ladder height, and open in the centre in the shape of a wine glass. Fruits are produced in heaviest numbers on growth that is 3–5 years old, after which productivity tends to decline. Since olives break freely into new growth when pruned it is relatively easy to cut out older wood and thus maintain a balance. Despite their reputation for extreme hardiness olives do benefit from fertilising in winter after the crop has been taken off, when any pruning required is also done. Irrigation in the early years is also beneficial.

Punica granata
Pomegranate

The pomegranate is a very ancient fruit carrying immense symbolism in many Mediterranean cultures, particularly in relation to fecundity, prosperity and general proliferation. The prodigality with which it fruits and the quantity of seedy pips encased in sweet pulp in each fruit has given it prominence as a semi-wild harvested crop since ancient times. Interestingly, at least to garden historians, the pomegranate has a history approximately as long in China as in the Middle East and the Mediterranean.

Several forms of pomegranate in cultivation have been selected on the basis of fruit superior to the common variety. These originated in the former Soviet

Union and are worth searching out as their fruits are larger, more distinctly flavoured and more juicy. 'Rosaveya', 'Azerbaijani', 'Velez' and 'Horses Tooth' (all white flesh) are among those available in Western countries. 'Dura', from northern India, has sharp, almost bitter flesh that is very significant in the local cuisine. Those in general commerce are grown for their flowers – double red, double creamy white and a red double with a picotee edging of creamy white ('Madame Legrelle') – or for the novelty of a dwarf form. The double-flowering variants do not produce fruit. The dwarf form does, but the fruit's small size makes skinning it a tiresome task for the resultant quantity of flesh and seeds. There may be other selected fruiting varieties in countries such as Turkey where the fruit plays a significant role in the cuisine but it seems unlikely that these have been introduced elsewhere. Aside from eating the fleshy seeds fresh, they are also made into a syrup for cooking, and a liqueur called grenadine which is added to sparkling or still white wine, in much the same manner as blackcurrant or raspberry liqueur is to make kir.

Pomegranates are hardy trees that with a minimum of care can add a significant element of productivity and beauty to a garden. Even if the fruits go only to feeding wild birds they do so with distinction at a season, late autumn and early winter, when bird food is not freely available. In those places where Indian summers are common the fruits hanging on the defoliating trees take on jewel-like qualities as the bright enamelled-red skins glow in the sunlight.

Having a somewhat limited use in cookery most gardens need no more than one tree to meet domestic needs, and even then enthusiasm for the curious fruits tends to wane after the novelty has worn off. But then children find endless uses for them as bowling balls and other imaginary objects.

Mature plants respond well to heavy pruning and can easily be trained as hedges. This tends to limit fruit production but maybe that is not such a huge disincentive.

Ziziphus jujuba
Jujube

The Jujube is a small tree from the warmer parts of

The Jujube tree has an ancient history of cultivation beginning in China more than a thousand years ago and still growing strong. Also known as the Chinese Date, *Zizyphus jujube*, is best known for its candied fruits. Though slow growing it makes a good garden tree with few requirements for maintenance other than shaping. Photo courtesy Bill Macaboy

Mediterranean region. It is deciduous and each leaf node bears a pair of thin, sharp spines for armament. It is not immediately thought of as a fruit of the first order, for its relatively small succulent fruits do not transport easily and have a leatheriness of skin that ensures they do not find a place on supermarket shelves. Thus it is relegated to cultivation in home gardens by those who appreciate its sweet, juicy fruits, especially when they are candied by stewing in a heavy sugar syrup.

Given its hardiness and ease of culture it could even be thought of as having weed potential, although its early introduction to both California and Australia by enthusiastic acclimatisers keen to discover new crops and develop new markets seems so far not to have resulted in problems. David Fairchild is scarcely remembered today but in the early years of the twentieth century this very significant plant hunter was employed by the US Department of Agriculture to scour the globe for crop plants that would be useful in the USA. His four fascinating books describe his years of sailing, trekking and pony riding in far-flung Asian provinces, South and Central American outposts, across the wilds of Africa and through the Middle East, and to Polynesia, Australia and New Zealand. The jujube was one of many exotic fruits he introduced to Florida and California, where he reported it as developing into a flourishing new agricultural industry. Did it survive American involvement in World War II? Sometimes it seems a shame that oranges, grapefruits and lemons won out for we are missing out on a greater variety of tastes and textures.

Maybe, like the date groves of Coachella Valley in California and Marree in South Australia, there will be a revival of the jujube as determined growers rejuvenate old plantations and develop market niches for gourmet foods and exclusive, luxury export crops.

More than any other influence it is the time taken for exotics to become thoroughly absorbed into local cuisine that marks the rise, fall and rise again in favour of such fruity gems as the babaco, the tamarillo, the Chinese gooseberry (kiwi fruit), the date and maybe yet the jujube.

The trees are easy to establish on any soil of reasonable structure and composition and are reported by Fairchild as fruiting in eighteen months on grafted varieties; he doesn't say what the trees were grafted onto but since his plants came from collections made on his behalf by Frank Meyer in Chinese orchards it seems likely that wild seedlings were used as hosts. Meyer, another latter-day American plant hunter, introduced the Meyer lemon to the West, a dwarf variety he found growing in Beijing that is cold tolerant, thin skinned and sweet. Jujube trees are prone to suckering and need to be managed so that this tendency is well controlled; they are drought tolerant and can be cultivated in large tubs, though this greatly reduces their productivity.

We can only wonder how the jujube from the shores of the Mediterranean made its way to China; most likely seeds were carried there as a dried or semi-dried food along the Silk Road following the establishment of the spice trade in Greek and Roman times.

To enjoy jujubes it may be necessary to wait for a year or two for trees to come into production, assuming that some enterprising rare fruit nursery can supply stocks. In the interim between planting and fruitfulness search out Chinese dates in Asian markets and specialty food shops, for they are one and the same thing. Candied and packed in loose blocks, they are a fine delicacy.

Citrus hystrix
Kaffir Lime

The Kaffir Lime, *Citrus hystrix*, is a red-hot favourite with foodies and keen cooks. Its unusual and distinctive leaf form is best appreciated close up. Like all citrus its dark green foliage is a foil for a wide variety of other colours. Thoughtful picking of leaves will keep the small tree compact.

A small tree, usually no more than 3.5 m (12 ft) tall and very bushy, resembling a shrub. It has short stiff spines along the stems, compact growth and leaves that are divided into segments. A native of the far south of China, Vietnam, Cambodia and Laos, the Kaffir Lime's leaves and juice are widely used as flavouring agents in the cuisines of those and surrounding countries. These flavours have entered the Carib cookery of the West Indies and the Fusion foodie cultures of the West that have adopted Pacific Rim styles to develop flavour combinations using new ingredients and new techniques.

Being a tropical to subtropical plant the Kaffir Lime is not usually cultivated in Mediterranean climates except in very favoured, frost-free locations where the soils are rich, friable and well watered. Even so it is a useful culinary plant and easily accommodated in a large pot or tub. The fruits are thick skinned and roughly corrugated but picked fresh and used immediately produce a sharp juice that adds to the sweet–sour contrast so often called for in Asian cookery. Incidentally the leaves can be frozen and used successfully later; a handy thing to know when growth slows in winter and it would be unwise to strip a tree of its foliage. When the tree is growing strongly it can be picked regularly for daily use or freezing but picking should cease when growth slows. Heavy watering and regular feeding will ensure growth is strong and leaf production is plentiful.

Tub-grown plants can be maintained in good growth for many years provided it is remembered that the tree needs a steady supply of fertiliser and a consistent degree of soil moisture year round. Obviously summer watering will be a concern for Mediterranean gardeners, as it is for any citrus tree. Every three to five years the potted trees will need root pruning to maintain vigour. By removing the plant from its container 5 cm (2 in) or so of roots and soil can be carefully shaved off the outside of the root ball. The plant can then be returned to its pot and carefully packed in with fresh potting mix. Give the whole lot a thorough dousing with water to eliminate air holes in the soil mix and to settle it close around the roots. Resist the temptation to tamp, bang or pound the soil around the exposed roots; it will cause too much damage. Do this maintenance task at the end of spring as the weather turns warm and sunny. A light dose of foliar fertiliser could be applied to stimulate new root and top growth.

By far the biggest pests are scale, sooty mould and aphis – all associated with the activities of ants. At the outset the drainage hole of any container intended for citrus should be screened against ants by coving it with fine bronze or stainless steel flywire. This must be checked every time the root ball is pruned. An ant powder will also help control the ant farmers and prevent them from carrying their 'milk' aphis and scale onto the trees. Other preventives, such as oil-based sprays and systemic pesticides, can be used as necessary but always with caution.

It is from the Kaffir Lime that the thin-skinned Tahitian and Caribbean limes (*Citrus* x *aurantifolia*) have been developed. Only the fruits of these are used, for juicing, the leaves being poorly flavoured and coarse in texture.

I have been unable to discover the reason for the common name Kaffir Lime, though I could believe it has racist overtones associated with the slave trade and the sugar plantations of the West Indies.

Ceratonia siliqua
Carob

Limbing-up ancient shrubs can be a better alternative to removal and replanting. This century-old Carob, *Ceratonia siliqua*, has been carefully pruned to show off its wonderfully gnarled trunk.

A multi-purpose tree that has provided fodder for goats, sheep and donkeys for several thousand years at least; more recently its fruits have provided a substitute for both chocolate and coffee drinks and in post-colonial states it has also found utility as a hardy and stout hedging plant.

It is a plant which repulses the unknowing and fascinates those who understand just how useful it has been and is. More than that, the plant provides beauty in areas where not much else is capable of producing such a lush deep green. Of course it is common. It is found everywhere as a hoary hedge plant, or as pollarded street trees in dusty country towns. It stands solitary where farmsteads once stood; it is found in old mining towns around school yards and cemeteries; it is seen carved and clipped in old German settlements and in the towns settled by Italian, Greek, Spanish and French immigrants, but more recently it has found favour with a few garden designers working within the possibilities of climate and soil.

The only detraction, and it is a short-lived annoyance, is the rather sickly, cloying perfume given off by the inconspicuous flowers that appear in spring. Otherwise the carob is a thoroughly meritorious tree; drought tolerant and disease free, long-lived and providing good solid shade.

Although the carob has a reputation as a food

source for grazing animals this use seems to be limited to countries in the Old World. Touted in the nineteenth century as having great potential as fodder, especially in times of drought, it seems rarely to be used for that purpose today. The foliage as well as the long bean-like pods can be eaten. Health-conscious types have taken to powder of the dried carob bean as a fair substitute for coffee and chocolate and the evil stimulatory effects of caffeine. If mortar and pestle work are in your health-giving regime then harvesting a few kilos of carob beans from feral trees may be Nature's way of satisfying cravings for something sweet and rich without risking heart palpitations, blurred vision, heavy breathing and sweaty palms.

How may it find use in a modern Mediterranean garden? Like the olive this utilitarian plant has been overlooked by designers as a source of structure and height. It makes a wonderful hedge, tough, dense, green to the ground and able to break into new growth when cut hard to old wood, thus making rejuvenation relatively easy. It is also reliable in exposed and difficult situations and is particularly adaptable to coastal conditions where soils may be poor and very thin. As buttress hedging it is a great windbreak and can be grown as high as 4 m (14 ft) and still be maintained with compact, close-knit growth down to the ground.

It may also find more decorative uses. While it cannot be recommended for fine topiary work (its leaves are too coarse and its growth too vigorous), it can be clipped into simple cones, domes, balls or blocks, and grown into standards. And it could be trained as a hedge on stilts to magnificent effect; equal to linden trees and half the trouble, and suited to life in Mediterranean gardens.

More solid and upstanding in appearance than its graceful cousin the Date Palm (*Phoenix dactylifera*), the Canary Island Palm (*Phoenix canariensis*) is nonetheless an impressive, stately tree when well maintained and groomed.

Phoenix dactylifera
Date Palm

Thought to be native to the cradle of civilisation, the southern reaches of the Euphrates and Tigris rivers in what was called Mesopotamia before it became Iraq, the date palm is not really a tree at all but like the Ombu (*Phytolacca dioica*) of Uruguay has a cell structure more closely related to herbaceous plants. Since prehistoric times *Phoenix dactylifera* has been cultivated in Egypt and Palestine, and from there spread along the southern shore of the Mediterranean to Algeria, Tunisia and Morocco and then across into southern Spain with the Moors. More recently, in the 1900s, plantations were established in California and Arizona, and also in South Australia.

Groves established in Western countries have had a chequered career, partly because of the labour involved in fertilising the flowers of such tall trees, and partly because of the challenge of harvesting the fruits. These problems today appear to have been overcome but even so, does the date palm have a place in garden design, even of the large and self-sufficient sort? It seems such a doubtful proposition. Its simple form just goes up and up and up, and it doesn't cast a great deal of shade. Yet it does have a certain ruggedness about it. Dates are recognised residents of deserts and as such immediately set off a whole range of intellectual linkages, going from visions of camel trains and endless sand dunes to Moorish architecture and hookah pipes. A plant so rich in associations must offer designers something to work with. And so it does. Who could ever forget that astonishing park in Barcelona, composed simply of date palms planted on a squared grid and set in a few hectares of raked sand? It is so simple and so effective on both the aesthetic and practical levels. It looks wonderful, especially when the sun is shining and the trees cast a moving pattern of shadows onto the sand. Morning and afternoon, and at night, the space under the trees is thronged with residents from the surrounding apartment blocks playing volleyball, soccer, petanque, chess, dancing to music from boom boxes, chatting, dreaming, strolling, airing babies, courting and eating picnic meals. In the old Moorish quarter of Palma di Mallorca it is common to see the heads of ancient date palms rising above the rooftops of the houses, springing from central courtyards and soaring up three or four storeys, while on the promenade along the walls below the cathedral paired palms weave a sinuous line in concert with patterns in the cobbles and paving blocks.

So the examples exist and simply need building on wherever the trees will grow, and where mature specimens can be relocated from derelict groves and gardens. If the equally tall, heavyweight Canary Island Palm, *Phoenix canariensis*, can be handled by crane and backhoe, so can the lighter and more graceful date palm.

Dates can be propagated by seed but in the hope of eventually getting some of the luscious fruits it may be thought worthwhile obtaining named cultivars selected for the high quality of their fresh fruit. There are varieties known for their qualities as dried fruit as well as those whose fruit is soft or hard, sweet or dry and those with highly charged names such as 'Bridegroom's Fingers'. In the Arab states dates are thought of as a staple food, indeed one group is known as bread dates, but in Western countries they are universally thought of as dessert fruits, to be eaten with coffee and nuts at the end of a meal. Dessert varieties are sweet and semi-hard, and there are other soft dates that appear as solid blocks of compressed fruit. The two most often found on Western tables are 'Deglat Noor' ('Daughter of Light') and 'Medjool'

('The Unknown'), the most widely planted types in America and Australia. Offshoots from them may be available from specialist rare fruit tree growers.

Opuntia ficus-indica
Prickly Pear, Indian Fig, Tuna

Loved in southern Europe for its succulent fruits, the Prickly Pear, *Opuntia ficus-indica*, has a more sinister reputation in warmer subtropical climates where it became an invasive pest in the early twentieth century. Responsible gardeners can enjoy its form and fruits by exercising care to ensure there is no chance of an escape to the bush.

Gardeners new to Mediterranean conditions are often bemused to find the Prickly Pear planted in gardens and along roadsides in the vicinity. They may be even more surprised to find the prickly red, orange, yellow or purple fruits offered for sale in markets and fruiterers. And, no doubt, some will look askance and screw up their noses when they find them served up as an accompaniment. They need not be worried, the fruits are succulent, mildly flavoured and sweet.

The prickly pear has a long history as a fruit, and as a defensive hedge, in Mediterranean climate countries and into the subtropics and tropics, where some varieties were also cultivated as host plants for the cochineal bug from which the well-known red colouring agent was extracted. The fruiting kinds are so well established that it is no longer possible to determine from whence the plants originated; so widely spread since ancient times that they are virtually endemic in those climatic areas where they thrive.

Opuntia ficus-indica is not the only prickly pear that is edible. *Opuntia robusta* and *O. tuna* are also widely cultivated as a food source, while some other species have localised uses for making jammy fruit 'leathers' and long-lasting semi-dried sugary pastes. Many other species are edible but are generally looked on as inferior wild foods because the flesh tends to be dry, floury and flavourless.

Generally the appearance of these cultivated opuntias is similar. Each has flattened, circular, jointed leaf pads that are grey-green or grey, bearing more or fewer long spines and small clumps of fine spines that are particularly irritating if they get caught in the skin. *Opuntia robusta* is perhaps the most decorative of the lot as it has large, thick, circular, silver-grey pads, silken yellow flowers and wine-red fruits. It is well armed too!

The plants can attain considerable size as they mature, hence their use in some cultures as hedges. They can grow as large as small trees and when managed this way respond well to the removal of wayward and unwanted growth. Propagation is usually by whole leaf cuttings that are removed from the mother plant, left to dry for a week or so, then 'planted' by being barely sunk in the soil and rested against a short stick. Leaf pads potted in sand will also make roots readily and can be transplanted directly to their growing positions. Pests are few, mainly scale and mealy bug – both farmed by ants for their sugary body secretions and relatively easily controlled by controlling the ants. Opuntias are not fussy about soil as long as it is free draining and never waterlogged, indeed their preference is for dry soils though not so arid that the fruits end up small and dry.

Pitayas are the fruits of several species of night-flowering epiphytic *Selenicereus* cacti – the climbing kind. Photographed in a Peruvian market, these exotic rare fruits are now being grown more widely in Mediterranean climates as a luxury cash crop.

They must have an open position in full sun all day and can withstand light frosts once established. Heavy hail can turn the succulent pads to mush so where hail is a frequent occurrence prickly pears are not a viable garden choice.

There is a slight risk that prickly pears could become weedy garden escapees, so care should be exercised. The serious pest prickly pears are much less attractive varieties introduced to populate cochineal farms – they have cylindrical jointed pads or thin deep green pads with long, strong spines – but it would still pay to be careful.

Besides the fruits the flat leaf pads are used for Tex-Mex cooking in which they are cut in strips or cubes and fried, roasted or stewed as a base for the stronger flavours of chilli, garlic and other herbs and spices. The prepared leaf pads are called *nopales* and the cooked pieces *nopalitos*.

Around 2000 other fruiting cacti have been introduced as food accompaniments in the developed world. Several of the climbing, night-flowering *Selenicereus* cacti produce large purple or yellow fruits which appear from time to time in the boutiques of purveyors of superior fruit. The fruit is filled with a juicy white flesh and plenty of small black seeds.

Diospyros kaki
Persimmon

Ideally suited for small gardens in all Mediterranean regions but the driest zones, the Japanese Persimmon is both beautiful and productive. The tree itself is low crowned and spreading, with dusky brown smooth bark and large shiny green leaves. In autumn the leaves turn brilliant shades of reddish orange and gold and then the glowing globes of the orange fruits are exposed. Apart from shaping the trees need no pruning and are pretty much disease free. They do best in deep, rich, well-drained soils and benefit from an occasional drenching during summer when the fruits are swelling.

Old garden lore was that the fruits were bitterly astringent, and so they are in some varieties – 'Dai Dai Maru', 'Hachiya' and 'Nightingale' (seedless) – but there are also excellent non-astringent forms such as 'Fuyu'. The astringent kinds rely on frosty weather to 'blet' the fruit to a stage of almost rotten soft ripeness

now a less obvious choice since the fruits have become much more attractive as food for humans.

Fruits vary remarkably, some being small, flat-bottomed spheres while others are the shape of huge peaches with distinctly pointed ends. As a general rule the larger the fruit the fewer a tree will carry. The trees benefit from careful cultivation with attention being paid to soil fertility and the judicious application of irrigation as the fruits swell and ripen through summer and autumn. Fertilising and mulching with straw and animal manures will also be repaid by strong growth and good crops. The wood of persimmons is rather brittle so the trees need to be sited out of reach of prevailing winds and weather, or sheltered by surrounding wind-resistant trees. Left to its own devices a persimmon tree may become lopsided as overladen branches bend downward under the weight of fruit; subsequent new growth

Persimmon, *Diaspyros kaki*, makes a fine small tree for Mediterranean climate gardens where soils are loamy and well drained. Fruit, autumn foliage and graceful habit make it ideal for mixed planting, as in this combination with *Yucca gloriosa*.

at which point they are edible and very sweet. The non-astringent kinds are eaten when they are crisp and sweet. Dozens of both kinds have been introduced in recent years and have found a very receptive market. Older gardeners may once have planted persimmons with a view to enjoying the flaming autumn foliage and preferring to leave the fruits to the birds. This is

may well grow in compensatory directions as a counterbalance. This means that the gardener who wishes a more regular appearance, and a tree less prone to branches splitting or breaking, must prune to correct imbalances. Otherwise no special treatment need be followed apart from keeping birds away from the delectable fruit. Gas guns at 2 m (7 ft) may be the answer here for hungry birds can be very determined.

Where persimmons are successful it is well worth trying to grow Nashi too. These Japanese pears are crunchy and very juicy, sweetly pear flavoured and thin skinned. There are numerous green or yellow smooth-skinned kinds available, and also several with russet-brown skin. Varieties include 'Nijisseiki' and '20th Century'.

Ficus carica
Fig

It wouldn't be wise to omit the edible fig from this little summary of useful plants for Mediterranean gardens. It is so accommodating and thrifty it even manages to self-sow in paving cracks and seed pans. Often the last relic of an abandoned farm or village, mining camp or mission, it is too often dismissed as something so common it is beyond consideration by smart gardeners. Yet who is the first to drool over figs stuffed with gorgonzola, wrapped in pancetta and grilled? Who bemoans the difficulty of buying good figs and wails about the cost? These self-same chi-chi folk …

In Mediterranean climates figs are easily accommodated in most gardens except where frosts are frequent and hard. In such situations the trees can best be managed in a sheltered courtyard or against a sunny wall. Even so they are pretty easy-going unless the growing tips that produce the fruits are frosted and the formative fruits damaged. While figs will grow under very difficult circumstances they produce the most luscious and succulent fruits when they are well treated with a mulch of animal manure applied regularly and afforded some supplementary watering to swell the fruits. They can be pruned very hard and will break away from below the ground or from low down on the trunk. Left alone they will grow into large-spreading, low-crowned trees, probably too high for easy harvesting. Thoughtful trimming and pruning will bring them down to heights that are easily, and safely, accessed for picking.

Figs are deciduous and may even drop their leaves in extremely hot or dry weather but generally they are hardy and resilient, subject to very few diseases or pests, and tolerant of a wide range of growing conditions.

The fig is rarely looked at from a design point of view, yet each tree is a strong character in its own right, formed by the weather and the winds, gnarled by time and distinctively different in the manner in which branches are thrown against the sky or against the earth. It may be very surprising to pay close attention to the leaves. There is a remarkable diversity that never really strikes the casual observer until attention is drawn to their being broad and simple, or deeply divided into fat lobes or pudgy fingers. Seen alongside each other the contrasts become immediately apparent. Why had not this simple difference been observed before? How easily we can be deceived by our own unseeing eyes.

One fig is probably enough for any home garden so what is the choice to be made? Basically there are black figs, brown figs and green figs – sometimes over-optimistically described as 'white figs'. For truly luscious eating and an almost degenerate appearance the black figs are highly recommended. 'Black Ischia', 'Negro Largo' and 'Violette Seper' are among the best. For jam-making the brown and green kinds produce conserves that are a very appealing light brown in colour. 'Brown Turkey', 'Brunswick' and 'White Marseilles' are rich in sugar and flavour and make terrific jams with or without the addition of bitter almonds or ginger.

Carissa species
Natal Plum

There are at least three *Carissa* species that have found a use in Mediterranean gardens, especially those of the settlements made during the colonial era. Most often they are found as overblown survivors, boundary markers, hedges and windbreaks in and around old estates and farms. Typically the plants have small, round, deep green leaves, green young bark, huge long straight thorns, and small white starry flowers that are followed by plum-like fruits that ripen to bright red, deep plum or golden colours. The fruits are very juicy and refreshingly sweet, according to some enthusiasts for rare and subtropical fruits; others perhaps more discriminating are less charmed by them. Just maybe the best use of them might be in fermenting a kind of potent jungle juice from them, as certain tribes of baboons already know how to get drunk by gorging on them.

All these plum-like fruits grow on densely branched shrubs that are unfussy about soil but require well-drained conditions free from hard frosts. They are subtropical plants well adapted to a distinct hot, dry season in their Indian and East African homelands. Apart from occasional infestations of scale they appear to be relatively disease and pest free. The shrubby growth can easily be hard trimmed to make stout animal- and tourist-proof hedges up to 4 m (14 ft) tall and 1–2 m (3–7 ft) thick, depending largely on the degree of security the garden owner may require. Even ancient hedges can be satisfactorily rejuvenated by being given a thorough clean-out of all growth back to a basic framework of trunks and main branches.

Carissa grandiflora, Natal Plum, is widely planted as a low hedge or groundcover. Prostrate varieties circulate from time to time under commercial names such as 'Nana', 'Compacta' and 'Emerald Carpet' but there appears to be little appreciable difference between these and cutting-grown plants from old gardens. The starry white flower resemble a large jasmine flower and is sweetly scented. The flowers appear sporadically throughout spring, summer and autumn and give rise to a steady supply of bright red succulent fruits.

Carissa carandus, Karanda, is a larger plant in all its parts than the more frequently seen Natal Plum. It is occasionally found growing as a high, thick hedge where its very long, strong thorns protect property and privacy. With pale yellow-green foliage and red-black fruits it is sufficiently different from the former to be easily recognised. A native of India, *Carissa carandus* is a member of that interesting group of lesser known subtropical fruits now receiving the attention of rare fruit specialists. Much work has already been done by Dr Chiranjit Parmar of India and members of the California Rare Fruit Society.

Carissa edulis, Egyptian Plum, is a smaller, more straggly edition. It has a food history as venerable as those of its African and Indian counterparts and yet somehow managed to avoid the attentions of pioneering plant breeder Luther Burbank, an American noted for his dedication to new kinds of fruit.

5 Scent makers

Scent makers are one of the greatest joys of making a garden in a Mediterranean climate. Plants that in other places must struggle and persevere to flower half-heartedly will grow beautifully outdoors with hardly a care on our part. Wisteria, lavender, orange blossom, Burmese honeysuckle, salvias, scented-leaf pelargoniums and half a thousand more thrive in warmer and drier climates than those where writers speak of all such things as cold sensitive, needing winter protection and benefiting from both glass and heat.

To go into the garden early in the morning, or just after dusk, and take in the air – what an experience, to be engulfed in the perfume of a nearby shrub or climber. Building scented plants into a garden is a vital inclusion to the palette of available resources. While advocating acceptance of the natural cycles and weather patterns of the Mediterranean climate regime, which means gardens becoming relatively static during the hottest and driest months, need not mean the garden is completely lacking in interest. Quite the contrary; it is exactly the right time for plants with scented leaves and perfumed flowers to give a refreshing lift to an otherwise quiet season.

Thus the plants listed here come into play, not only in summer but at other seasons too. I find it necessary to smell every possible new admission to the garden and tend to choose plants as much on scent and leaf shape and colour as on flower colour. After all, flower colour quickly passes as different things blaze forth and then fall; foliage goes on and on and on – forever in the case of evergreens – and scented leaves and the perfume of flowers add a further dimension of delight.

Wherever the opportunity presents itself, choosing a perfumed plant should not to be missed.

The setting for plants with perfumed flowers is important if the perfume is to be appreciated to best advantage. Perfume is an evanescent thing; in itself it is attractive to be struck by unexpected nose-pleasing wafts as you go about a garden, but its presence can be enhanced, contained if you like, by siting plants where their perfume won't be dissipated by constant breezes and where walls or surrounding protective banks hold it in the air, in effect concentrating it. Even then the perfume may not last long on the nose but it will be noticed more when such a site is first entered. In the case of trees and large climbers the perfume will most likely spread over a wide area when conditions are still.

Not listed here are the really small plants that give perfumed delights when they can be smelled at close hand. With plants such as *Ferraria undulata*, *Cyclamen purpurascens* and *C. hederifolium*, hyacinths, jonquils, tazetta narcissus and other small, low things, I suggest growing at least some in pots raised so their perfume can be enjoyed at nose level.

Plants with scented foliage need to be positioned where passers-by can brush against the leaves or rub them between the fingers, thus releasing the aromas contained in the volatile oils in the leaves. As a general rule, the harder the growing conditions the more pronounced will be the scent of the leaves. However, some sensitivity is needed in individual cases. For example, the numerous pelargoniums with scented leaves are fairly tough but observation will show that *Pelargonium graveolens* (Rose Geranium) is much better able to withstand hard, dry conditions than

P. tomentosum (Peppermint Geranium), and while *P. crispum* (Lemon-scented Geranium) is as tough as old boots *Pelargonium* x 'Mabel Grey' (also strongly lemon-scented) is nowhere near as hardy.

Thought should be given, too, to plants not usually considered notable for the perfume of their flowers. One group that immediately comes to mind is the tall bearded irises. Complex hybrids, they are not consistently perfumed, indeed some are completely lacking olfactory appeal, but others – the blues, lilacs, purples and plicata (stitched) forms, it seems to me – can be well endowed with a delightful but elusive perfume that carries something of violets in its makeup. Make it a rule to always smell such flowers before choosing them for your garden. It really is the only way to tell.

Apart from plants with foliage that bears a pleasing scent there are many others that may smell medicinal, doggy, acrid, herbal, grassy, astringent, pungent or even foetid (of rotting flesh). Some of these may appeal for reasons of novelty or because of a preference for things that smell sweet or spicy, in a manner much like taste and food preferences. Wormwoods, or *Artemisia* spp., are thought of by some as doggy or stinky and therefore avoided, while others find them medicinal and quite pleasant, an essential part of the atmosphere of a Mediterranean garden, especially after a summer thunderstorm has wetted the foliage and released their refreshing scent to the air.

Azara microphylla

There is no common name for this endearing small evergreen tree from South America. It is really marginal in drier Mediterranean climate areas, but where summer thunderstorms and downpours can be expected at the slightly damper end of the scale it will do well enough, as long as the soil is neutral or slightly acid. It will stand light frosts but hates being waterlogged. A well-drained sunny situation suits it perfectly. Rather pendulous growth with light brown bark and tiny green leaves, toothed and glossy, are pleasing features of the plant, but its most endearing feature is rarely noticed by any but the most curious and observant – in the dark days of winter the tree produces masses of tiny yellow flowers hidden under the small leaves. The flowers have a strong vanilla-chocolate perfume that is especially noticeable early in the evening. What is most pleasing is the manner in which the perfume drifts unseen in the garden; the late stroller walking through a patch is caught by surprise in the gathering darkness. 'Just where does that marvellous perfume come from?', people ask as they walk by in the lane. Maybe the impression of the perfume is emphasised by the cold night air but it is always sought out by those who smell it.

The dimensions of the tree are quite small, usually about 5 m (17 ft) tall and everything squared away within a footprint of approximately the same size. The dark, shiny leaves make an excellent foil for other colours and the generally graceful habit makes it highly acceptable in almost any garden situation. The timber is fairly tolerant of wind and while extended slender branches may snap the tree is rarely subject to any more significant loss. The emergence of new growth at the points where loss has occurred suggests that it would respond quite well to any heavy pruning or shaping that might prove necessary. The roots do not seem to be any problem; another reason why it could be considered, especially for small gardens and courtyards.

There are other kinds of azara, with larger foliage and more prominent golden yellow flowers, but for my mind none approaches *Azara microphylla* for grace and delicious perfume. Everything about the tree seems to be in perfect scale, and just right for gardens.

Since the tree flowers in mid-winter, another bonus point, and is green for the remainder of the year it may benefit from companion plants that perform at other times. The branches would come down to the ground if allowed to, but if they have been taken up 2 m (7 ft) or so the under-space could be utilised with a flowering shrub or two such as *Ribes speciosum*, a beauty from California, or *Kolkwitzia amabilis* from China, or even a dwarf flowering almond. In the foreground a simple belt of tall bearded irises, chosen for perfume and sympathetic colour, would find a good home, and if coupled with interwoven *Allium christophii* would result in a long display of flowers, silver, sword-shaped leaves and the drying starbursts of the allium flowers.

A contrary approach could be to build on the intense deep green of the azara's leaves and add more greens to the picture. *Santolina virens* would be a good starting point, to which could be added *Ilex cornuta, Grevillea quercifolia, Laurus nobilis* 'Angustifolius' (Willow-leaved Laurel), *L. nobilis* 'Aureus' (Golden-leaved Laurel), myrtle and rosemary. This combination might benefit from being clipped into domes or balls but only after due thought; this is a great idea but can be overdone if repeated *ad nauseum* throughout a garden. It looks better if some contrast can be contrived to allow the idea to sparkle against a plainer setting – plants growing in natural shapes, say prostrate plants in this example, or against boulders or paving.

If the azara were to be planted in the outskirts of a garden where little maintenance was the objective, a simple high groundcover of pelargoniums with scented foliage could make an effective and tough combination. Stick with the taller growing bushy kinds, eschewing those of smaller stature derived from *Pelargonium crispum, P. odoratissimum* and *P.* x *fragrans. Pelargonium quercifolium* (and its numerous forms), *P. radula, P. vitifolium* and *P. cordatum* will do very nicely. All the maintenance required will be to trim back growth to an acceptable height from time to time, and to remove any branches that die of old age.

Gardenia thunbergia
Tree Gardenia

Gardenia thunbergia, the Tree Gardenia, is a tough shrub found in many old gardens. Conspicuous grey-barked woody 'pears' are long-lasting reminders of the heavy annual display of sweetly-scented white flowers. Slow growing but very hardy and reliable in most Mediterranean climate regions. Photo courtesy Bill Macoboy.

Despite its reputation for being slow, the Tree Gardenia is a plant that every gardener should try somewhere. Its growth is steady, if that puts it in a more affirmative light, and a small plant will grow at a satisfactory rate if given some care and attention. *Gardenia thunbergia* was named in honour of Carl Thunberg, a Swedish physician-botanist who worked for the Dutch East India Company at their diplomatic mission at Nagasaki, Japan in the late eighteenth century. The adventurous life of Thunberg is worth reading as a travelogue and history, as well as for the plants he discovered and introduced to the West.

Plants from Japan do not immediately spring to mind as highly suited to life in Mediterranean climates until some of the country's highly specialised microclimates are taken into account. It is a land of much volcanic activity with soils derived largely from that source. Some are rich and fertile volcanic loams, others impoverished composites of ash, cinders and pumice stone. The southernmost parts of the Japanese Archipelago are subtropical in nature and plants such as *Cycas revoluta*, well known in Mediterranean regions, hail from these parts and their poor soils. *Gardenia thunbergia* is another. And it does just as well as the cycad in cultivation.

Gardenia thunbergia fell from favour around the turn of the nineteenth century when cheap town water supplies enabled more highly water-dependent plants to be grown. Like many other truly hardy plants it languished in out-of-the-way corners of old-fashioned gardens. Rediscovering its excellent qualities has taken some time. It is both attractive and reliable. It makes a stout bushy shrub or small tree, according to the manner of pruning, and can reach about 4.5 m (15 ft), perhaps taller if it is limbed up and well cared for, and about 3 m (10 ft) across. The branches and trunk are covered in a smooth pale grey bark, almost silvery white, and over this is laid a dense canopy of broad spatulate leaves (trowel-shaped, if you prefer). The creamy white flowers, heavily scented, are spangled across the bush off and on throughout the year, varying from almost none in cold weather to plenty during and after long periods of warm weather. Some of the flowers will be pollinated and set woody, pear-shaped pods the same colour as the bark. Each flower lasts about three days, deepening from creamy white to deep yellow as it matures.

Though the Tree Gardenia responds quite well to

shaping, trimming and pruning it is slow to grow into the shape that may be required so the tendency is not to treat it as a subject for hedging or making standards. I have seen standards on offer recently that looked rather hurried, the effect possibly of a too-hasty approach and too little understanding of how the plant grows. In really hard alkaline conditions there may be need to address an unsightly yellowing of leaves. This is easily done with a decent loose mulch, say stable litter, and a dose of Epsom salts watered in – about a large spoonful to a 10 litre (2 gallon) bucket of water.

Propagation is usually by semi-ripe softwood cuttings with mist and warmth but seed is also an option, especially for home gardeners.

Like some others listed here, the Tree Gardenia might best be looked on as a quiet background plant, hardy and evergreen, with a special season all its own that relates more to perfume than a stunning riot of glorious colour. Its capacity is not to astonish but to create a sense of calm and sweet repose at a time of year when extremes of heat and dryness can upset the inner balance that generally allows us to cope with Mediterranean style summers. Those fortunate to have swimming pools or shady terraces will find *Gardenia thunbergii* a useful addition to poolside and near-terrace plantings where the perfume can be enjoyed while seeking relaxation. Growing it in a large tub would be a possibility, especially where space is limited or where frosts may necessitate some winter protection. It is certainly much more easily grown than the derivatives of *Gardenia augusta,* and its subvarieties 'Radicans' and 'Florida'. Unlike them the Tree Gardenia needs neither high levels of humidity nor specialised soil conditions to thrive.

Syringa x persica
Persian Lilac

It amuses me to read of the lengths to which some people will go to enjoy the perfume of lilacs in late spring. In California, in particular, this pursuit seems almost a statewide pastime among gardeners determined to succeed with the lovely French hybrids developed in the late nineteenth century by the Lemoine family and other nurserymen. Inducing late summer dormancy by leaf reduction seems to be the

Syringa x persica, the Persian Lilac, is a tough and ancient shrub that will grow happily where the more complex, large-flowered French kinds will not. Its delicious perfume and arching growth make it ideal for pathside planting.

most successful method of ensuring flower bud formation but is it worth it, I wonder, when I see (and smell) Persian Lilac?

This old-timer has been about since the great gold rushes in Australia and California. Hoary old trees still blossom year after year amidst the remains of mining camps and cemeteries deserted since the lodes ran out – almost a hundred years ago in many cases. It is simply a lilac, beautifully perfumed, simple of flower and easy in growth. There's nothing flash about Persian Lilac. It is all lavender and old lace, the flowers a quiet lilac-grey that fades to almost white as they age. There is no doubling, no strong colour, no startling bicolour effects – just solid old-fashioned charm. There is also a white form, but that is a little less vigorous, and harder to source. With such abundance

Syringa afghanica 'Lacinata' is a low dense shrub with masses of small lilac-purple flowers in spring. As the name suggests it is a plant that will prove hardy in Mediterranean conditions. The flowers are well scented too.

and ease of culture, why would trouble with fussy types be necessary?

Looking a little further afield into the realms of botanists and collectors we find several other lilacs equally hardy: *Syringa afghanica* 'Lacinata', *Syringa* x *diversifolia*, *S. josiflexa* 'Bellicent' and *S. wolfii*. All produce massive panicles of blooms, strongly perfumed, and are willing growers too. No fuss needed, please! Each variety should be treated simply. All that is really necessary to promote maximum flowering is to shear off all spent flower spikes immediately so that the strong new growth that emerges just below the panicles can get through the dead twigs. Leaving it won't hurt; the plant just looks incredibly messy.

Syringa x *persica* will grow to about 3 m (10 ft) tall and as much across, with tall arching growth springing from the base. Every now and then the leading shoots can be thinned by completely removing one or two of the oldest stems – these look barky while younger stems are smooth. Not much taller are *Syringa josiflexa* 'Bellicent' and *S. wolfii*, which both produce pink flowers, clear pink in the case of 'Bellicent' and mauve-pink in the latter instance. *Syringa* x *diversifolia* is a spreading bush about 1.5 m (5 ft) tall, with small, finely divided leaves and masses of white flowers in spring. Depending on which botanist is consulted the latter may be found as *Syringa* x *persica* 'Alba' and the darker lilac *S. afghanica* 'Lacinata' as S*yringa x persica* 'Lacinata'. Not very helpful in finding what you want in nursery catalogues, is it? But there you are; some botanists like to split up plant families into numerous species based on minor botanical points of difference,

others prefer to keep them lumped together, taking the broad similarities as having greater scientific import than numerous minor variables.

That aside, all these lilacs are hardy and not too fussy. They appear to gain some benefit from occasional light frosts but are well worth experimenting with in frost-free locations where the weather is still quite cool in winter. They are worth growing in Mediterranean climates because they flower, make their new growth spurt and cease their active growth cycle before the annual summer dry begins. Thus, though in full green leaf they are not growing during the long, hot summer months and need no or minimal irrigation to keep them going.

Hardy lilacs such as these make good companions for other Mediterranean climate plants such as lavenders, wild roses and cistus, rosemaries and artemisias. Planted in mixed groups with an eye to foliage combinations and flower colour they are very effective. Despite not being David Austin English Roses, and therefore somewhat out of favour, I find that the genuine old roses like 'Mme Hardy' and 'Raubritter' are an easy addition and very attractive in combination with these plants. Being once-flowering they do not require summer irrigation. Indeed, the dry summer period is ideal for ripening the wood of new shoots, thus almost certainly ensuring a good crop of flower buds the following year. Also suitable are *Rosa moyesii* 'Highdownensis' and *R. nutkana* 'Plena'.

Trachelospermum asiaticum
Chinese Star Jasmine, Confederate Jasmine

While a greenhouse and conservatory favourite in cooler, more temperate climes, *Trachelospermum asiaticum* finds its real home in the gardens of warm, dry climates where it truly thrives and does wondrous things. Sometimes used as a wall shrub to cover unsightly but necessary pieces and bits, and occasionally found as a not terribly convincing standard, it is most often found doing what it does best – being a climber. Chinese Star Jasmine is a strong, close-jointed, evergreen, bushy climber that while vigorous is by no means rampant or invasive. Dark green leaves are oval-shaped with a slight point and give a good account of themselves, covering the

Sedum x 'Autumn Joy', providing a solid block of colour and growth with minimal summer irrigation, has achieved greater acclaim for the architectural appearance of its dead flower stems in the winter garden. Enjoy it year round.

substructure of branches and twigs with a dense canopy. From each terminal leaf cluster a small bunch of starry white flowers is produced from summer into autumn. These have a very telling perfume, sweet, somewhat resembling jasmine but with citrus highlights and notes of spice – sounds like a description of chardonnay. Where the perfume can be concentrated by walls or by reflected warmth from paving it creates a zone of rare delight. For planting on walls and fences around swimming pools it seems almost perfect – well, it does shed leaves and drop finished flowers but in a general sense is a very clean plant. It responds to clipping very well, the long lead growths producing numerous stubby side-growths when headed back. For effective cover in any sort of hedge after pruning, a thickness of 60–75 cm (24–30 in) seems about the ideal. This would need the support of chicken wire or some other sort of strong mesh and it could be as high as needed. Given adequate care and a modicum of pruning, *Trachelospermum asiaticum* can reach the eaves of a two-storey building quite comfortably; the only real limit to growth is the height a gardener is willing to scale to do the trimming from time to time.

The base of any hedge can present a challenge as the foliage frequently peters out at ground level, leaving a blank where greenery is called for. Chinese Star Jasmine is not a great offender in this regard but still the odd gap will appear as plants age. Regular pruning and trimming can help, but should any holes appear they are easily dealt with. By good fortune it is not an aggressively-rooted plant so other things can

be grown successfully close under its skirts. Typically, catmint (*Nepeta* hybrids) is called into play. Other options are *Sedum* x 'Autumn Joy' or 'Gooseberry Fool', or dwarf agapanthus, blue or white, which flowers at the same time as the jasmine. Slightly larger plants like *Heliotropium arborescens* 'Lord Roberts' or *Artemisia* x 'Powis Castle' would also be good. Any of them could be interplanted with spring bulbs to give a colour show at another season.

There is a variegated form of Chinese Star Jasmine but it is an insipid plant, neither one thing nor the other, the variegation being mottled and muted, not sharply defined. There is also a variety with quite pleasing soft apricot yellow shades at the heart of the flowers. Even though the flowers are not as prolific as in the plain white form they are still carried in numbers large enough to make a good showing. In this 'gold' form the growth is slightly less vigorous and also slightly less dense.

Maintenance of a hedge of Chinese Star Jasmine is simple and easy. In Mediterranean climates the plant usually has two periods of active growth at the conclusion of which the hedge can be trimmed back to the required dimensions with shears or hedge-trimmer. The first growth spurt, in late spring, can be very vigorous, producing a mass of long new growths and numerous short shoots from growths trimmed the season previous. The long growths in particular need cutting back, unless they are wanted to increase the length or height of the hedge, in which case they should be tied into place before pruning begins. The second growth spurt is less vigorous and comes as the flowers fade toward the end of high summer. It may well be more vigorous if the plant has been irrigated but that vigour can be reduced by simply cutting back – or eliminating the irrigation. The second cut is needed to keep things tidy and to keep growth compact.

As the years go by the hedge will become thicker, carrying more dead stuff inside the green covering of leaves, and a more severe cutting back may be thought necessary. Fear not. Cutting back a mature hedge by as much as 50 per cent seems to be possible with no ill effects provided all danger of frost is past. The best time to do this is in late spring or very early summer, before the flowers develop. The plants will quickly reshoot from old wood and thick trunks and most likely will flower well. The second lot of regrowth may be noticeably more vigorous than usual but that can be dealt with at the second pruning.

Brugmansia suaveolens
Angel's Trumpet

While the members of the genus *Brugmansia* have been recently proscribed by drug educators, public safety bureaucrats, insurance risk assessors and other non-gardening experts, they have a long history as greenhouse plants in Europe, and an even longer history as medicinal plants among South American Indian tribes, a history only now being explored and exploited by Western pharmaceutical companies.

Yes, the plants are poisonous and everyone who grows them has to take responsibility for exercising care in regard to the safety of humans and animals. That caution being understood and exercised, Angel's Trumpet can be considered for the qualities of use to Mediterranean gardeners. The flowers are by and large spectacular, and most are perfumed – some highly so – and the plants are reasonably hardy given a modicum of irrigation during the most intense summer heat. The plants have a natural tendency to drop their large leaves when the weather gets hot and dry, and to cease flowering. They retain the smaller leaves, being not truly summer deciduous, and quickly put on new leaves and recommence flowering once the extreme heat has passed.

Since the mid-nineteenth century gardeners have

been familiar with three sorts of Angel's Trumpet – *Brugmansia suaveolens*, *B. sanguinea* and *B. arborea*. Still to be found in many older gardens, they have recently enjoyed a slight vogue among those wanting to create subtropical effects or looking to recreate colonial cottage gardens. But now, despite the dire warnings of officials, a whole gamut of new brugmansias is being introduced. Without doubt the increasing popularity is due to the publicity given to them by Ulrike and Hans-Georg Preissel.

Working their way from specialist collectors and breeders to wider cultivation are a large number of cultivars that will engage the attention of gardeners with new colours – yellow, cream, pink, rose, apricot, orange, red, dwarf forms and double flowers. 'Ecuador Pink' and

Grand Marnier' was foremost among the new kinds of *Brugmansia suaveolens* to be introduced to Mediterranean gardens. A tall, upright shrub, its high, spreading canopy displays the long apricot trumpets to great advantage.

Brugmansia versicolor 'Ecuador Pink' is a newcomer that will quickly win favour with gardeners in warm, dry climates. A modicum of summer irrigation will ensure plenty of flowers and strong growth in the open garden or in large tubs.

'Grand Marnier' (apricot) are two of the vanguard, but watch out for 'Pink Favourite', 'Goldtraum', 'Roter Vulkan' and 'Herrenhäsen Gärten', among others.

Brugmansias enjoy warm conditions and deep, free-draining soils well enriched with compost, a combination not always easily achieved in Mediterranean environments. Where soils are mean, impoverished and shallow they can be grown well in large tubs in sheltered sites. All-day exposure to full sun may be rather too hard on them, since the large leaves and the trunks are liable to dehydration and sun-scorch. But where they can be afforded some shelter and shade for part of the day, Angel's Trumpets are happy and will flower well from early summer into autumn.

In the open garden they prefer similar conditions, quickly growing into upright small trees with a high spreading crown from which in due season a mass of large, pendent flowers will appear. The perfume is strongest at night and is most often thought to be musky, spicy and sweet. It can be overpowering for sensitive noses, however, so the plant should be sited with thought. But where it can freely perfume the evening breezes, place it for maximum enjoyment.

Brugmansia suaveolens is the most widely grown and known, but think of it as an introduction to a group of plants that offers opportunities for some exciting design and planting. The white kinds, hardy and easily propagated, are widespread in commerce. When the newer kinds follow them, gardeners will be able to utilise their considerable flower power and fine colours to build more colour and perfume into their plans.

See Ulrike and Hans-Georg Preissel, *Brugmansia and Datura: Angel's Trumpets and Thorn Apples*, David Bateman, Auckland, 2001. ISBN 1-86953-474-3

Camellia yuhsienensis

In tendering this particular camellia as one of my ten top perfumed and scented plants it must be understood that it is done on behalf of those fortunate enough to live in Mediterranean climate regions that have some summer rainfall rather than in those that have almost none. Provided the soils are neutral to slightly acid, some camellias will grow very well in these areas.

Once established many camellias will survive well without additional summer irrigation. In my experience these tend to be the old nineteenth-century hybrids, the older Reticulata hybrids and many of the Sasanqua, Hiemalis and Wabisuke cultivars. The more recent, complex inter-specific and widely out-bred hybrids seem less hardy in these conditions. In Mediterranean gardens where camellias do flourish it is not unusual to find trees well over a hundred years old doing magnificently; indeed, one plantation high on a steep, exposed hillside facing west continues to do well after 150 years plus. It receives no irrigation at all and hasn't since the plants were established. Watered only for the first few years, they have withstood the long annual dry season, serious bushfires, being eaten by goats, sheep and horses, and total neglect for at least the last 75 years. These are, of course, old Japonica hybrids, some of them bred in Japan, some in France, Belgium and Italy, others in Australia when the nation was in its infancy. By contrast *Camellia yuhsienensis* is a newcomer, discovered and introduced from China in 1965. It has proven itself to be thoroughly hardy.

As camellias go this particular one is pretty typical. It has the usual broad, pointed, smooth leaves, mid-green, glossy and lightly toothed along the margin. Growth is more compact and close jointed than in most other camellias but the bush is still vigorous. The significant point of difference is that numerous flower buds are carried by this particular form (selected by Ross Hayter to represent the species), appearing in all the leaf axils and terminals on new growths made after flowering the previous year. The buds open to produce a long succession of charming white, ruffled single flowers that are delightfully perfumed. The plant was introduced with the expectation that it would make a significant contribution to breeding camellias with perfumed flowers.

It was with some slight sense of frustration that I discovered the species has been subsumed (lumped in) with *Camellia grijsii*,* a species that superficially bears no close resemblance to *C. yuhsienensis* – at least from this gardener's point of view. The botanical similarities must arise within the flowers – they do have some observable commonalities, being ruffled, single, white and perfumed – but the flowers of *C. yuhsienensis* are approximately three times larger at least than those of *C. grijsii*. The foliage bears no close comparison, in *Camellia grijsii* being quite small, no bigger than the first two joints of an average-sized

Among the many camellia species recently introduced, *Camellia yuhsienensis* can be recommended for its mass of white perfumed flowers and dense evergreen foliage. Requiring deep mulching and summer irrigation until it is well established, it will thrive in cooler microclimates in Mediterranean gardens.

adult thumb, noticeably toothed with the upper leaf surface deeply and heavily veined. The contrast with *Camellia yuhsienensis* could hardly be greater.

Since its flowers are perfumed *Camellia grijsii* finds a place in my garden where it is equally as hardy as *C. yuhsienensis*. It grows upright and almost columnar, a handy shape in a family dominated by Christmas pudding-shaped plants; its form being more open than most of the genus gives it a lightness that is also a pleasing variation.

These shrubs are not to be mucked around with. Pruning and trimming should not be necessary in most cases, though once in 20 years they may need to be cut hard to keep them with their allotted space. Generally they grow back strongly. Growing in pots, no matter how large, seems an exercise in futility since the bushes never achieve their potential and suffer from the least lapse in attention in very hot weather; flowering is reduced and growth becomes stunted by die-back and loss of leaves.

As plants that grow in clearings and at the edges of forests, camellias prefer that sort of mixed setting in gardens where they have plenty of room to grow and air movement is free, but where they also enjoy some filtered sunlight and the protection of surrounding trees and shrubs. This in itself suggests the soil should preferably be fairly deep and capable of supporting trees of a reasonable size. By nature camellias have a dense, shallow root system that enables them to coexist with other deeper rooted plants. In Mediterranean conditions this means that by the end of the dry summer the root mass will be pretty much dry and impenetrable, making it extremely difficult to grow any companion plants in the understorey without heavy irrigation. Therefore a semi-woodland setting where the ground is covered with a mulch of dead camellia leaves seems a sensible way to go. Here and there it may be possible to establish small colonies of tough *Epimedium* spp. and really tough wild bulbs like *Asarum proboscidium* or *Arum italicum* 'Pictum'.

There are other tough camellias with perfume. The numerous Sasanqua hybrids come to mind but they are most often noted for the dusty or foxy smell of their flowers. These are mainly old Japanese cultivars, or hybrids derived from them, and while they are as a rule tough and reliable in more favoured Mediterranean climate areas they would scarcely rank alongside *Camellia yuhsienensis* or *C. grisjii* for the quality of their perfume. 'Scentuous', 'Pink Scented' and 'Improved Pink Scented' are three charming recent Sasanqua introductions worth consideration, as are one or two older kinds, the old Higo camellia 'Nioi Fubuki' being perhaps the best. It has single white flowers with occasional pink veins and some cresting of the central boss of stamens – its name in translation, 'Scented Wind', says it all.

*See Chang Hung Ta and Bruce Bartholomew, *Camellias*, Batsford, London, 1984. ISBN 0-7134-4660-9

Amaryllis belladonna
Belladonna Lily

Of the garden favourites that have survived since the days of eighteenth-century colonialism, South Africa's Belladonna Lily would have to be the most widespread of bulbs. Its constitution is such that it survives and thrives in Mediterranean climate regions in both hemispheres. A traveller to any old gold mining area outside the Klondike would most likely be able to spot its leaf clusters, flower stems or dormant bulbs.

With a multitude of common names – Naked Ladies, Aunt Eliza, Belladonna, Easter Lily – the hardy *Amaryllis belladonna* has established itself in many an old churchyard, cemetery, public park and private garden. It is found in massive clumps, existing well enough on whatever nature provides in the way of moisture and sustenance. Where tent cities and shanty towns once housed hundreds or thousands of hopeful miners, clusters of Naked Ladies remain to show where hopeful housewives tried to create gardens as a sign of a permanent home. Elsewhere they are all that remain of farms long ago abandoned when bitter experience disproved the old belief that rain followed the plough.

That it is so hardy and reliable is at once a great incentive to make good use of *Amaryllis belladonna* in its several forms, and at the same time a disincentive to the fashion conscious. But can your garden afford to be without it? Its qualities so well match conditions in Mediterranean climate gardens that strictly speaking it is an essential. Flower colour is limited but effective, especially if the creamy white cultivar 'Hathor' is massed, or one of the rich hot pink forms tinged with gold at the centre. Foliage is strong in form, though being deciduous the effect is not available year round. And the flowers have a rich and heavy perfume that permeates the air around them.

There are numerous hybrids, much confused by all but those who specialise in the family Amaryllidaceae. Given the ease of growing these bulbs it is easy to understand why plant collectors and enthusiasts have tried to broaden the range available. This admirable effort has not been particularly productive as some of the other species and near family members (genera) are less amenable to cultivation in gardens. What frustration, to grow such stunning beauties as *Brunsvigia josephinae* only to discover that nine years out of ten it fails to flower! Perhaps even in a dry garden they get too much of a good thing? Exposure, exposure, exposure seems to be at least one of the significant factors for success. Maybe when breeders get a few more generations down the track they will strike it lucky and realise a successful merger of the astonishing forms of *Boophane* and *Brunsvigia* with the willingness of *Amaryllis*.*

All too often the common amaryllis is badly used in gardens. It exists somewhere in an out of the way corner where it grows and flowers without making any demands on the skills or time of the gardener. Its clumps get larger and larger, growing as they will and in no way deployed to fulfil the ideas of a creative mind. Growing amaryllis as self-sustaining groups of gap-fillers is too limiting. How about trying them in a more formal way? A path lined either side with just one colour form would carry far more visual weight that the usual mish-mash of mixed forms that flower at different times throughout the autumn. The creamy white 'Hathor' would look very telling used in such a manner, the more so if the colour was linked to other plants in the background with white, cream or yellow flowers, fruits or foliage. A picture that comes to mind would be such a path passing beneath a towering golden gleditsia underplanted with cream variegated periwinkle and a cream iris Spuria hybrid against a further background of silver-leaved Alba roses – *Rosa* x *alba semi-plena* and *Rosa* x *alba maxima*, which are as tough as any rose can be and flower prolifically in early summer. No floral fireworks here but a very pleasing picture that takes advantage of the almost naturalised way these plants will grow in Mediterranean climates while also imposing some design organisation.

*See John Manning, Peter Goldblatt and Dee Snijman, *The Colour Encyclopedia of Cape Bulbs*, Timber Press, Portland, Oregon, 2002. ISBN 0-88192-547-0

Prostanthera ovalifolia
Purple Mint Bush

Prostanthera is an Australian genus that ranges across the southern and eastern part of the continent, generally finding homes in open bushland and in forest clearings and large glades where there is good exposure to sunlight, though with the benefit of some protection and high dappled shade for part of the day. As water-wise plants they are good given similar conditions but they are not plants for extremely exposed situations, or for settings at the dry end of the Mediterranean climate spectrum. Even so they manage well with very little summer irrigation as long as the soil is reasonably deep and well covered with a

Prostanthera ovalifolia, Purple Mint Bush, is a beautiful and hardy shrub, easy to grow and easy to care for. It can grow happily under tall trees, as it does in the Australian bush, or in more open positions.

deep, coarse, open mulch, in nature made up of shreds of gum tree bark, gum leaves and small twigs. As an underplanting to already established trees they perform well.

Prostanthera ovalifolia is the mint bush most common in gardens, making a fine shrub about 3 m (10 ft) tall and 1.5 m (5 ft) wide. Its habit is somewhat arching, not enough to be described as weeping or pendulous, but still attractive. Growth is twiggy and fine with small dark green oval leaves. The leaves are strongly aromatic, releasing their minty scent when crushed, or drenched with rain. In spring the bushes are smothered with thousands of small, open bell-shaped flowers making a dense mantle of lilac-purple. Flower colour varies, and there are colour selections that range from white to rosy pink. If anything these tend to be slightly less vigorous. There are smaller growing mint bushes too. *Prostanthera rotundifolia* is probably most likely to be found and as the name implies has round leaves. It achieves about 2 m (7 ft) in height and maybe a little more in diameter, with lilac, mauve or almost white flowers.

All prostantheras need a well-drained position and are relatively unaffected by frosts unless they are hard and frequent. They benefit from a light tip pruning all over once flowering has finished. This helps keep the bushes compact and prevents them splaying apart from being top heavy with growth. Mint bushes tend not to be very long-lived; 15–20 years should be considered a good life span, but what they lack in longevity they certainly make up for in prodigious flowering.

They seem so right in their natural bush habitat under well-spaced eucalypts that it is difficult to imagine a better placement – yet a few more contrived settings could be designed that would pick up their dense texture, graceful habit and extravagant flowering. There are numerous other Australian native plants with lilac-mauve flowers that could be introduced to a design based on that colour,* as well as white-flowered plants and those with complementary colours. *Dianella* would be a hardy companion, as would *Scaevola* or Fan Flower, and the purple and mauve species of *Eremophila*, the emu bushes. Of similar stature and suited to intermingling with these lilac-mauves are the white daisy-flowered *Olearia floribunda* and *O. microphylla*. There are also some hybrids derived from New Zealand species of *Olearia* in shades of pink and mauve. All are hardy and reasonably drought tolerant.

In gardens where stronger form is required the mint bushes, when kept compact by tip pruning, would associate well with other plants that have naturally strong growth forms. *Correa alba* would be a prime choice here. Its low, rounded bushy form, compact and made more so with an occasional clipping, would create a more controlled feeling, perhaps even with hints of European formality if the plants were laid out that way rather than in the more random pattern of a bush garden. As informal hedges prostantheras are a good choice, especially if having no thorns or hard growth are important criteria, with the bonus of perfumed flowers and scented leaves. Trimming them formally would be counterproductive as it would simply reduce the number of flowers.

*See Geoff and Bev Rigby, *Colour Your Garden with Australian Natives*, Kangaroo Press, Sydney, 1992. ISBN 0-86417-492-6

Salvia dorisiana
Peach Sage

Of all the sages that could be included here this is neither the most hardy and drought tolerant, nor the most flamboyant; neither is it lush. It sits somewhere in the mid range of salvia performance, well behind *Salvia apiana*, behind *S. leucantha* but ahead of *S.*

mexicana and well ahead of *S. gesneriflora*. Salvia buffs, of whom there are many, will more than likely recognise these species and their relative dispositions in regard to environment and habitat. The genus *Salvia* is very wide ranging, existing on every continent but Antarctica and found in tropical, subtropical, temperate, Mediterranean and cool climate regions. Some are low ground-hugging annuals, like *Salvia lyrata*; some are groundcovering perennials, like *S. coccinea*; yet others are shrubby and woody, like *S. tiliifola*, and some are towering perennial giants – think *S. gesneriflora*. Members of the salvia family are found in deserts and at the edge of rainforests: a most adaptable and diverse group.

The Peach Sage offers Mediterranean gardeners an intermediary plant – a softwooded perennial, shrubby in habit, evergreen with scented leaves and colourful pink flowers. It is not as hardy as some but can get by with a small amount of irrigation, especially if it is grown in a position where it receives some protection from the strongest sunshine and greatest heat. It is somewhat frost tolerant and will, nine times out of ten, sprout from below ground level if the top growth is severely damaged. As the name suggests the Peach Sage has leaves strongly redolent of peaches or, if you are olfactorily challenged, fruit-scented. The scent is released when the rather sticky leaf surfaces are touched or brushed past, and also released to the air in hot weather. The impact is very noticeable if there is rain about or humidity is high.

The foliage is light green, roughly heart-shaped and slightly hairy. The square stems are also green. Flower spikes appear towards the end of summer and last well into early winter. Indeed, in mild climates flowering will continue until new growth takes over in spring. In these circumstances the plant can easily build up successive growths to over 2 m (7 ft) tall and sprawl almost as wide. In less favourable settings it will reach about 1.5 m (5 ft) tall and as much across. The growth in this situation is more compact, the stems thicker and shorter, and the plant less likely to sprawl. Any pruning should be undertaken while the weather is warm and likely to stay that way for six weeks or so to give the plant time to get new growth made and hardened off. Plants respond well to pruning but grow less vigorous as the centres get older and woodier. It is sensible therefore to make cuttings every few years and renew plants before they become tired. Cuttings

of hardened green growth are quite easy to root, seed is a possibility if it can be harvested before the seeds pop from their calyces, and side-stems will often make roots of their own accord if they sprawl low enough to touch the ground. This habit makes *marcotage* (layering) also possible. Simply put this practice involves pegging down to the earth a suitable side-growth and waiting until roots are formed. Most salvias are obligingly quick in doing this.

Since the main attraction of growing the Peach Sage is the scent of the leaves, it makes sense to plant it close to paths where this quality can be enjoyed without tramping over other plants to get to it. In milder Mediterranean areas where heat and dryness are ameliorated somewhat by summer thundershowers, *Salvia dorisiana* will assort well with cistus, especially the smaller growing forms, and Algerian irises, dwarf agapanthus, tall bearded irises and, in favoured

Hummingbird Sage, *Salvia spathacea*, is a willing coloniser forming dense mats of growth and producing spires of claret-coloured flowers over a long period. Like many sages its leaves are redolent of spices, dust and aromatics.

locations where a cool root-run is made possible by nearby paving or large rocks, training the smaller flowered forms of *Clematis viticella* over the bushes is an attractive option. Pink forms would suit best. Look out for 'Abundance'. One of the not-climbing-but-flopping clematis could be just as good. *Clematis integrifolia* 'Alionushka' which is an excellent shade of pink would be my first choice. Management of the clematis in either case is very simple: cut back all stems to less than 10 cm (4 in) above ground every winter. The plants will renew themselves vigorously and produce masses of flowers in early summer.

Other salvias as companion plants would be fatally dull next door to the Peach Sage, but elsewhere in the garden room could be found for those with scented leaves. *Salvia rutilans* comes to mind. Redolent of ripe pineapples, it has bold red flowers, not scarlet but bright enough. *Salvia elegans* is similar but with honeymelon-scented leaves. I like the pungent aroma of the Hummingbird Sage, *Salvia spathacea*, and also that of *S. apiana*, but noses more sensitive than mine may find them astringent and too pharmaceutical.

See Betsy Clebsch, *The New Book of Salvias*, Florilegium, Sydney, 2003. ISBN 1-876314-18-4

Cymbidium tracyanum

Incredible as it may seem to some, I include this orchid with its strong sweet perfume as it is one of that hardy breed from which tens of thousands of hybrids have been made. While many of the latest varieties will only prosper and flower outdoors with a great deal of care, in Mediterranean climates some of the original wild forms and their close hybrids will manage quite well under a tree, at the rim of the drip-line. *Cymbidium tracyanum* and its hybrids are among them. These are generally identified by their perfume and greenish-yellowish flowers heavily spotted and lined with deep red-brown marks. The flower stems are usually erect and arching, carrying around fifteen open, somewhat spidery flowers. It is the perfume that makes these cymbidiums worth trying, especially if a suitable microclimate afforded by a shaded watery grotto or contrived watercourse will produce humidity and still allow the plants reasonable exposure to the sun,

Cymbidium tracyanum was around for a century or more before the large-flowered hybrids came along. It is hardy and will grow outdoors with minimum protection and fuss. It needs some exposure to the sun to ripen its growth and produce its deliciously perfumed green flowers.

without which they will not produce their late autumn flowers.

Though not advocating the widespread use of large water features in Mediterranean gardens I happily concede the attractions of some small dipping well, dripping grotto or tinkling runnel. During the hottest weather these will induce a cooling sensation and give birds a place to drink and bathe, and who could deny the desire to splash the hands, arms and face with waters from such a construction? Shaded by trees and planted up with xerophytes such as bromeliads and tillandsias, taros, crinums and flowering gingers, a little patch of dampness is a welcome thing.

Susana, Lady Walton, made much use of water features in her garden 'La Mortella' on dry, dry Ischia in the Bay of Naples and developed a series of small, lush-seeming gardens around three fountains and along a very slender canal. The arrival of piped water under the bay from the mainland tempted Lady Walton into a style of gardening more water dependent than we might contemplate today as a model for the Mediterranean ethos, but the environment she created certainly established the setting that enabled her husband to imagine and compose great music. Even more exotic are the gardens made for Yves Saint Laurent at his 'Villa Oasis' at Marrakech in Morocco. Here too much use is made of water, in the form of traditional rectangular reservoirs surrounded by palm groves and underplanted with lush-looking xerophytic foliage plants such as yuccas, papyrus, asparagus 'ferns' and the ubiquitous bougainvillea.

Where the orchid finds a home there may be room also for a few more really hardy xerophytes, in particular the bromeliads, of which there are hundreds of astonishing species and hybrids, and dozens of genera.* Not all bromeliads are suitable for Mediterranean gardens because some are tropical plants that require high levels of humidity to thrive. The realisation may prove disappointing if your first reaction is that only the tropical types appeal, yet there are numerous kinds that will be entirely suitable and equally colourful and exotic looking. The genus *Billbergia* offers many hardy choices, as do *Aechmea*, *Neoregelia*, *Nidularium*, *Hohenbergia* and *Portea*. With the larger types such as *Vreisia* it can be more challenging to discern species likely to survive away from the tropics, as with the numerous *Tillandsia*

species and some *Dykia*, inhabitants of specialised microclimates best left until experience is gained in dealing with the easy kinds.

Other orchids besides cymbidiums could be tried with reasonable chances for success. *Zygopetalum* are pretty reliable in lightly shaded spots where a minimum of water can be supplied to keep the pseudobulbs plump during the hottest and driest months. Smaller flowering kinds such as *Sarcochilus*, *Dendrobium*, *Oncidium*, *Coelogyne*, *Miltonia* and *Cattleya* all offer species and hybrids well able to grow outdoors in suitable microclimates where they can be given the necessary periods of rest and growth at the right season.

*See Werner Rauh, *The Bromeliad Lexicon*, Bok Books International, Durban, 1990. ISBN 0-947444-42-4

A silver-scaled bromeliad from the coastal cliffs of Mexico, this *Dykia* species is allied to the equally lovely *Dykia marnier-lapostollei*. Dykias and tillandsias are air-plants that will prove happy in well-lit but sheltered areas in Mediterranean gardens providing they are misted from time to time in hot weather.

6 Silver superstars

The thing about plants with silvery foliage is that to a large degree they have been done to death by garden designers and fashionistas eager to replicate the Mediterranean style made so chic in England and the wetter parts of Europe as a result of recent water shortages and possible changes to world weather patterns. On these bases has been raised a virtual empire of good practice that ranges from feel-good sunny design to 'natural' hayfields and futuristic gardens of rusted junk, beach pebbles and scavenged botanical flotsam; all grown dry, of course.

One of the earliest precursors of these arty developments was the silver garden. It all began with the knowledge that silveriness was a plant survival mechanism, whether caused by the presence on leaf

At 'Wigandia' William Martin combines yuccas, flaxes, palms, Mexican Horned Poppy (*Argemone mexicana*) and Jerusalem Sage (*Phlomis fruticosa*) with Gymea Lily (*Doryanthes excelsa*) at centre rear in a rich tapestry of foliage and colour.

surfaces of a covering of hairs or a layer of waxy deposits. Both prevented leaf damage, either by protecting from the scorching sun or by reducing transpiration. Plants with these attributes came to be accorded almost mythological veneration as plants for difficult situations – in gardens in cool, wet climates! Indeed so great was their drawing power that those which proved themselves difficult in non-Mediterranean climates gained further panache by being regarded as a challenge worthy of any good English gardener. Mrs Desmond Underwood, in her 1971 book *Grey and Silver Plants*,* makes quite a point of the superiority of these plants. Written barely a generation ago, and already the idea is almost a cliché … what ignominy to have befallen obliging plants that are such good performers in climatic conditions where those protective mechanisms do come into play and are intensified by the exposure.

Perhaps I am too hard on Mrs Underwood; after all, she did bring to attention a group of plants that might otherwise have languished, and has aroused us to the potential of plants better able to withstand the conditions under which we garden than they did in her experience. At 30 years distance there is room to take a broader view.

Whoever would have thought, on first seeing *Calocephalus brownii* growing wild on the coast of southern Australia, that it would take so handsomely to a garden setting? All dead patches and fallen centres, a scruffy wild thing tortured by sea winds and salt air, a mess of growth and a tonsure of lumps, bumps and bald patches – yet the potential was noted and the transition made from wilderness to garden. Left to its own devices it will return to its old habits but with a little care and a haircut now and then it serves a garden well.

Equally unlikely are the ramshackle saltbushes (*Rhagodia* and *Atriplex* spp.) in all their worldwide variety. Despite their botanical diversity most come pretty close to being pretty ordinary xerophytes – tough, tough, tough, and drought tolerant too, but not much more – until they get in the hands of a creative person whose inward eye can discern the potential for a certain degree of domestication. Not the sort that seeks to turn a plant into what it is not by gigantism, flower doubling, colour gaudification or gene manipulation; rather the sort that leaves things simple and seeks to keep them so.

Then too, traditions practised elsewhere for different reasons may find a useful application in Mediterranean climates. For instance, pollarding is an ancient European practice usually applied to woodlot trees or street trees. More recently it has been advocated for maintaining the special juvenile features of various plants for the purposes of garden design. The technique has been applied to the Powton Tree (*Paulonia tomentosa*); annual pollarding means a new crop of stems appears each growing season, ensuring a continuing supply of its huge, decorative juvenile leaves. Several Australian eucalypts have been treated the same way, especially those species that have intense silver juvenile foliage with a leaf form more interesting than the usual lanceolate gumleaf shape. This technique needs to be tried more widely in Mediterranean climates to better understand how it may help build the gardening vocabulary of those places.

Let us now consider silver-leaved plants.

*Mrs Desmond Underwood, *Grey and Silver Leaved Plants*, Collins, London, 1971. ISBN 0-00-214056-X

Euphorbia rigida

Travelling by day train from Avignon to Barcelona, observant travellers will note the changing flora as the salty lagoons of the Camargue give way to the rocky outcrops of the mountains on the Spanish border. Towering giant reeds (*Arundo donax*) and feathery tamarisk trees are replaced by desiccated brooms, dusty gorse and olives, dead pale fennel stems and silver-grey euphorbias. As the train nears the border it winds close to the coast, skirting cliff tops and ducking in and out of tunnels to give a near view of the dry, stony landscape. Easily identified flashing past the carriage windows is the typical form of *Euphorbia rigida* – or something very close to it.

Both leaves and growth appear rigid and stand in bold contrast to pretty much everything else around them. In truth the growth is really not that rigid, it just looks that way. The entire plant is covered in a dense silver-blue, half powdery grey meal and half grey wax, that serves to preserve it from the extremes of reflected heat from the rocky environment that forms its habitat. The leaves are narrow and sharply pointed, supported

Euphorbia rigida is but one example of a numerous and very useful tribe, especially for Mediterranean climate gardeners. Planted *en masse* or treated as a single specimen it is a telling addition to any sunny garden corner.

by stems about 75 cm (30 in) tall. The plant is made up of numerous stems arising from a common base so that it looks much like a small shrub. Like many euphorbias it is winter flowering, a feature that allows the swelling and ripening of seeds before the harsh, dry summer takes hold. And like most euphorbias the flowers are a curious affair – if you look closely – of yellowish green arranged in a compact terminal head.

Sounds pretty much like most other euphorbias gardeners meet, doesn't it? Greeny-yellowy flowers, silver leaves and silver stems. So what? Why would you plant it unless you were a euphorbia freak?

Seeing the possibilities of *Euphorbia rigida* requires a fresh mind and a willingness to experiment. It is a very hardy plant. That's one good point. The colour is attractive and compatible with many others; a second good point. The plant has substance and solidity without being dumpy; a third good point. And its form

is architectural and structured without being monumental or overscaled – just like its cousin *Euphorbia characias* subsp. *wulfenii*. It can stand alone or in a broad swathe of its kind, but it also associates happily with other plants. Five points to recommend it. That's good enough for me.

Planted *en masse* it can sometimes look a bit sparse on the ground. Its habit is upward with not a lot of sideways spread. Even planted in staggered or random patterns there can be an impression of too much open space at ground level. This may be okay for a large-scale landscape treatment but is probably not satisfactory in a home garden where coverage of bare earth is usually preferred. To fill some of the bare patches other euphorbias could be employed to sustain the silver-grey colour base while adding some diversity in foliage form. Keeping things simple, just one additional species – *Euphorbia myrsinites* – would serve to cover the bare earth adequately. Gardeners intent on a richer tapestry could consider adding at least three different species: *Euphorbia nicaeensis*, *E. nicaeensis* subsp. *glareosa* and *E. cyparissus*.* Each offers something different. The Nice Spurge (*Euphorbia nicaeensis*) hails from the northern Mediterranean coast along the Riviera and around to Spain. It is a pleasant trailing plant with numerous stems radiating from a central stem with a spread of about 30 cm (12 in). It and its larger subspecies from Turkey and around the Black Sea mix well together, covering the ground with a mat of silver-leaved stems and small heads of typical flowers. If a more abundant and softer infill were called for, the Cyprus Spurge (*Euphorbia cyparissus*) could be a useful option, especially where conditions are really difficult, such as where the soil is rocky and filled with surface roots. It too is silvery grey all over with small airy heads of typically coloured flowers and feather-fine leaves. Its greatest asset is also its greatest drawback: it colonises widely, the more so where soils are watered and good. It really needs harsh conditions to keep it in check, though it is shallow rooted and easily controlled by pulling, scuffing and smothering with mulches. But it does need watching. Where it can be allowed to roam at large it will, and does a thorough job of covering difficult ground. It is a true perennial, briefly deciduous and hard as hobnail boots.

*See Roger Turner, *Euphorbias*, Batsford, London, 1995. ISBN 0-7134-7071-2

Santolina pectinata
Lavender Cotton

This fine small shrub is treated too unkindly by many of those gardeners duped by the low maintenance school of slack horticulture. There's really no such thing. There's always something to do in a garden,

Often featured in old-fashioned cottage gardens Lavender Cotton, *Santolina pectinata*, is proving adaptable to more architectural modern styles of gardening too, as this plat garden shows.

whether it's picking up blow-in rubbish, tying up tomatoes or fussing like a fanatic over some rare succulent of minuscule proportions. Some choose to work with green things, others play with mechanical toys, some maintain a balance between the two – but most, I fear, find the toys more appealing. This leaves a lot of fine plants to look after themselves until they are subjected to some cruel treatment in a vicious assault in the name of gardening made once a year. Sadly but not surprisingly many plants do not respond well to this once-all-over short-back-and-sides way of doing things. *Santolina pectinata* is one of them.

It well repays a more considered approach; not that it is all that fussy, it simply needs attention in its own season rather than in that brief time between the football Grand Final and the beginning of the tennis season. Its needs are simple: a sunny position, well-drained open soil and a darn good clipping all over at the time of flowering. Just exactly when, before or after *floraison*, is important only if the bright yellow button flowers will give offence to sensitive colourists and designers. But cutting back by half to two-thirds is

important to keep the growth vigorous and the bush compact. Allowed to go untrimmed it will fall open and then fall apart, at which stage repair is more difficult and potential garden impact greatly reduced. Lavender Cotton will grow in lightly shaded positions as long as it is not overcrowded or heavily overshadowed by other plants. In general plants live between ten and twenty years, by which time they will be decidedly iffy about reshooting when pruned and liable to developing odd dead patches. Propagation couldn't be simpler; short side-growth cuttings taken and treated in the same manner as for lavenders. Where stems touch the ground it is highly likely that roots will form anyway. It is a simple matter to separate these from the mother plant and relocate. Cutting back the top growth of such plantlets will assist in their secure re-establishment as independent plants.

Aside from *Santolina pectinata*, there are several other santolinas in general circulation. At a distance there is not much between them but for minor variations in stature and the way in which the leaf edges are lacinated. *Santolina chamaecyparissus* is often met with in catalogues and plant displays. Its leaves are more deeply cut along the margins than those of Lavender Cotton and in hard conditions it is more compact; coralline might be the best way to describe its appearance – it looks rather like branching coral bleached silver-white by the sun. It also produces the questionable bright yellow button flowers. Somewhat less dazzling is the cream-flowered *Santolina pinnata* subsp. *neapolitana* 'Edward Bowles', a real mouthful for a very fine plant. There is some uncertainty about exactly which species this cultivar should be attached to, so just make sure you get 'Edward Bowles' and your eyesight should be safe from a golden glare. It requires the same conditions and treatment as others of its kind.

At the risk of being a bore I will say santolinas can be clipped into tidy domes and buns … but they have a long history of being used to construct the intricate interwoven patterns of the very low hedges known as 'knots'. Rediscovered in fairly recent times by garden historians and their followers, such as Rosemary Verey, the knot has enjoyed a brief vogue but has a disadvantage that applies in Mediterranean climates as well as temperate zones: it dies of cold, it dies an ugly old age and it needs frequent renewing to maintain any clarity of pattern. Whether you are laying out lover's knots, your initials or the municipal coat of arms, it is a lot of effort to maintain santolinas grown this way. I'll take the domes and buns any day!

The lavender cottons have reputed homoeopathic qualities that relate to their capacity to repel bed bugs, fleas and such-like little critters. This may be so but who wants to sleep on twigs and dried leaves? Better use them then to make tussie-mussies and other nosegays which can be appreciated without irritations and restless sleep.

Helichrysum petiolare

One specimen of *Helichrysum petiolare* has always been enough for me, but it is also very useful planted *en masse*, as seen in combination with *Rhagodia spinescens* in chapter 3, Structure makers. One plant gives sufficient coverage to fill an area 2 m (2 yd) square and then some, so it is valued in my garden and I recommend it to you with few reservations. It is frost tender, the leaves are scorched by the cold, but the woody structure generally remains unaffected – or at least retains enough sound wood to regenerate when days and nights warm up. It also has yellow bobble flowers, unfortunately rather horrid in their dirty colouring and scruffy appearance, so I make it a rule to give all stems a clipping when they show signs of running up to flower in early summer.

As a plant with silver foliage it is quite useful. It grows well in full sun or part shade, and apart from requiring a well-drained situation is not fussy about soil. Its habit is a low intertwined network of silver-felted branches and twigs that support rounded leaves, about thumbnail size, covered in a dense silver felting.

The bulk of the plant appears impenetrable so it is a surprise to find that some other plants of lesser habit can successfully coexist with it. By accident I found a scarlet-flowered California Fuchsia (*Epilobium californicum*) had managed to insert itself in the heart of the helichrysum. Its leaves, a slightly different shade of grey, do not intrude on the solid silver of the helichrysum and the scarlet flowers add a wonderful surprise in late summer when the garden needs a lift.

As a groundcover *Helichrysum petiolare* is one of the best for Mediterranean gardens. Each plant has an impressive ability to cover a large area and where a simple effect is wanted this is an ideal candidate. What is more, left alone it will cover an even larger wilderness area, or it can be clipped loosely or cut hard to make formal designs. A note of caution: it is wise never to cut too hard into the basewood, as this creates a risk that the plant may not reshoot and die instead. The embarrassment of creating such a large hole in a garden is best avoided. Should such a disaster occur, a replacement plant will quickly establish itself though the impact created by the mature plant will be lost for a season.

Plants-people will know that there are at least two other forms in general cultivation – a lime-green or 'golden' version, *Helichrysum petiolare* 'Aureum', and a variegated kind. Both are less vigorous and less hardy in Mediterranean conditions than the species; they are highly susceptible to leaf burn and scorch in strong sunshine and are equally at risk in frost, hail and cold, wet weather. They seem best left to the situations where they are most often found – in hanging baskets outside English pubs.

Speaking of hanging baskets reminds me that although such things are very difficult to maintain at a presentable level, there are other treatments that allow a special kind of colourful planting to be tried. The experimental nature of developing the idea is where the main attraction lies. In the Mediterranean garden, spot colour in key areas can be supplied by using very large pots or half wine-barrel tubs. Be sure to have some wheels fitted on a steel frame to hold each one; when filled with soil and plants, containers this size are too heavy to lift. Play with the idea of making lush bedding-out schemes in miniature to fill them. Here the weaker forms of *Helichrysum petiolare* come into play along with masses of other foliage and flowering plants. Use trailing plants and spiky sword-shaped leaves to liven up the picture and create a varied scene. Easy colourful things, annuals mainly, will kick the idea along further and lead to new planting plans from year to year. Do not be tempted to keep the planting going from one year to the next; that is just too dull and boring. Renewing the planting every year makes it fun to dream up new combinations.

A plant as vigorous as *Helichrysum petiolare* calls for careful placement and a sense of scale. It can be the dominant plant in a design, which is the way it has been described here, but where it is but one element in a larger scheme it looks best where strong and big and bold foliage forms are set against it. A more expansive association could include blue palms (*Butia capitata*), cycads with bluish leaves, *Opuntia robusta*, *Callitris glaucophylla*, *Cupressus cashmeriana* or even a Blue Cedar (*Cedrus atlantica* 'Glauca')

Artemisia canescens

There would be those, many perhaps, who would not look twice at this diminutive artemisia. In fact there would be a goodly number with whom it would fail to

Minute and feathery *Artemisia canescens* is deceptively delicate. The tough roots and stems hidden beneath its finely cut leaves will see it safely through summer dry spells and offer shelter and shade to other fine Mediterranean plants such as the wild crocus and

register at first. It is just a blur of insignificant grey fluff that sits low down in the garden and stays there, hardly spreading from its original spot and not capturing anyone's eye. Its flowers, though present over early summer, are nothing to look at either, and don't stand out from the basic mat of foliage.

Yet it remains a firm favourite with me. It is reliable and hardy and acts as a great foil for many other more colourful plants. More important than that is its usefulness as a nurse plant. Barely more than 10 cm (4 in) high and slowly growing to about 1 m (3 ft) across over some years, it gives just the right amount of protection to those special plants that do best when afforded a little shade at the roots and some protection for their stems from the scorching sun at midday. In seeking to establish a number of wild peonies from Mallorca, Greece and Nepal it has proven ideal. Studying photographs of these plants growing naturally I came to understand that they did not occur in splendid isolation but in the company of grasses,

subshrubs, perennials and small bulbs. Endeavouring to replicate such a plant community led me to experiment with the idea of making my own version of the garrigue. So it was that I came to interplant seedlings of *Peonia cambessedesii*, *P. hellenica* and *P. emodi* with pieces of *Artemisia canescens* and other similar low herbs and perennials. Together with several thymes, a few savories, an erodium or two, a santolina and *Tanacetum densum* subsp. *amanum* (syn. *Chrysanthemum haradjanii*), an approximation of home has been established wherein the peonies can grow with shade and protection for their roots and their dormant buds are easily able to penetrate the loose thatch of plants, leaf out and flower in the sunshine above. It seems to work very well and is an idea capable of almost endless variation. It could be worked in a more pure attempt at the real Provençal biotype; it could be reduced to a very simple association or vastly enriched with an increased range of plants. And in the thick of it all, interweaving and tying together the whole, is the barely noticeable *Artemisia canescens*.

Propagation is very easy; almost any piece removed from the plant – even broken off roughly – will make roots if pushed into the soil. It also roots along its trailing stems where these touch the ground, and coarsely chopped prunings will take root if returned to the ground as loose mulch. It is winter dormant at which time it should get a hard cutting-back, leaving stems only a few centimetres above the soil level. It is easily controlled by pulling up the trailing stems. It is not at all deep rooted. Unfussy as to soil, it looks best where it is kept compact by dryish conditions and full exposure to the sun.

Rather more leafy but of similar habit and stature is *Artemisia stelleriana* with silver leaves that resemble those of a small chrysanthemum. It would intermingle well with the plants listed above, as would *Helichrysum angustifolium*, the Curry Plant, with its pungently scented needle-like silver leaves and low sprawling growth. Although a bit of a runabout, *Artemisia ludoviciana* 'Valerie Finnis' would add further variety of leaf form to such a grouping.

At least from the Mediterranean perspective all of these would be a better bet for longevity and sustainability than the many softer silver plants recommended by Mrs Underwood and her compatriots. The likes of the softwooded silver senecios, the kind used so often in nineteenth-century

'Valerie Finnis' is a form of *Artemisia ludoviciana* that honours an English gardener and nurserywoman. Though selected from cool climate stocks it has proven as hardy as the wild forms from California, where it is also known as Cudweed.

style bedding schemes in public parks and zoos, are too water dependent for our purposes as Mediterranean gardeners, as is in my experience the silver-leaved convolvulus, *Convolvulus cneorum.*

Other 'silvers' often touted in European garden magazines and books are the architectural thistles. They all need a setting in scale with their majestic size. They just cannot be cramped, for then they look silly and swamp everything else, only to die back in late summer leaving a huge hole that is impossible to fill at this driest of times. Planted with forethought, the prickle-free Globe Artichoke, *Cynara scolymous*, is a good addition to the range of silver plants; however, its prickly wild relative *Cynara cardunculus* is perhaps unwise if the former is available. Of the stately Arabian or Crusader's Thistle, *Onopordon arabicum*, what can be said in its favour? It is a declared weed in many countries; it is very prickly, and its prolific seeds are spread far and wide by the least summer breeze. Unless every care is taken – religiously mind you – that no seed is broadcast it should be avoided. 'One year's seeding is seven years' weeding' should be the watchword here.

Yucca rupicola subsp. *pallida*

Of all the plants available to Mediterranean climate gardeners the yuccas seem to find themselves in some sort of horticultural limbo. Why? Is it because they are still very much the province of specialist collectors of cacti, succulents and other xerophytic plants? Is it because they haven't yet been sufficiently used by designers and landscapers? Are there not supplies in a range sufficiently wide to attract the attention of nursery crawlers and other hapless plantoholics? They are not hard to grow so it can't be that. And they are easily raised from seed and cuttings and suckers. Micro-propagation works well too, so building up stocks can't be a reason.

I am at a loss to understand why yuccas are so overlooked. I buy every one I can get, often in twos if that is possible, and I recommend them frequently. They really are too good to be missed. Curiously, and encouragingly, the four large nurseries I know that do propagate yuccas report that sales of their limited stocks are quickly taken. So the plants are going somewhere; they just don't show yet. Roll on the day when they add their special attributes to our gardens and landscapes.

The special attribute applicable to this chapter is the silver-blue colouration of the leaves of some species and subspecies. As a rule these have been selected and reselected over successive generations so nursery stocks are fairly uniform, although the wild populations might show considerable variation from plain green to grey-green to grey to silver to silver-blue. The silver-blue colouration comes from a waxy bloom on the leaf surfaces; the greater the density of the wax the more intense the colour. The waxy bloom is dislodged by rain and by being touched so it is not indelible but where plants can be sited to minimise such weathering they will look quite striking.

First choice would have to be *Yucca rupicola* subsp. *pallida* which, as the name implies, is pale due to a dense bloom that creates an intense silver-blue covering. Each leaf is about 1 m (3 ft) long and 7 cm (2¾ in) wide at its broadest point. Sword-shaped, and equipped with one sharp terminal spine, the leaves are held in a more or less erect rosette. The identifying feature of this species is the way each leaf has a simple twist or curve. Botanical information is a bit sketchy, those lumpers and splitters at work still, but *Yucca rupicola* and its sub-tribe are centred in Texas.

This yucca is stemless; it makes no above-ground trunk and increases by offsets made underground after flowering. In most cases these offsets will not be prolific, so the plant once established and flowering more or less maintains itself. The flower spikes appear annually if the plant is well established in conditions to its liking. Each spike is approximately 2.5 m (8 ft) tall and simple in construction, with creamy white bells tinged green on the outside ranged along its length, either solitary or in small clusters.

American authorities suggest that this yucca is being used increasingly in landscapes around its Texan habitats and that it has outstanding ornamental characteristics that should see it more widely distributed. We can fervently hope so.

Continuing in the blue-leaved vein, there are two other yuccas that will reward those who seek them out with good colouration, pleasing foliage and hardy constitutions. These are *Yucca thompsoniana* and *Y. recurvifolia*, two quite distinct plants united by their silvery foliage. Again the degree of silveriness seems to depend pretty much on the care with which seed parents have been selected in succeeding generations, though some natural populations may have higher percentages of silver-leaved plants than others. Current literature does not offer much help to the uncertain but seed collectors' field notes sometimes highlight particular collecting populations as noteworthy for their foliage. That leaves the intending purchaser with the task of risking a mixed bag or specifying that silver-blues only are wanted.

Yucca thompsoniana is considered by some experts to be an outrider population of *Y. rigida* that is sufficiently different to warrant attention from discerning gardeners. It makes a compact hemispherical head of thin stiff leaves that are twisted in some seedlings and straight in others. This is probably a variable we can accept; quite the contrary with variations in leaf colour though. The bright white bell-shaped flowers are carried in panicles on a spike less than 1 m (3 ft) long. Usually the plant remains a solitary rosette and in great age can attain a stature of 3 m (10 ft) or more.

Yucca recurvifolia is also tree-like and often abundantly branched, and may also develop new basal trunks. The leaves are broad and tend to recurve gently. Leaf colour varies but the better forms are a distinct leaden grey-green. In cold locations new leaves often assume purple tones, an attraction in itself over the winter months. Flower spikes are tall and carry cream blooms; a telling picture when a mature plant is in bloom.

Eucalyptus cinerea
Argyle Apple

This small to medium-sized gum tree could have gone equally as happily into the chapter on shade makers, but since its silver foliage is its most outstanding feature it sits well here. Authorities list several other eucalypts as 'apples'. There is no explanation offered for the common name but that little mystery need not detain us here.

Aside from having foliage that is distinctly silver, in fact not far off white when the tree is viewed from a short distance, what is most attractive is that it frequently – in fact, most often – retains its juvenile leaf form into maturity. The juvenile leaves are 'orbicular, amplexicaul, opposite' which means, if my observations are right, very rounded, overlapping and in pairs; the pairs of leaves appear to be almost continuous around the stem, a striking effect that is of great appeal to floral artists and flower arrangers. So in a small garden the tree can serve two purposes, one indoors and one outside. Even so it may be too large in a small space, in which case it can be pollarded as advocated for several other species with attractive juvenile foliage. One offshoot of the attraction of the leaves for the cut-flower trade is that the Argyle Apple has been widely grown as a plantation crop for cutting that is exported to Japan, the Arab States, Europe and the USA. As far afield as Israel, where it is also grown as a field crop, it satisfies a demand for unusual and lasting stuffing for bouquets and arrangements.

Its garden uses are almost as versatile. It is hardy, drought tolerant and frost resistant once established; its habitat is part of Australia's Snowy Mountains so it is well adapted to harsh conditions. Generally the tree is well shaped in cultivation unless damaged or badly trimmed and has an upright habit free of side-branches for 2–3 m (7–10 ft). The white flowers are not particularly significant, though nectar-eating parrots and other birds love them in their season. The small fruits in clusters of three are round but not noticeably apple-like. The grey-brown bark is rough with strong vertical furrowing and offers a pleasing contrast with the leaves above; altogether a rather handsome gum tree.

Obviously this is a tree that shows to best advantage when grown in association with plants of a

Pollarding is hardly known in Mediterranean gardens but look how effective it is in encouraging new growth with silver juvenile leaves on the Argyle Apple, *Eucalyptus cinerea*. Cut low down annually at the onset of autumn, it grows away strongly.

Echeveria elegans has no common name in English but is such a beautiful plant that it's worth learning the Latin name. Fabulous overflowing from a terracotta pan, great as a garden edging, and splendid as groundcover too.

similar scale. It could make an effective partnership with *Leucodendron argenteum*, the South African Silver Tree, and with *Pyrus salicifolia* 'Pendula' where space permits, while on a more intimate scale it could pick up the colour associations with *Agave americana*, *A. vilmoriniana* or *A. attentuata* – especially if one of the more strongly glaucous forms could be acquired. As these trees can be sensitive to too much water, growing too strongly, getting out of form or even collapsing from root rots, it makes sense to underplant with things that do not require heavy summer irrigation. Were further decoration wanted, equally drought-resistant companions could be sought from any number of the larger artemisias – 'Faith Raven', 'Lambrook Silver' – or even the smaller 'Powis Castle'

and 'Poquerolle'. Titivating could take the form of broad swathes or fat clusters of *Echeveria elegans*, *E. crenulata*, *E. secunda* or *E.* x 'White Rose'.

Other combinations could be tried – partnerings with trees and shrubs with strongly contrasting leaf colour, for instance; perhaps the purple-leaved plums (*Prunus* x *blireana* et al) or the much abused red-leaved *Photinia*, bronze New Zealand flaxes, the dark-leaved kinds of *Coprosma* and *Pittosporum*. Where conditions allow further variety could be added by diversifying into other silver plants – the likes of *Plectranthus argentifolius*, the Silver-leaved Coleus, the dark *Echeveria* x 'Black Prince' or *Sansevieria* 'Silver Leaf'. But in my view these bold contrasts already appear in one form or the other in many gardens, most often as a result of happenstance. Finding suitable companions for the Argyle Apple and developing from them a plan based on silver foliage would be a greater challenge and the result more novel – for now.

Salvia apiana
White Sage

On the bare rock of the road cuttings leading from Carmel to Carmel Heights on the Monterey Peninsula in California grows a silvery shrubby plant, coated in road dust and grime, exposed to the full glare of the sun and blasted by reflected heat from a hard white limestone so dense it's almost marble. It is *Salvia apiana*, the White Sage.

The specific name refers to the attraction the flowers have for bees; an attraction that is put to good use by apiarists in the extensive wild populations that cover much of the chaparral country. For gardeners the White Sage has other attractions, namely intensely silver-white leaves that make quite a handsome small shrub, strongly aromatic and releasing their pungent scent when brushed against and when hot, dry winds blow – a remarkably refreshing discovery on a hot day. Tall spires of white flowers emerge in spring, growing to 1 m (3 ft) or so and flowering over six to eight weeks. And it is bone hardy.

I cannot imagine why some gardeners, perhaps more refined than I, do not like this plant. It is just too

From the steep, dry hillsides and stony roadside cuttings of the area around Carmel in California, White Sage, *Salvia apiana*, is a clean silver-white bullet that electrifies any garden scene. It has pungent foliage too, so place it where it can be touched.

reliable and useful to be ignored. In the most unpromising situations it will grow and give a good account of itself. Why reject it?

Salvia apiana is not particularly fussy about soil but it should be free draining. To give some indication of just how unfussy it is I can say that my greatest success has been with a plant set directly into the decaying stump of a dead apple tree. Perfect drainage, almost no nutrients, dry conditions, and still it has grown beautifully. Situation is important as the plant needs full sun to develop its characteristics to best advantage. The woody parts of the shrub are naturally kept compact by hard conditions and to keep that compactness is desirable as the hollow stems can give way and fall if growth becomes soft and elongated. Pruning can remedy this; the plant will recover well but will not take repeated prunings. It is fairly short-lived, after about ten years looking really decrepit and producing fewer flower stalks, so it is wise to plan for replacements. Fortunately it comes easily from seed and with any luck there will be at least a few volunteers to be moved to where they are wanted. Growth almost ceases during the summer months, the plant entering a state of aestivation (summer dormancy) until cooler wintry weather arrives. For Mediterranean gardeners this habit is a bonus. No summer irrigation is our aim and the White Sage will help us achieve it.

Effective plant associations can be diverse, each of them pleasing in their own way. In California White Sage grows alongside *Yucca whipplei* and *Artemisia californica*; a natural association which is replicated by many gardeners, both those who are enthusiasts for native plants and those who favour more eclectic approaches. But like my version of the garrigue, the imitation chaparral is by no means the end of the story. White Sage mixes very well with a wide variety of other Mediterranean climate plants including *Lavandula* x 'Seal', *Yucca thompsoniana*, dwarf agapanthus, *Teucrium pulverulentum*, *Marrubium libanoticum* 'Scallop Shell', *Tulbaghia fragrans* and a selection of hardy spring bulbs. (It is tempting to include a selection of the many new cultivars and colour selections of lavender that have been much promoted in recent years; however, they are not all entirely hardy in the traditional sense of lavenders being tolerant of dry soils and sunny situations. Sadly, many of them are better suited to cooler and damper summers than Mediterranean climate zones provide, and equally sadly many do not seem to live beyond two seasons.)

Given other opportunities to deploy *Salvia apiana* I could see it set out formally as the centrepiece of an arrangement of square beds framed with clipped santolinas, teucriums or low artemisias. In a different arrangement, looser and more fluid, the sage would be used in a manner resembling fields of lavender, following waves of contour or laid out in grid patterns. With just a light pruning after flowering the bushes could be made more uniform and regular in shape.

Poa labillardieri

Selected forms of this Australian native grass are as intense in their silver-blue colour as more widely distributed forms of *Festuca* and *Carex*. *Poa labillardieri* is perennial, reaching about 75 cm (30 in) and making a strongly arching clump of thin round leaf blades. At flowering it gets to 1 m (3 ft), maybe a little more, and makes a striking garden picture. While it is most often used to recreate natural-looking watercourses and grassy bushland savannas, this silver grass melds

This selected form of *Poa labillardieri* is renowned for its silver-blue colouring. Cut the plant hard after autumn and be prepared to replace it every two or three years to best enjoy its form and colouration.

nicely with more conventional perennial borders and mixed plantings. It is just the sort of plant needed to make a satisfying end point, say where paving changes direction or a piece of garden begins or ends. Its versatility doesn't end there. *Poa labillardieri* can make a very effective foil to stronger growing plant forms such as those of agaves, aloes and yuccas, and it also

offers a solid base on which to build a grass garden – if you are not concerned about the presence of snakes or the potential for bushfires.

Intending growers outside Australia would be well advised to seek assurances from suppliers that only selected silver forms will be supplied. There is much potential for grievance due to variation in the quality of the silveriness and the high percentage of plain green forms that arise from seed-sown supplies. In the revival of interest in native pasture grasses it is finding such a strong market among farmers that seed supplies are hard to find, even in the small quantities that would give an entrepreneurial nurseryperson an opening.

Cultivation is quite simple; small divisions of mature plants or seedlings should be grown on in pots until well established and planted out where they are required. With one or two waterings over the first summer they should be sufficiently well established to survive future seasons. After flowering it is best to cut the plants down quite hard, by about two-thirds at least, taking away all the dead leaf blades and spent flower stalks that would otherwise soon build up into a dense, stifling thatch. This allows new growth to emerge and fill out the shape and form of the plant. Gradually the base of the clump will reach about 60 cm (24 in) diameter, after which it will begin to decline, dying from the centre outwards. At this stage it is smart to dig up the whole thing and start again.

Poa needs an open, well-lit situation to develop its best grassy form. In too shady a spot, or where it is too wet, growth will quickly become etiolated and instead of a grassy silver fountain there will be a floppy mess that does nothing for design or appearance. No fertilising should be needed; the harder the grass is grown the better will be its health and argent display. There are no obvious pests for *Poa labillardieri*, though in close quarters and dampish conditions it is possible that rusts could infect the plants. Otherwise it is easy care.

Those with a quirky sense of plant humour could find it amusing to use the silver poa in a design that could be termed 'following the manner of Martha Schwarz', the creative American designer. Without wishing to suggest she would do this, it is possible to conceive of the grass as a kind of giant shaving brush that would, if each clump were trimmed so the foliage was mostly upright and slightly splayed, give rise to some very unusual garden effects. Combined with strong colours and forms such abstractions would give a lot of us something to think about. And that's good for all of us. Mind you, it wouldn't be half as challenging as seeing agaves and yuccas with eggshells impaled on the end of each leaf, as is sometimes seen in Mexico.

Poa labillardieri has one more excellent quality to recommend it to gardeners, and that is that it stays where you put it. Unlike some other silver grasses – *Elymus arenarius* 'Glauca', Blue Lyme Grass, in particular – poa is not wildly invasive, nor even mildly bothersome. It is perfectly peaceable.

Further information on grasses see John Greenlee, *The Encyclopedia of Ornamental Grasses*, Rodale, Emmaus, Pennsylvania, 1992. ISBN 0-87596-100-2

Lavandula x 'Seal'

Of all the lavenders that could be suggested as garden worthy in Mediterranean regions, this particular cultivar is, in my experience, superior to most others in terms of hardiness, reliability, longevity and beauty. Along with *Lavandula stoechas*, Italian Lavender, and its several forms including *L. stoechas* subsp. *pedunculata*, which are sufficiently resilient to self-sow and naturalise, this hybrid is one of the few lavenders that are good doers in mixed company in dry situations.

'Seal' is not a new introduction, having been around for at least 30 years and moving in and out of catalogues as interest in various aspects of lavender culture took hold among gardeners, herbalists, homoeopaths, craftworkers and cottage gardeners. Thought to be a selected cultivar of the hybrid *Lavandula* x *allardii*, it is characterised by vigorous growth to about 1 m (3 ft) high and 1.5 m (5 ft) across, with a strong woody frame and a dense coverage of silver-grey leaves, long and fairly narrow with small indented teeth towards the leaf tip, and very tall unbranched flower spikes holding aloft strongly scented purple spikards. It is preferred by craftworkers who make such lavender-based products as lavender fans and the objects like folded umbrellas that are used to perfume handkerchief drawers. As a garden subject 'Seal' is a plant of distinct stature and presence,

The Italian lavender, *Lavandula stoechas*, is among the hardiest of the clan and now available in an increasingly wide range of colours and forms; most retain the tough characteristics of the wild form pictured here. It grows best when grown hard in full sun and with minimal summer irrigation.

particularly when it is covered with hundreds of flower spikes in early summer.

Maintenance is simple: prune immediately after the flowers have been harvested, or when the plants have finished flowering. Pruning can be as hard as necessary but cutting into old wood with no signs of active growth can be a little risky, especially if the plant is old – say more than seven years. The best and safest strategy is to prune every year so that no drastic cutting is needed. Plants can generally be expected to live in good condition for ten to fifteen years, after which they generally collapse from the centre out exposing the bare heart of the branch structure. They may well live beyond this state of senility but clearly this appearance may not be suitable for the garden.

Lavandula stoechas subsp. *pedunculata* is instantly recognised by the long colourful 'flags' at the top of each spike. Several selected forms are getting about, some darker coloured, some with larger peduncles – all are reliable in Mediterranean conditions.

Replacement is easy; simply make short cuttings of side-shoots by tugging each shoot gently downwards so it breaks away from the parent plant with a 'heel' from the main branch attached. Dibble these into a free-draining potting mix, water attentively and watch for signs of decay, removing failed cuttings before rots spread. After about six weeks the cuttings should be rooted and can be planted out where they are needed.

As an internal hedge *Lavandula* x 'Seal' gives a good account of itself, for its dimensions and habits of growth form an effective barrier, too tall and too wide for all but the most determined youngster to get over. Its density is a deterrent to dogs and cats and visually it makes an effective break between parts of the garden without disrupting a longer view. Otherwise, its broad, rounded form has the solidity to anchor a piece of garden or border or to make an effective contribution to formal arrangements of gravel and clipped shapes.

Skimming through various books about herbs, scented plants and silver-leaved plants, readers will come across several other lavenders recommended for inclusion in garden schemes. Be aware that these books may not be written from the point of view of Mediterranean gardening; some are for collectors who want to have a representative selection of all lavenders, or for those seeking advice about the best kinds for different commercial enterprises or for homoeopathic use. Not all lavenders are equally hardy, long-lived or attractive as garden subjects. It is tempting to consider the likes of *Lavandula pinnata* and *L. lanata* with their appealing silver-white, much-divided leaves. It is only too easy to dream up planting schemes based on these apparent beauties. They are worth trying but are specialised plants and may not prove as hardy as required by the rough and tumble of Mediterranean circumstances. This may seem incongruous considering that they both inhabit places usually thought to be Mediterranean – Spain and the Canary Islands – but *Lavandula lanata* comes from mountainous areas and *L. pinnata* from the humid atmosphere of the otherwise dry islands. Each in their own way has adapted to unique climatic conditions that may be hard to approximate in gardens. Their habits of growth, while compact, are also open and somewhat sparse, so while individual leaflets are fascinating close up they are perhaps less convincing as an element of a garden plan.

Ballotta pseudodictamnus

Ballotta pseudodictamnus sprawls and snakes about in the most difficult soils and driest spots – and always looks trim and perky as long as its annual crop of flowering stems is cut down before they have time to make the plant look scruffy.

This Cretan native does not at first jump out as a plant of the first silvery order. It is a small woody perennial that reaches about 75 cm (30 in) across within a few years. Its stems and leaves are covered with a dense, long-lasting silver felting, or fur. Each year the woody framework produces long stem growths that are well clothed in leaves and finally produce clusters of small lavender flowers in the leaf axils. These would hardly be described as startling, or even showy, but they do add to the charm of the plant. The flowering stems last for several months after the flowers have faded, maintaining the show of silver well into early winter, by which time a hard pruning will restore the bush's compact form and make way for the new growth even now emerging from the base and along the older twigs and branches.

With me the ballotta grows at the base of a dwarf conifer, the kind that reaches 4.5 m (15 ft) after 30 years and can't be trimmed or pruned without destroying its shape. Here it is bone-dry soil most of the year, the conifer greedily soaking up every drop of available moisture. By mid-summer this situation is baked by

the western sun every day – and still the ballotta does its thing and looks good. In fact it outdid some nearby *Euphorbia rigida* so well that it replaced those at the base of the conifer, which now has an underskirt of ballotta. It is a pleasing plant by virtue of its thrift and appearance.

I haven't grown it in conditions that could be thought any easier, but I am certain it would prove adaptable to almost any situation that was sunny and dry most of the time. It would be a very useful addition where spring bulbs are grown. In its winter state of reduced size, due to pruning, bulbs would easily be set between plants of ballotta, grow, flower and go down again before the longer summer growth spread out and covered the ground between the bushes. The bulbs could be as simple or fancy as you wish; preferably they should be early flowering so there would be little chance of growth overshadowing their ripening foliage. Have you ever thought of trying to naturalise some of the hardy wild tulips? *Tulipa saxitalis*, itself a native of Crete, is one that comes readily to mind. It has lilac-pink flowers, somewhat starry in shape, with a yellow central patch at the heart of each bloom. Red-flowered *Tulipa hagerii* could be an option, and lilac *T. aucheriana* another. Fortunately these bulbs are becoming available in quantity and at prices that make bulk planting possible. As natives of Turkey these species tulips, and others, are much hardier and more easily grown than the elaborate large-flowered hybrids.

Cyclamen hederifolium is commonplace on sheltered hillsides in southern Italy, Greece and Turkey. It is colourful and easy for gardeners in most Mediterranean regions so long as it is not baked under the summer sun. With no-dig gardening practices its seeds will soon self-sow over a large area.

Another option could be to underplant the ballotta with corms of wild cyclamen, choosing the autumn and winter flowering species *Cyclamen hederifolium* and *C. coum. Cyclamen creticum* could be an interesting choice too. It has very small flowers with narrow, twisted, white petals and a delicate perfume. It is very hardy provided that the resting corms are not exposed to the roasting rays of the sun. In habitat they live under shrubs and among grasses and rocks where they have the protection of dead growth and fallen leaves in summer. Even before the first rains of autumn *Cyclamen hederifolium* will be showing its pink or white flowers well before the leaves appear. Searching out one of the scented strains selected by specialist bulb growers would be worth the trouble if you are the sort of gardener who likes to see and smell lovely things while you work on your hands and knees. Given conditions to their liking, wild cyclamen will self-sow freely and quickly colonise a wide area wherever suitable shelter from adjacent plants exists.

It is said that flower arrangers like long flower-bearing stems as backgrounds to mixed arrangements in the manner of Constance Spry, the English florist so influential in the 1950s. The stems of the ballotta have an attractive sinuous quality that would find much the same uses as Bells of Ireland (*Mollucella laevis*), although smaller in scale. It is reputed to dry well too, but as I have no enthusiasm for dust-gatherers I have no experience to report on here. And anyway I like it perfectly well as nature intended – in the garden.

7 Surprising super specials

Many newcomers to Mediterranean gardening bring with them with some unshakeable preconceptions; other long-established residents of Mediterranean climate zones have equally well-cemented ideas about what might or might not be possible in their locality. In my gardening I have taken an exploratory approach, preferring to experiment with plants to see what they will do in my conditions. There have been some pleasant surprises, surprises that I think are worth sharing. My concern is not to show off what I can grow that others cannot, nor is it to make a catalogue of impressive rarities, or to hint that I have some secret and superior skill. What I want to suggest is that everyone who gardens in Mediterranean climate regions should try a few experiments. These could begin, as mine did, by developing an understanding of the match between patterns of plant growth and patterns of weather, and of the survival features of plants that grow naturally where we live. When we appreciate the importance of storage roots and stems, of growth that takes place during the wet, rainy months, and of plants that rest over the hottest months, we then have a framework for considering how best to garden where we are, and to do so with some well-founded sense of experimentation and excitement.

Armed with this framework of understanding we can go shopping for plants; plants we know for certain will grow, plants we have every reason to expect will grow happily, plants we believe have the necessary attributes to give them a good chance, plants we think might have a chance in a suitable microclimate, plants we hope will have a chance in a suitable microclimate with some additional irrigation and attention. There is another category too: plants we know haven't got a hope of surviving. Should these be bought? Yes, why not have the pleasure of their flowers for a month or two, as long as it is understood that they will be temporary inhabitants of our gardens, just as we understand the temporary qualities of potted cyclamen, potted annuals, indoor azaleas, poinsettias at Christmas, forced hyacinths in autumn and tulips in winter. So, go to it with a will and explore for those marginal plants that may, or may not, succeed in the conditions you can provide.

Peonia suffruticosa
Tree Peony

Of all the plants tendered in these pages the Tree Peony may well be the most surprising, as it is mostly thought of as the pampered inhabitant of an altogether different category of gardens – *tres riches* rather than Mediterranean. Yet by guesswork and observation I have concluded that it is quite reliable in all but the driest Mediterranean regions. My first observations were made as a child as I walked to school along a dusty main road through market gardens and orchards – stone fruits, loquats and oranges. One house had a straight row of a dozen or so low stumpy bushes that in late spring put forth a show of deep wine-coloured flowers. Some years later I knew them to be tree peonies.

Many years afterward while researching for my book *Gardens of the Sun* I drew up a list of

Tree peonies have strong, far-reaching root systems well able to withstand warm, dry conditions once their growth spurt has slowed after flowering. This white Tree Peony (*Peonia suffruticosa* hybrid) is flourishing at 'Filoli' on the southern outskirts of Berkeley, California.

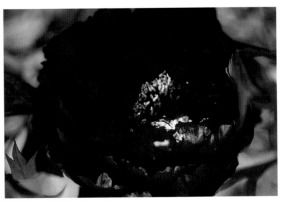

'Black Panther' is one of the modern Tree Peony hybrids that is gradually making its way into gardens everywhere. Such unique colouration demands placement where the lustrous petals can be seen backlit by sunshine.

characteristics that would be good indicators of plants best equipped to cope with Mediterranean type climates. Among these was having a sturdy, far-reaching root system, and this is why the Tree Peony gets my recommendation. It has a very stout root system of this type which allows it to thrive in some unlikely looking places. Once established it can survive hot, dry summers surprisingly well with its thick root-trunk acting as a water storage system and its far-reaching roots acting to collect soil moisture over a wide area. I find it produces a burst of new growth at flowering time and after that ripens the new growth and developing seed pods over the rest of summer. While the leaves may look decidedly ratty and scorched by summer's end the plant is, despite its weather-beaten appearance, in good shape for peak performance next spring.

Grown as field crops in parts of China, tree peonies look pretty much the same as they do in the wild. Whether to be harvested for the medicinal properties of the roots, or to be dug, potted and forced into flower under glass for sale in the big cities, the plants are not mollycoddled in the manner advocated by some authorities, who confuse the high cost of the plants with some imagined state of extreme constitutional delicacy that simply isn't proven by experience. It is as well to understand, however, that tree peonies do not thrive where the roots of trees and other shrubs compete aggressively for available moisture and nutrients, nor will perform well where they are overshadowed by taller plants. Achieving healthy,

strong-flowering growth is a careful balancing act between giving the plants what they must have and preserving the flowers from sun and wind for the besotted gardener's pleasure. In the end the plants must come out the winners here. If the flowers are to be enjoyed as long as possible the best course may be to pick them and enjoy them indoors.

The name Tree Peony is a little misleading as the plants do not make a genuinely permanent stem and branch structure. Instead they make a woody structure that may last seven to twelve years, maybe longer, but eventually entire branches are liable to die mysteriously. Usually they look fine going into winter dormancy but the buds fail to swell in spring and it becomes worryingly apparent that the branch has died. There is an upside to this depressing event in that strong new shoots usually surge from the surviving structure within a week or so of the awful realisation dawning. There is a hint in all this for those wishing to maximise the chances for success with Tree Peonies: pruning encourages strong replacement growth. So instead of treasuring a plant with only one stem take your heart in your hand and prune it back by a half to two-thirds and see if the plant doesn't send up two or three strong new shoots.

Numerous named tree peonies are listed in the catalogues of specialist dealers but such are the vagaries of propagation and the pressures of demand that it is common for not all varieties described to be available every year. This need not be a huge concern to anyone other than collectors who want one of everything, especially if it is rare or costly. Seedlings are also offered for sale by wholesale propagators. These can be quite attractive, being mostly semi-double, or semi-single, with or without dark red central flares at the base of each petal, warm pink or pale pinky white.

Plectranthus alba

Plectranthus are fairly common plants, related to salvias and lobelias, and popular for filling up awkward spaces under trees and shrubs where shade is a disincentive to many more colourful plants, and where intense root competition ensures that a lot of plants won't thrive. Semi-succulent four-sided stems and rough-surfaced green leaves, sometimes with purplish tinges on the undersides, make shrubs that range between 1–2 m (3–7 ft), sometimes reaching 3 m (10 ft) in sheltered positions among other shrubs. There are other forms that grow flat against the ground, or are pendent, hanging over banks and down garden walls. A few have glossy leaves. In some countries these trailing forms are known as Swedish Ivy. Short spires of rich blue or purple-blue appear in mid-summer and continue until cold winter weather slows growth. Being more or less succulent, the plectranthus tribe are frost tender and can be felled to the ground by even light frosts, especially if they recur several times while the plant is in a weakened state. Capable of withstanding periods of dry weather, the plants may flop and their leaves droop for days, even weeks at a time, but given a light shower or sprinkle from a hose they revive quickly and can then withstand further dry periods.

Plectranthus are so easy to propagate anyone can do it; simply snap off a section of stem with at least two leaf nodes, the joints where leaves and stem attach to each other, and plant in situ. A few light waterings will usually see the cuttings make roots and grow away happily enough. They have no significant pests or diseases and are very satisfactory as background plants, needing almost no care or maintenance other than an occasional pruning to keep them from becoming leggy with old growth and bare stems.

The white-flowered *Plectranthus alba* is less commonly seen in gardens than the blue and purple types, but is well worth any trouble involved in obtaining it. It stands out in shaded settings where the deeper coloured kinds tend to recede into the darkness unless things can be arranged so that for part of the day at least the flowers are in sunlight. It is as well to treat these plants as subjects for mass planting rather than for dotting about here and there in a mixture of things. Their simple charms are thus amplified rather than being lessened by being thrown into competition with larger, brighter flowers. At other seasons the mass of dark leaves, the bulky solid shapes of the shrubs could be set in handsome contrast with clumps of clivea. Given that they will most likely not be flowering together there is an opportunity for the foliage to act as a foil for the cream or deep red hybrid cliveas now coming into wider cultivation. Or again, the plectranthus could be set together with broad sweeps or long ribbons of hardy hellebores, particularly *Helleborus argutifolius*, itself so good for dryish shade. Another good companion of similar constitution would be the Peppermint-scented Geranium, *Pelargonium tomentosum.*

An excellent, far-roving groundcover, the Peppermint-Scented Geranium, *Pelargonium tomentosum*, covers itself in a dense mound of boldly shaped leaves that are strongly perfumed.

Lupinus arboreus
Tree Lupin

I imagine there will be those who find the inclusion of the Tree Lupin rather a puzzle: in parts of New Zealand it is almost a weed, elsewhere it is hardly known at all – in Australia for instance. It is not long-lived, nor is it consistent in colour, two demerits for some, and it is not really a tree but merely a shrub – a further demerit.

The Tree Lupin, *Lupinus arboreus*, makes a great addition to a Mediterranean garden in late winter and early spring. The creamy yellow flowers, somewhat variable in their depth of colour, and silver-grey leaves provide a great foil to brighter yellow flowers as well as to lavender and purple shades and lime greens too. Photo courtesy Clive Blazey.

And yet this old-timer has a long history of finding favour among discriminating gardeners from Gertrude Jekyll onwards. Why, one might well ask?

It grows quickly, filling awkward gaps, screening unsightly places, it is hardy and unfussy as to soil – though it is intolerant of badly drained and shady places. Being short-lived it finds a role as a shelter plant in exposed situations and when its work is done two or three years from first planting it can be ripped out with no great loss. Like all legumes it has some function in fixing nitrogen in the soil, enriching even the poorest dirt and rendering it more amenable to other plants. It is easily propagated from seeds which are produced abundantly. And it is easily controlled by hand pulling; the heavy seeds do not travel far unless carried by animals or birds so environmental control should be no problem.

Aside from its general attributes of hardiness and utility the Tree Lupin has, in its flowers, an asset for gardeners who generally find yellow a bit hard to cope with. I like yellow, but apparently there are those who find the colour a tad too raucous and crude. So the creamy yellow of the Tree Lupin's spires offer a toned-down version of sunshine that can lift a piece of garden from being dull without hitting one between the eyes with shafts of chrome yellow. Another softening feature of this low shrub, to around 1.5 m (5 ft) is its silver-grey foliage. Clothed to the ground with leaves the plants always sit comfortably in a garden, doing their bit in late spring and at all other seasons

In a difficult spot, shaded by deciduous trees in summer and growing in rocky shale, *Yucca gloriosa* 'Variegata' and *Euphorbia characias* subsp. *wulfenii* make a pleasing picture year round and are perfectly at home as partners in a simple planting for low maintenance and low water use – in fact they get no water in this situation.

contributing a solid base and background for other plants. It could be teamed up with California poppies – the apricot and brick pink strains would look good; and a few stray runners of a similarly coloured nasturtium falling through the superstructure of the lupin would look great. It could also be teamed up with any of the silver-leaved artemisias, *Teucrium fruticans* or *Chrysanthemum ptarmicaefolium* – all shrubs that assort well together. Contrast could be found with *Yucca glauca*, or even *Agave vilmoriniana* if there were space enough for the octopussy spread of its broad rosette of swirling leaves. A choice could also be made for the garden artichoke (*Cynara scolymous*), although this tends to collapse suddenly after flowering, leaving an enormous gap for four months until autumnal rains bring forth a fresh crop of its huge leaves.

If the Tree Lupin were selected for permanent inclusion in a garden scheme it would be wise to take account of its relatively short life span by ensuring there are always one or two youngsters growing on to take over the starring role. Plants up to twelve months old can be transplanted with reasonable success provided the deed is done with care and the transplant treated with supplementary water until it shows signs of fresh new growth.

The white perennial tree stock, *Matthiola incana* 'Alba', is found occasionally growing in sandhills and on rock faces on the coasts of many countries: it was an early and willing botanical tourist. As a garden plant it is easy, accommodating and charming, living for three or four years before needing replacement from self-sown seedlings.

Matthiola incana 'Alba'
White Perennial Tree Stock

Martyn Rix, the English botanist and author of many admirable books, kindly sent me seeds of this plant after I admired it in his garden at 'Rose Ash'. Since growing it successfully it has been passed on to numerous gardeners in Australia and elsewhere. When I first noticed it in Martyn's garden I recalled seeing something similar in mauve-pink growing naturalised on the cliff faces and rocky shores around Encounter Bay in South Australia where Nicolas Baudin and Matthew Flinders met as they mapped the southern coast of the continent for their rival governments. This is what sparked my interest in the white form. I wondered how long the plant had been established in an area now thick with holiday houses, one of the earliest sites settled by colonists after they arrived in 1836.

Loosely described as a 'tree', *Matthiola incana* is no more than a perennial with a permanent shrub-like framework arising from a single stout stem. It lasts about six years before the whole structure becomes too woody and begins to fall apart. Where it can be grown really hard, in imitation of its coastal habitat, it might well last much longer, though as it grows older it also gets more decrepit and ugly to look upon – all sticks and stalks with a few clusters of dusty grey leaves on top. Best to start again frequently, I should think. Every two years would not be too often. The large seeds are freely produced and easily self-sow and germinate in great numbers. Young seedlings

Crambe maritima or Sea Kale is one of the forebears of the cabbage and curly kale family. A denizen of pebbly sea shores around the Mediterranean coast, its strong leaf form and sweetly perfumed flowers recommend it to gardeners everywhere.

could be moved from around the mother plant and relocated as desired without undue setback.

Pierandrea Mattioli (1500–1577), after whom the genus is named, was an early Italian herbalist-cum-botanist-cum-physician and author noted for his translation into Italian (as opposed to scholarly, academic Latin) of the herbal of Dioscorides, by repute doctor to Anthony and Cleopatra.

The White Tree Stock finds company in my garden with other reliably hardy perennials of the not-overdeveloped type; the likes of *Anthemis* x 'Sauce Hollandaise', *A.* x 'Sussanah Mitchell' and *A.* x 'Mrs E.C. Buxton', along with the tall *Sedum* hybrids 'Hestor' and 'Matrona'. These all have sufficient of the wildling about them to make a relaxed and uncomplicated composition that remains in form for a long time and to which the various plants add their flowers from time to time. In the same vicinity there are also plantings of *Salvia argentea*, the Silver-leaved Salvia, and *Crambe maritima*, Sea Kale. The latter has sweetly scented, creamy white flowers, and both have excellent silver-coloured leaves, but we shall come to them later

Crataegus tanacetifolia
Tansy-leaved Hawthorn

The Tansy-leaved Hawthorn is a delightful small tree with heaps of character and a real tree presence despite its diminutive size. At 4–5 m (14–17 ft) tall and pretty much the same across it forms a pleasing lollipop shape with a lovely trunk covered in shaggy silver-grey bark with strong vertical fissures. The leaves are broad and spatula-shaped with deeply cut ends. Most telling is the dense covering of short, fine, grey-silver hairs that adds a lovely depth of grey to a garden of silver-leaved plants, highlighting the whiteness of many of them. The tansy reference is to the supposed resemblance to the leaves of the herb tansy (*Tanacetum vulgare*) but it is a rather far-fetched likeness; suffice it to say the leaves are cut, or lacinated, but not to the point of delicacy or fragility. Deciduous in winter, and with a dense cover of small white flowers in spring before the leaves unfurl, its chief highlight, apart from overall colour and character, is the heavy crop of light orange haws that ripen in late summer and persist until the birds clean them up.

You may conclude that this is a tree I greatly

Hawthorn trees are dependable performers in many areas with Mediterranean climates. The Tansy-leaved Hawthorn, *Crataegus tanacetifolia*, is one of the better ones – moderate in stature with rough stringy bark and silver-grey leaves.

admire. You are right. It is also a tree that, in my estimation, is much overlooked by garden designers, garden owners and landscapers.

How may it be put to good use? How may it be planted to good effect? First, it is a true tree form in its manner of growth, producing a well-defined trunk and superstructure so it is very useful in cramped conditions where a larger tree could not be accommodated. For courtyards and small inner-city gardens it is a strong contender, the more so as it has at least four seasons of interest, four changes of garb – naked branches in winter, a flurry of white flowers in spring, a crown of silver-grey leaves throughout summer and a heavy crop of haws in autumn. Like all deciduous plants the Tansy-leaved Hawthorn has drawbacks, in that it drops its leaves and may also

Hawthorns have haws, roses have hips and sloes have sloes but whatever they are called berries are an added bonus to any flowering tree or shrub. These are the haws of *Crataegus tanacetifolia.*

Clematis viticella 'Etoile Violette' is one of an attractive and numerous group of small-flowered hybrid clematis. Easier to grow than their larger flowered cousins, these make up in numbers what they lack in size

drop berries if the birds don't find them first. But at least the mess is made only for a few weeks of the year and is relatively easily dealt with, at least by those who are compulsive and obsessive about a few stray leaves.

The regular growth habit of this tree also recommends it for semi-formal planting schemes where consistent growth is needed from specimen to specimen to maintain the idea. A little judicious winter or summer pruning could further enhance the impact of regularity and form.

It is also the sort of tree that can be drawn into a subterfuge very successfully – where the effect of an orchard or grove might be wanted but not necessarily the care and work of maintaining apples, pears, plums and such like, nor dealing with the mess of fallen fruit that comes about when there is a mid-summer glut and the things can neither be given away nor processed into a sufficient diversity of flavours to warrant a flurry of bottling and preserving. The Tansy-leaved Hawthorn makes a perfect orchard tree without actually being one; it needs no spraying or fancy pruning techniques and is even pretty well proof against the disfiguring depredations of the cherry slug, thanks to the dense covering, front and back, of silvery leaf hairs.

Clematis viticella
Old Man's Beard, Virgin's Bower.

Any kind of clematis is often viewed by gardeners in warm, dry climates as problematical, probably not worth bothering about. Yet quite a few species are native to the Mediterranean climate zones, which should suggest that there are a few possibilities to be considered. *Clematis viticella* is one such species. Besides the wild form there are numerous garden hybrids that offer even more variety to those willing to take a punt and make a few minor efforts to effect reasonable chances for success. Clematis are like many plants in that they prefer situations where their root systems are enveloped in cool soil. Moisture is

'Perle d'Azur' is one of the *Clematis viticella* hybrids that can be relied on to perform well in most Mediterranean climate regions; simply prune hard in winter, fertilise, mulch and stand back.

so that its base is lightly shaded for about half of each day. Observing these few tips should ensure *Clematis viticella* and its hybrids are successful in many more Mediterranean gardens.

Clematis are mostly climbing plants that scramble about by the habit of their leaf petioles (stalks) twining around the twigs and stems of other nearby plants for support as they head skyward. *Clematis viticella* is a purple-blue-flowered climber of low stature, generally attaining no more than 4 m (14 ft). The flowers may be open, starry and somewhat bowl-shaped or more closed and bell-shaped. Frequently the flower has a broad paler central stripe that shows inside and out. Other forms of the species have uniform flower colour but show a marked seersucker texture on the upper petal surface. Given such a variable range of characteristics it is hardly surprising that the hybrids also show a great deal of variety; a feature of the species that gives gardeners a wonderful choice. Check out 'Alba Luxurians', 'Carmencita', 'Etoile Violette', 'Perle d'Azur' and 'Betty Corning'.

See John Howells, *Trouble Free Clematis: The Viticellas*, Garden Art Press, Woodbridge, UK, 1998. ISBN 1-870673-24-7

Clematis texensis

Another kind of Old Man's Beard or Virgin's Bower, this particular clematis is just as hardy and reliable in Mediterranean climate gardens where its requirements for a cool, shaded root-run and a degree of soil moisture during the hottest months can be met. Having grown the species and its several hybrids I have found no significant differences between them so far as their tolerance of warm, dry climates goes. As the name implies the wild form is found in Texas, growing on the edges of woodlands where the plants can scramble up shrubs and trees or among the high grasses found in such locations. The flowers are typical of clematis, being composed of four (sometimes six) strongly recurved petals that are thick, rather like orange peel but less fleshy. As *Clematis texensis* grows and flowers with the rains (and snow melt) of spring and early summer, it is semi-dormant by mid-summer when, having ripened its seeds and dispersed them, it makes little further active growth but puts its energy into

necessary when the plant is in active growth but after that it can exist quite comfortably in a state of suspended animation; a state in plants called aestivation. Among Mediterranean plants this is a quite common pattern of growth, a mechanism by which they get through the driest and hottest months until cooler, wetter conditions return. Gardeners wishing to capitalise on this survival technique can do so by adapting a few simple garden techniques. A mulch of flat paving stones, roof tiles, slates or stones can assist survival, as can a super mulch of coarse shreddings over the top of the stone mulch. These simple steps will alleviate the impact of most summer weather. As further insurance plants can be given a soaking once a month over the hottest part of the year. A final aid to survival would be siting the clematis developing growth buds for the following season, eventually becoming dormant in autumn. Except in the driest regions these characteristics of growth mean that the plants are reasonably well adapted to Mediterranean climates.

The wild form is variable from seed, the preferred forms reported as being bright wine red to darker wine in colour, but the seedlings I have raised have always turned out to be rather pale pearly pinks that fade to almost white. It is still a worthwhile plant, and one can always hope for self-sown volunteers to arise with more desirable colouring. Neither the wild form nor the garden hybrids are as vigorous as many other clematis and generally make only 3–4 m (10–14 ft) growth annually. Left alone the plants will grow longer and longer, with ugly woody stems supporting sparse active growth and few flowers. The best treatment is to cut the vines to the ground every winter. This will stimulate strong new basal growth, good foliage and ample flowers.

While the plant is well equipped to climb with leaf stalks that act as twining tendrils it grows equally well as a scrambler over low subshrubs such as artemisias, lavenders, cistus, sedums and even low thymes, oregano, erodiums and such like. Grown this way the flowers can be set against foliage that shows them to advantage and displays them in a way that goes beyond the traditional uses for clematis. Low bushes and groundcovers also have the advantage of providing a good source of shade and cool soil conditions for the clematis's roots.

Recommending named varieties can be problematical unless a good supplier is close at hand. For most of us it will be a matter of catch as catch can; the selection will probably be very limited. Fortunately all are good garden subjects and can be looked on for a fine touch of colour and interesting flower form. Scan specialist catalogues and mail order suppliers for 'Sir Trevor Lawrence' (dark purple-red), 'Ladybird Johnson' (dusky red), 'Etoile Rose' (cherry pink with lighter edges), 'Princess Diana' (bright deep pink), 'Duchess of Albany' (clear rosy pink) and 'Gravetye Beauty' (rich red).

For more information see Mary Toomey and Everett Leeds, *An Illustrated Encyclopedia of Clematis*, Timber Press, Portland, Oregon, 2001. ISBN 0-88192-508-X

Lonicera hildebrandiana
Burmese Honeysuckle

I have always been very pleased I have been successful with this large and beautiful climber from the Himalayan foothills of Burma. Now about 30 years old and well established, the plant was a complete mystery when I bought it. Reference to (English) garden books at the time described it as tender, needing care until old wood was ripened and barky. The Burma tag didn't help either, suggesting high humidity and frequent rain could easily be required for success. Happily it has proven quite hardy, tolerant of dry periods and though vigorous not so thuggish that it smothers everything it touches. And then there are the flowers! These were downplayed somewhat in those first references; as a greenhouse resident or denizen of only the most sheltered Cornish gardens it was likely to have its flowering savaged by chilly weather, but in Mediterranean Adelaide it is generous and glorious. In early summer the first slender trumpets extend, changing from creamy yellow to deep golden yellow over the three or four days each flower lasts. About 15–20 cm (6–8 in) long, the flowers form a small cluster, opening sometimes singly, sometimes in pairs, occasionally in threesomes but never altogether. The display builds until the impact is overwhelming, a mass of golden flowers, perfume across the whole garden, and a huge surprise for visitors, most of whom have never seen such a thing before.

Unlike its many small cousins this giant honeysuckle seems not to be colonised by the armies of grey aphids that regularly smother the rest of the clan.

Tough enough to survive without mollycoddling, *Lonicera hildebrandiana* can easily host support acts too; the likes of roses 'Buff Beauty' and 'Graham Thomas' seem no hindrance at all, and they manage to flower happily together. By good fortune *Clematis* 'Jackmanii Superba' also flourishes in the same setting, so from time to time its blunt-pointed purple stars enliven the yellows and golds of the roses and honeysuckle. Nothing much will thrive under such a tangle despite the fact that the underskirts of the honeysuckle are de-thatched of dead twigs and branches every year, although a dense mat of *Vinca minor* 'Elizabeth Cran' and *Hedera* 'Buttercup' fight it out with convincing gusto, adding plummy winter flowers and golden leaves at ground level. The golden-leaved form of oregano was also there but having lost the tussle it won't be replaced. The Mediterranean garden is no place for weaklings.

Perfect for throwing over an ugly shed, or over a strong, high pergola, Burmese Honeysuckle is one of those garden characters over which it is impossible to wield any but the most subtle influence. It would have to be very much doubted that such a free spirit could be tamed by harsh shaping and pruning, indeed, it could only be expected to sulk and withdraw the favour of its prodigious flowering. While not a plant for a small garden this is nonetheless a much under-utilised climber that should find a home in many more gardens.

Bauhinia variegata 'Alba'
White Orchid Tree

This small tree has a decidedly tropical appearance, its flowers most often said to resemble some kind of exotic orchid, and its leathery, liver-shaped leaves having the air of some glaucous foliage plant from India or Columbia. Lucky us that it is entirely hardy in Mediterranean gardens where winters are gentle, free of hard frosts and chilling, blasting gales. In fortunate instances farsighted street planners have planted avenues of this spreading, shady tree. It can be briefly deciduous in winter but this seems not to have any impact on the flowers which come with the first leaf break. Those forms which show flowers before the foliage expands are to be on the whole preferred, as the flowers are shown to greatest advantage against a blue sky and a haze of green leaves as yet still furled.

There are several rosy pink and pinky lilac forms about, but the pristine beauty of the white form is to my mind superior. With pale green nectary stripes down the centre of each petal the whiteness is emphasised to a state of refined glamour; just like a cattleya orchid in fact. Individual seed-raised trees can vary in the quantity of flowers produced so while the large 'bean' seeds are easily raised it may be good sense to seek out plants propagated from cuttings of the most floriferous kinds.

Young trees tend to be rather rambunctious and wayward in the vigour and direction of growth. Their teenage years can be fraught with misunderstood diversions from the path to uprightness, and no amount of discipline or standardised treatment seems effective; they will do their own thing come what may. A whole avenue of two dozen such trees has proven completely unanswerable to the firm ministrations of the pruning saw, the secateurs and even the stake! Left to grow unchecked they will form a low spreading crown that by sheer strength of personality eventually makes skyward, at which time tactful parents can encourage matters with some gentle trimming and removal of extraneous bottom growth. It is worth it in the end to see an avenue clothed in white butterflies, or even to see just one tree against a bright blue sky – surely a case for exclaiming 'O frabjous day! Callooh! Callay!'

Such a glorious sight really needs no accompaniment, but solitary settings are unusual in gardens, especially the small urban gardens in which most of us have to find creative satisfaction. Still, it is not in itself a punishment to be so confined. It should exercise the mind to discover what may be made of such a space without the imagined benefit of a limitless horizon. Putting my imagination to work I have settled on several pathways to follow. Bear in mind that I have a whole avenue of 24 such trees to play with, so from end to end I have the opportunity to do a number of things. At one point I am planting burnt orange-red lantanas under the bauhinias. I see these clipped into Burle Marx freeform shapes, a bit lumpy and bumpy but definitely with an art moderne feel. At a further point 'trees' of *Aloe plicatilis* in square burnt umber pots stand between the orchid trees, with *A. aristata*, *A. humilis*, *A. brevifolia* and *A. longistyla* clustered at their bases. And at yet another point the white-flowered bauhinias are themselves backed by creamy flowered Australian Native Frangipani (*Hymenosporum flavum*). I could see that there would be equally interesting prospects with plumbago, iochromas and other blue- and purple-flowered plants.

Cyclamen coum

In this tiny plant we have one of the greatest gems of the Mediterranean climate garden. Though very small it is tough and a marvel of variety and detail in leaf and flower. Widely distributed in Greece and Turkey,

One of the greatest treasures of the Mediterranean garden is the diminutive *Cyclamen coum* which is found wild in many parts of Turkey. With a great variation in silver-patterned leaves, and flowers from white to dark wine red, it is a winter charmer.

Cyclamen coum shows an immense degree of variation, so much so that several distinct subspecies have been described. Found naturally in crannies between roots and rocks under the shelter of deciduous trees, and on open sheltered slopes away from day-long direct sun, these small succulent bulbs, really tubers, are an easy subject for most Mediterranean gardens. Some of the selected forms show all-silver leaves and hot pink blooms with propeller-shaped petals, yet others are white or bicoloured, and at least one form is a dark wine red. These beauties can be maintained in a garden setting with care but are best taken care of, and displayed to greatest effect, by being grown in shallow clay bulb pans. As the plants are naturally gregarious, and freely self-sow, they can be planted in quite large bulb pans with every prospect of filling the pot with new seedlings in a few years. Preferring a gritty soil with leaf mould and an annual dressing of compost in early autumn before growth begins, the small tubers sit half-buried, their roots reaching down into the soil and their tops clear so that their leaves easily emerge above the mulch.

Propagation is possible by carefully cutting the tubers into sections, each with a growing point, and carefully drying the cut surfaces before replanting in very free-draining potting soil. Treated this way and very carefully tended it is possible to reproduce plants vegetatively, but it is much simpler and easier to raise plants from seed. After flowering the seeds mature within a small round capsule behind the dead flower. As the seeds reach maturity the capsule begins to split. At this stage the seeds, which are rather sticky, can be carefully extracted and stored in small envelopes. Named forms and cultivars will not come true but are nonetheless well worth growing. Seed should be planted as fresh as possible in gritty compost and barely covered with a layer of fine gravel to discourage the growth of mosses. By soaking the seeds in tepid water, renewed every day, and sowing after a week of being so treated, germination will be speeded up. Single leaves will appear after a few weeks and a tiny tuber will form to carry the baby plant through to the following year. Self-sown seeds will appear alongside flowering plants in the garden as

Crocus tommasinianus 'Ruby Seedlings' show just what is being missed by those who don't try a few of these delightful winter-flowering bulbs. Often considered the province of specialist alpine plant collectors, the more common sorts are quite easy to grow in garden conditions.

long as the soil is not disturbed by digging. Ants may carry seeds away so that plants appear unexpectedly where conditions suit.

The plants are in active growth from autumn until early summer, reaching a peak of flowering in late winter. As a groundcover for shady places they are hard to beat, even though not evergreen. Planted in drifts or colonies and allowed to self-sow they are spectacular, if diminutive. They assort well with hellebores, looking at home with *Helleborus lividus* and *H. odorus* which flower about the same time and provide a good colour combination. Other small bulbs can be interplanted to increase the flower power and the charm that small flowers give. Try them in cool sheltered spots with snowdrops (*Galanthus* spp.), crocus, species tulips

and species daffodils, especially hoop-petticoats.

In pebble gardens, and at the edges of gravelled areas, the tubers will establish and flower happily. Otherwise plant individual forms in bulb pans and bring them forward for displaying when they are in flower – even in leaf, as many silvered and patterned forms look great. The bulbs do not mind root-filled soils as such conditions are frequently found where colonies grow in their habitats. Generally found in open areas of mixed evergreen and deciduous woodland, *Cyclamen coum* is accustomed to a covering of fallen leaves; however, care needs to be taken over some of the fancy-leaved selected forms, which seem susceptible to sundry rots in damp situations where they are continuously covered with wet leaves.

Good companions are found in the numerous selected forms and subspecies of *Cyclamen hederifolium* which, while not as varied as those of *C. coum*, are nonetheless most attractive. They add to the length of the flowering season by flowering before *Cyclamen coum* in autumn, often beginning quite precociously in late summer.

For further information see:
Brian Mathew and Neriman Ozhatay, *The Cyclamen of Turkey*, The Cyclamen Society, UK, 2001.
Christopher Grey-Wilson, *Cyclamen: A Guide for Gardeners, Horticulturalists and Botanists*, Batsford, London, 1997.
Christopher Grey-Wilson, *The Genus Cyclamen: A Kew Magazine Monograph*, Timber Press and Christopher Helm, 1988.

8 Successful succulents

At the Mexican restaurant Jardin de St Juan, in St Juan Bautista in California, a collection of hardy cacti is attractively displayed on steps leading down to the patio; an idea that could easily be copied.

The recent revival in interest in succulent plants, due in large part no doubt to the movement for sustainable gardening in Mediterranean climate regions, has produced several books that offer a broad survey. Here will be found just ten plants from all those thousands; a selection based solely on the directions my own interests in this vast conglomerate of plant genera have taken me since I first began growing them as a youngster.

Ranging as they do from tall tree-like plants to wide-spreading dense thickets and sparse trailing stems, down to plants so small and well concealed by the camouflage of mimicry that they can scarcely be seen against their backgrounds of pebbles, sand and dry grass, succulents give ample opportunity for exploration and discovery. The larger growing kinds, and those more favoured by specialist growers and fanciers, are dealt with elsewhere. What appears here are plants that help define my special

interests, not so much as a hoarder of rarities or a specialist grower with secret knowledge but as a person who simply appreciates the unique qualities each has in form and foliage.

Names can be a challenge here as frequent botanical revisions and much debate among taxonomists seems to ensure that names are often outdated and confused. At least as a beginning it is best to choose plants on their direct visual appeal. Later you may choose to search out particular kinds, in which case you will most likely have to rely on the advice of specialist growers who should be able to help unravel the name you have noted from its many synonyms and attach it to the plant you think you want. Study groups abound and pronounce upon each new revision with grave authority and occasionally with some sceptical humour.

Succulents are highly adapted plants, particularly in relation to their methods of survival, but they are not generally capable of existing in a furnace or in conditions of utter drought. Most in fact need attentive watering (and a little feeding) to ensure they look attractive year round. The most highly adapted genera, such as *Lithops*, *Conophytum*, *Pleispilos* and several others, all commonly known as Stone Plants or Living Stones or Pebble Plants, require a long dry rest period and watchful attention to ensure they don't rot through being watered at the wrong season. Most of the rest are fairly adaptable as long as drainage is excellent and the soil open and gritty.

As signature pieces in my garden I have several collections of small pots arranged so they can be enjoyed close up by anyone who passes; this is most likely to be me or my wife so the plants so displayed are a reflection of our particular fascinations. There is something rather naïve about such a collection, perhaps an echo from a remote childhood or a reflection of an even more distant era when every veranda and porch had its collection of jam tins and holed wash-basins planted with succulents. Chosen purely on their appeal to the eye, these plants represent our own journey and old friendships.

Haworthia comptoniana

This is but one of a large and complex family of small succulents from South Africa. This particular variety is one of a group distinguished by the leaf ends having

Haworthia comptoniana has glassy windows that fascinate children and adults too. A small collection of these succulents is easily and attractively housed on a table-top display where youngsters can eye it at close hand.

a 'window' of clear tissue that allows sunlight to penetrate to the inside layer of the plant's skin; here is where the chemistry that uses sunlight to produce food for the plant occurs. In some species the clear part of the leaf tip is quite small while in others it covers the entire tip, as in the case of *Haworthia comptoniana*. The plant makes a compact rosette of closely packed, thick, succulent leaves, often with the leaf tips arranged in a roughly flat surface that shows at ground level. In nature the plants are found sheltered by an overgrowth of sparse shrubs and dry grasses, occasionally in more exposed, rocky settings. When they are in active growth the leaves are usually green and in the dry season they assume bronze tints. The roots are also succulent and contractile, withdrawing the plant into

the soil somewhat during the dry months. This is less commonly observed in potted plants but it does help us understand why the plants behave as they do, and sometimes we observe this feature in our growing of them. The flower stems are thin and since they do not produce flowers of any remarkable beauty can be removed by a gentle sharp tug without any great loss.

Propagation of such tiny treasures – they are only about 6–8 cm (2½–3 in) high and 10–15 cm (4–6 in) across – is a matter of patience more than anything else. Each rosette will eventually produce offsets, in some cases many, many offsets, in others very few. By exercising great care individual leaves can be detached from the stem of the plant; note 'detached' and not 'pulled' – it must be done gently so as to not damage the leaf tissue. Having been left to dry for a few days these can be induced to produce 'babies' by being rested on barely damp sand in a shady but well-lit place. This usually takes a month or two. Should nothing happen it may be that the all-important base plate of the leaf was not successfully removed with it. To ensure success it is a good idea to let the parent plant dry and almost wilt before attempting to take off leaves for propagating. Common sense dictates that the bottom-most leaves, those not shrivelled and still sound, are taken for making leaf cuttings. Mature rosettes damaged by crushing, even partially beheaded, will often throw a crop of new rosettes from around the base – too risky a process to be seriously considered as a reliable method of increase, but handy to remember when the cat springboards from your stand of pot plants.

There are many other glassy-tipped 'windowed' haworthias to choose from, each appealing in its own way. While some forms are very rare and endangered in the wild by the depredations of indigenous gatherer-collectors who look on them as a means of income support, there are others that may be had for reasonable sums and at no risk to the biodiversity of South Africa. Check out cacti and succulent shows for the following: *Haworthia retusa, H. tesselata, H.* x *maughanii, H.* x *truncata, H.* x *cuspidata, H. cymbiformis, H. cooperii, H. mirabilis*, and their several variations and subspecies.

Charles L. Scott, *The Genus Haworthia: A Taxonomic Revision*, Aloe Books, Johannesburg, 1985.
ISBN 0-620-079474-6

Bruce Bayer, *Haworthia Revisited: A Revision of the Genus*, Umdaus Press, Hatfield, USA, 1999. ISBN 1-919766-08-1

Rhipsalis species

Rhipsalis is a genus of very odd cacti; they generally live in trees, hanging down from the branches, or dangling off jungle cliff faces; they grow in forests but not in deserts; they have no thorns and no leaves; they mingle in the treetops with bromeliads and orchids, and are graceful and attractive in their habits.

These are epiphytes, or air plants; they appear to live on almost nothing but fresh air, clinging to trunks and branches with hard, wiry roots that serve to anchor them securely against hurricanes and thunderstorms. Such food as they get comes from the few rotten leaves, bird droppings and the like that gather in the crotches of the trees they live on, or in rocky crevices.

I find they make fine subjects for hanging baskets, much more easily cared for than fuchsias, begonias and geraniums. Admittedly their flowers are not nearly as brilliant as those of the more traditional hanging basket plants but their varied foliage forms last year round and to my way of thinking about garden display are much to be preferred for this reason alone.

Those familiar with the growing requirements and habits of Christmas Cactus, *Schlumbergera truncata* (syn. *Zygocactus truncatus*) will be able to manage *Rhipsalis* without any difficulty. Depending on which kind can be found in growers' lists, the plants will broadly resemble a cluster of elongated, slender, pendent green pencils, some of which branch profusely, others sparsely. In a few the 'leaves' are flattened somewhat and in one variety the leaf segments are flattened and pinched, creating a squared appearance to the stems. As a rule the flowers are very small, white or yellowish, and short-lived. The following crop of small berries can be very attractive, giving rise to common names that refer to imagined similarities with white or red mistletoe or pink pearls.

Like the majority of succulents rhipsalis are easily propagated by simple stem or leaf cuttings, so simple in fact that children can do it and succeed. Follow the usual procedure for propagating succulents: secure cuttings with at least one growth point (node), allow them to dry off for a few days in a shady spot, put in a barely damp potting mix with a high sandy grit ratio to other constituents such as leaf mould or peat, and wait. Sometimes the leaves will need the support of a short cane or stick to hold them upright while the roots form at the base but otherwise there is really nothing much to it.

Being epiphytes, rhipsalis do not need much root room, or a rich potting mix; keep them confined to small pots or baskets and feed from time to time when in active growth with a diluted ration of soluble fertiliser. They grow best in conditions that resemble their jungle homes – plenty of bright light but no exposure to the scorching rays of the sun and good air movement at all times.

Species worth trying in frost-free settings, hanging under trees or pergolas, are *Rhipsalis alternifolia*, *R. clavata*, *R. capilliformis*, *R. burchellii* and *R. cassutha*. Names will almost certainly vary from supplier to supplier so it pays to check descriptions, though not one could be said to be a dog.

Cryptocereus anthonyanus
Rick-rack Cactus

Called St Anthony's Cactus in some American countries, perhaps for its supposed resemblance to an ancient instrument of torture connected with the death of the martyred saint, this elegant epiphytic 'air' cactus grows long leafy stems that are deeply and alternately indented, thus giving rise to the common names Rick-rack Cactus and Zig-zag Cactus. Somehow it manages to convey a sense of exoticism through its appearance. It is certainly a great addition to any small collection of hanging basket plants, and is easy to grow and manage in most Mediterranean zones.

Well-established plants will trail down a metre or so with several dozen leafy, jointed stems. Flowering is relatively easy to manage provided the orientation of the plants is not altered while the buds are developing. This is a peculiarity of a number of epiphytic cacti, including the Christmas Cactus and Crab Cactus (both *Schlumbergera* spp.). It does seem like an old wives' tale but appears to have some foundation in experience. The flowers are a little variable, ranging from creamy yellow and white to

The Rick-rack Cactus, *Cryptocereus anthonyanus*, creates a very exotic jungly look without the need for high humidity or tropical temperatures. Combined with hardy orchids, bromeliads and foliage plants, it will transform any patio into a lanai.

flushed apricot and pinkish tones. These variations may be as much to do with growing conditions as they are to species differences.

The only serious problems to successful cultivation of epiphytic cacti are posed by infestations of scale and mealy bug, which are best avoided by careful inspection of newly acquired plants, good growing conditions and quick treatment if the pests appear. Avoid oil-based sprays and aerosols as they too often contain ingredients destructive to the waxy leaf surfaces of these plants. Other damage may come about from hailstorms. Hanging baskets can be quite heavy so they must have secure, strong attachment points. Should baskets come tumbling down there is not only the risk to personal safety but also that of serious damage to the all-important foliage of the plants.

It is said the fruits of many kinds of air cacti are edible. Indeed, several are found in food and vegetable markets in Central and South America, and even in the more exotic foodie markets in the USA, New Zealand and Australia. Interesting – yes; tasty – hmmm? The few fruits that may appear on a home-grown plant would be better considered an amusing side-benefit than a seasonal crop.

Having achieved a level of competence with these easy and interesting beauties, it is but a single step to move on to trying out the much larger-flowered hybrid *Epiphyllum* cacti with their satin-sheened, gaudy, orchid-like flowers. Finally, *Marniera chrysocardium*, Fishbone Cactus, could be attempted. Even though it is much larger and much more tropical in its appearance it is well worth the minimal effort of growing it. This plant is named for the great French Marnier-Lapostolle family of plant hunters and botanists whose private botanic garden 'Les Cèdres' at St Jean Cap Ferrat on the Riviera is renowned. Being larger in all respects that the others mentioned here it requires room to grow and careful placement to avoid damage to the leafy stems. The flowers are large, creamy white, scented and open at night.

Fockea edulis

A very curious plain-looking plant; a sort of scrubby, scrappy, twining climber, *Fockea edulis* has on the face of it nothing particular to recommend it to gardeners seeking to add that touch of distinction to a collection of pot plants. However – there is a big however, and it is found under the soil – the roots form a massive turnip-like caudex (swollen root base) which when exposed becomes a great curiosity. There are no flowers to speak of, just tiny greenish-yellowish things, short-lived and starry. The plant's presence relies solely on the exposure of its underground parts. The vastly swollen root, elephantine, grey and wrinkled, can look most astonishing when carefully washed clean of dirt and raised well above soil level. The trailing, twining stems can be shortened back without harm once the annual growth spurt has matured. The overall impact is that of some curious sort of bonsai.

Young plants respond well to feeding and watering during their growing period and will quickly develop a

sort of grey canker – hardly a pleasing description, but these plants are not grown for their conformity to conventional standards of botanical beauty. They should be regarded as genuine curios of the plant world – the sort of plant that makes us wonder why it is so. Certainly children love to see such things, as do adults who have managed to keep an enquiring mind.

There are hundreds of other caudiciform plants that could be included in a collection of such vegetable curiosities; many are hard to obtain and not the easiest to cultivate. Among those that can be 'tamed' by most keen gardeners are the Pony-tail Palm, *Nolina recurva* (syn. *Beaucarnea recurva*), *Ficus palmerii* – a fat, stumpy-dumpling version of a rubber tree that likes warmth, and *Calibanus hookerii* – a tuft of grey, grassy horsehair growing out of an unpromising-looking grey disc, very, very strange and weird looking. Look out also for *Adenia* species, *Cyphostemma juttiae*, *Pachypodium* species and *Sinningia leucotricha* – this last grows out of a 'potato' that sits on the soil surface, producing large, silver, hairy leaves and bright red-orange tubular flowers that resemble somewhat a diminutive gloxinia.

Gordon Rowley, *Caudiciform and Pachycaul Succulents*, Strawberry Press, Mill Valley, USA, 1987. ISBN 0-912647-03-5.

Fockea edulis is a great curiosity that usually grows its swollen rootstock hidden underground. Taken out of the soil, scrubbed free of dirt and replanted at half-mast, it becomes an instant succulent bonsai.

marked caudex. Indeed, clever wholesalers are now growing young plants in tropical regions where they reach a good size within eighteen months, at which time they can be repotted and top-trimmed to create an instantly saleable plant in distant big city markets. Given reasonable care in keeping them away from cold winds, and some warm weather to help acclimatisation, these plants can be managed perfectly well as long as they don't get frosted. To some extent the size they will eventually achieve is dependent on how they are grown; given a free root-run they will become massive in 20 years or so, but restricted to pot or tub culture and regular top pruning they can be kept much smaller and still be healthy and vigorous. That this is so is hardly surprising when they are found in the wild occupying small cracks between boulders with the caudex spreading out over the rock surface like some

Lampranthus species
Ice Plant, Pigface

Lampranthus are a common feature of many Mediterranean climate gardens, and are increasingly found doing duty as soil retainers on freeway embankments. Hardy, drought tolerant, colourful and easy to grow, they have long been associated with gardening on the dry side – and all too frequently dismissed by the fussy as just too gaudy and far too common. Well, that is changing, and quickly, as people seek ways to reduce areas of lawn and replace it with something low, compact, dense, undemanding as to water and not much fussed about soil as long as water doesn't lie about after rain.

Often thought of as cottage garden flowers, the ice plants are found here and there dotted among mixtures of bulbs, annuals and hardy perennials such

Ice Plant or *Lampranthus* comes in colours ranging from white to bright red, orange, pink and yellow. In the case of *Lampranthus auranticus* the flowers glow brilliant yellow.

tree and shrub aloes and euphorbias. Obtaining aloes and euphorbias of sufficient maturity and size to replicate such a picture may be a difficulty to overcome, but creating the broad bands and slabs of colour should be no problem at all. A single pot-bought plant can quickly and easily become a dozen cuttings which, slipped into any garden dirt, will take root and grow away strongly in no time. They won't prosper in shaded situations, or where soils are poorly drained, but otherwise they are almost foolproof.

Knowing that the names of bought-in plants may well be unknown or confused, it is wisdom to purchase ice plants in flower to avoid unfortunate colour clashes and spotted dog effects. The colour range is not wide but there is an intensity of colour in many that explodes before the eyes. It is as well that the bright sunshine of Mediterranean climate regions reduces the impact of such brilliance but never let it scare you; a knockout colour scheme is character building – you will grow strong fending off criticism from your family and friends. Strong reds are found in *Lampranthus spectabilis* and *Drosanthemum speciosum*, bold oranges in *Lampranthus aureus* and *L. tricolour*, and glowing yellow in *L. auranticus*. There are several pink-flowered species too but somehow they seem just a tad wussy alongside the rest. After all, if you are stuck with a moniker as damning as Pigface there's little point in being shy about it. 'If you've got it, flaunt it', as Mae West probably once said.

as purple statice and sea lavender. However charming this may be, it does limit our perception of these adaptable plants, as does our habit of planting them and leaving them maintenance free to fend as best they can for themselves. A little care and grooming will be quickly repaid with a much smarter appearance.

Generally ice plants are found as unnamed mixed kinds sold as small rooted cuttings, or 'plugs', in the groundcover sections of nurseries and garden centres. They do not feature much in designer boutiques and stylish garden shoppes. What is needed is a fresh and bold approach to their more effective deployment in gardens and landscapes. The best model for this comes from the veldt, and from the botanic gardens of South Africa, where these simple succulents are found planted *en masse* in broad sweeps and massive blocks of colour as a background to the stronger forms of

Chorisia speciosa
Silk Floss Tree

Inclusion of this curious tree here could be argued as being inappropriate. Strictly speaking this is not a succulent, though its trunk is more or less swollen and acts as a storage vessel against survival in dry seasons. Although it is a tree it can be treated as a tubbed specimen, when flowering might be greatly lessened but the impact of its very odd trunk appreciated close up. It is found quite often in southern California where frosts are very slight or non-existent; it is seen often in northern Argentina and Uruguay; even in the North Island of New Zealand it makes an occasional guest appearance in gardens, but is hardly ever seen in Australia. Could it be that Australia's

The Silk Floss Tree, *Chorisia speciosa*, is a threefold wonder. Close up, its green trunk adorned with grey rhinoceros horn-like thorns is a hideous and awesome sight. Come early summer, stand back and admire its pink orchid-like flowers, and later experience great strands of silky threads as the ripe pods split open and shed their packing and their seeds.

genteel Anglo settlers were put off by its greatest feature? Were their English, Welsh, Irish and Scottish sensibilities offended by such a ghastly, dangerous sight? Perhaps so.

The surprising feature of this innocent tree is that from its apple-green trunk arise masses of thick, short grey spines that bear a likeness to a rhinoceros horn in miniature. A brutish sight if ever there was one, the sort of nightmarish thing that could lead to all kinds of childhood trauma. It does look ominous but is it threatening or dangerous? I don't know. I've never heard of anyone coming to harm from an encounter at close quarters, but a fertile imagination could easily raise up the most alarming prospects.

Looking on this tree as an experiment would be

the way to go, but it is definitely worth trying. It produces stunning pink flowers during its brief period of dormancy, which is even shorter in the case of the form 'Majestic Beauty' cultivated in California. The pear-shaped fruits which follow are filled with a silken white floss around the seeds which is released into the air when the seeds are dispersed, hence the common name.

Other trees with swollen trunks for water storage are also worth considering for Mediterranean climates, though they should never be planted in confined spaces where their eventual size would create problems. Native to Australia is *Brachychiton rupestris* (syn. *Sterculia rupestris*), the Bottle Tree, from the wet-dry monsoonal regions of the subtropical north. Despite its warm origins it seems to manage quite well in much cooler parts of Australia where is at home with long, hot, dry periods and heavy winter downpours. Grown in large, barrel-sized tubs these trees can be kept like giant bonsai for many, many years. Even larger are the famous Baobabs or Bottle Trees of Africa, *Adansonia* species. These are too big for most gardens and, unlike *Brachychiton*, take a long time to show the swollen trunk which is their principal feature. Almost as large but far easier to grow is the Ombu, *Phytolacca dioica*, previously mentioned for its curiosity value as a giant herb. The Ombu tree is a native of northern Argentina and Uruguay, where it is frequently found as a solitary specimen sheltering a farmhouse. It is reputed never to grow in groups but anyone who has visited the natural groves on the floodplains of the Rio Negro would understand that nature seems not to observe this tradition. Seedlings of such trees may be available from specialist nurseries dealing in succulents and cacti rather than from the usual garden centres.

Lithops lesliei
Living Stones

From one extreme to the other, big trees with swollen trunks to tiny succulents with nothing but a pair of leaves fused together with the appearance of a pebble! Just as folks in temperate and cool climates have their favourite pot plants so should we who live in warmer, drier climes. High among my recommendations for

Living Stones, in this case *Lithops lesliei*, make ideal displays in shallow pots and trays. Requiring only bright light (but not scorching direct sunlight) and a little water when they are actively growing, they are fascinating examples of plant life.

pot plant pets would have to be the fascinating *Lithops* from the arid deserts of South Africa. I have been fascinated by these little gems since I first grew them as a teenager and have recently renewed my acquaintance to share the delight with my grandson.

There are around 34 different kinds of living stones, extending to 87 if all the recognised variations are taken into account – and that's without going into the increasing numbers of selected variations treasured by sharp-eyed aficionados. Thirty-four species makes quite a manageable number as plant collections go, and there is no need to be obsessive about them unless the collecting mania hits; a small selection attractively displayed in shallow pans can be a unique signature to any Mediterranean garden. In really dry places where there is adequate protection from slugs, snails, ducks

and hailstones it is possible to 'play' with growing lithops in the ground, not something that can be contemplated by gardeners elsewhere.

Lithops lesliei is among the easiest to grow and also offers the attraction of having several distinct subspecies and cultivated forms. Found in areas where summer rains are common and often heavy, it tolerates a degree more excess water than some more particular hydrophobic varieties. Even so it must have a very porous soil with little compost and a high degree of grit, sand and small gravel or pebbles. It must also have a long, dry rest period over winter when it will get all the moisture it needs from fogs and dews. If too much water is supplied the plants will grow out of character, bloat, split and rot. Like all pets, lithops need an appropriate care regime to keep them in good form. While collectors often keep them in small pots as solitary clumps or specimens they look much better when grown as colonies in large, shallow terracotta seed pans. They need bright light and long hours of sunshine but care should be taken about exposing them to the full blast of the sun's rays. Such tiny things can easily get scorched or broiled and their appearance spoiled. This may not matter in the wild, where the plants have probably shrunk into the ground and become covered with sand, but it will not do for plants grown as garden décor.

The unnamed seedlings sold as novelties in garden centres and hardware stores are a mixed lot, probably hybrids and often not very distinctively marked. For an altogether more attractive display, look to specialist growers to provide the well-marked and more varied species and subspecies. As far as *Lithops lesliei* goes, watch out for subsp. *mariae* (gold speckled with clear pinspots), subsp. *venteri* (grey body with clear denticulate windows – like old worn teeth) and subsp. *luteo-viridis* (yellow body with greenish windows).The plain form, *Lithops lesliei*, if such may be said of so colourful a family, comes in a deep rusty brown with brown windows. Other robust types are *Lithops aucampiae*, *L. hookeri* and *L. pseudotruncatella.*

Gordon Rowley, *A History of Succulents,* Strawberry Press, Mill Valley, California, 1997. ISBN 0-912647-0

Steven Hammer, *Lithops: Treasures of the Veldt*, British Cactus & Succulent Society, Norwich, UK, 2001. ISBN 0-902-099-64-7

Aloe pearsonii

It is a risky thing writing about succulents in a wide-ranging book when there are already a number of books devoted to this group alone. But my selections can only be based on my own experience and preferences, which will almost certainly not be the same as those of other authors. I like this plant where others may find objections; it is not particularly rare or difficult to grow, it is not a miniature or a giant, nor is it cristate or monstrose – two aberrations often sought by specialist collectors – and it definitely is not a darling of garden makeover gents or a pet of landscape decorators. It is just itself. And that is why I like it.

Aloe pearsonii can grow to considerable stature in great age, given ample root room and space to grow. Confined to a pot, the best way of treating it, its charms are unaltered but its capacity for growth is held in check so that it stays relatively compact and small. By nature *Aloe pearsonii* is columnar, reaching 1 m (3 ft) or so, and making a clump of unbranched stems clad along their length in toothed reddish leaves marked with a few white spots. The narrow triangular leaves hang down and sometimes seem to be arranged in files. New growths appear from the base of the plant and slowly its columnar nature becomes apparent. It flowers in mid-summer, when yellow or more often orange-red tubular flowers appear atop short-branched or solitary stems.

Aloe pearsonii comes from Namaqualand, an extremely dry part of north-west South Africa. In its habitat it lives on exposed rocky outcrops and survives extremes of temperature and severe drought. It is very slow growing and resents over-watering or too much summer rain, which seems to make it almost ideal for Mediterranean gardens. Even so it needs excellent drainage that is best managed by growing it in a pot. It also needs plenty of direct sun to keep its characteristic upright, compact growth and to ensure it doesn't die from rot. As a pot plant for an exposed position *Aloe pearsonii* is a great choice and a pleasant change from the usual desperate, dusty denizens that occupy such

Aloe pearsonii finds a home in many specialist succulent collections, but it is time to move it into more general use as a fine specimen plant for pots and tubs where its exacting drainage and watering requirements can be effectively managed.

positions, a scrawny *Agave attenuata* or scruffy *A. americana*.

Some idea of the harsh conditions in which *Aloe pearsonii* thrives can be found by examining the potting mixture used for it by experienced nurseries. It couldn't be called potting soil for it comprises sand, pea gravel, brick dust and volcanic scoria – and still the thing grows well! Once a year, in early winter, a half teaspoon of slow release fertiliser should be enough to keep it in good shape.

For those not inclined to the larger kinds, the dwarf aloes can make a very attractive tabletop collection; just the sort of thing that could be massed in a large squat pot, glazed or plain terracotta, for display on a townhouse or apartment balcony. A good many of those available from specialist growers and markets will be hybrids of European or Japanese origin – though this does not make them any less attractive. Among the diminutive species favoured as parents by greenhouse breeders and growers, and good in themselves, are South African *Aloe variegata* and *A. aristata* and Madagascan *A. antandroi*, *A. bellatuloides*, *A. millottii*, *A. haworthioides*, *A. raughii*, *A. descoignesii*, *A. parvula* and *A. albiflora*.

Euphorbia decaryii

More than anything *Euphorbia decaryii* resembles to my mind a miniature grove of palm trees. Without any effort on the gardener's part it becomes a bonsai-like potful of grey trunks each with four or five grey-green palm fronds sprouting from the top. A childlike mind could easily add a toy camel or a tin donkey and create a perfect oasis for a windowsill or ledge. Mind, it would have to be a very tiny tray-garden, for this euphorbia is no more than 7 cm (2¾ in) high.

Coming from Madagascar it enjoys an arid climate, frost free, and light shade such as might be found under a scrubby bush or among rocks and dry grasses. The plant spreads slowly by short suckering stems until a dense thicket, albeit miniature in scale, is formed. It is a shallow rooted plant and can easily be accommodated in a bonsai type tray. The addition of a fine gravel to cover the potting soil and a rock or two with interesting shapes or colours will complete a picture of Arabian Nights charm. There are flowers too, but on such a small scale that the pale greeny-yellowy flower bracts are hardly significant.

Like all its kin *Euphorbia decaryii* has milky white sap that is a severe irritant to eyes and sometimes to skin, especially to the usual cuts and nicks that are part of a working gardener's marks of trade. Besides taking care of ourselves when handling plants such as these we also need to take care of the plants when taking cuttings, or dividing up established plants; they 'bleed' sap where they are cut or damaged and this needs to be given time to dry before they are potted up. This can be allowed to happen naturally over a period of days, or it can be encouraged by dipping the cut parts in fine dry sand. After that the new plants can be set in barely damp soil in a warm, well-lit place – not in full sun – and in time roots will form and the plants become established. Given their subtropical origins this euphorbia, among others, is best propagated in warm, dry weather around mid-summer before cooler weather brings on a period of semi-dormancy.

There are a good many small and dwarf euphorbias, each with their own peculiar attractions for pot gardeners. Most are reasonably easy in cultivation and offer a diversity of form that could be seen as oddball or cute. While most often viewed as the province of specialist growers and collectors, there is no reason why euphorbias should not become much more widely enjoyed by everyday gardeners in much the same way that sempervivums, crassulas, echeverias and sedums are already.

Euphorbia suzannae, *E. obesa*, *E. bupleurifolia*, *E. cylindrifolia* and *E. squarrosa* could be useful curiosities to add to a display, as well as the numerous forms and hybrids of *E. millii*, reasonably familiar as Crown of Thorns, with cheery red, apricot or creamy yellow flower bracts. These latter can be safely planted in the open garden in frost-free areas. Given room they will make spreading mats or shrubby growth. The fierce spines can be a drawback in gardens where young children play but even here they may find a place on dry retaining banks and awkward exposed spots where not much else will grow.

Pelargonium echinatum

Everyone loves a geranium but few would recognise this one as a close relative of the old-fashioned pot-plant and bedding-out kinds so common where a Mediterranean climate rules. *Pelargonium echinatum* is a succulent geranium to 15 cm (6 in) high and wide, with grey-barked stems and small spiny growths at each leaf node. During the growing season small grey-green leaves appear and also small stalks bearing white flowers with small wine-coloured markings on the two uppermost petals. The effect is quite charming even though the flowers couldn't compete with their modern cousins in size or colour.

This plant has been known in Western gardens and greenhouses since it was introduced from Ssouth Africa's Cape region in the late eighteenth century. There is even a hybrid, called 'Miss Stapleton's form' or *Pelargonium echinatum* var. *stapletonii*, which has pink flowers with the tell-tale darker markings. Both are well worth seeking out. Neither is rare but nor are they common, and they frequently turn up on trading tables and sales stands at geranium shows and cactus shows. Snap them up and you won't regret the few dollars they cost.

Succulent pelargoniums come in two basic kinds, those with succulent stems and those with succulent root systems. These latter are quietly attractive above the ground and only become highly interesting when their chubby, gnarled roots are exposed, in much the same way as *Fockea edulis* is displayed by knowing growers. *Pelargonium echinatum* is of the succulent stem kind. In many Mediterranean areas it could be successfully grown in the open garden as a small bush for it is quite hardy. Cultivation in pots has the advantage of allowing the small but beautifully marked

flowers to be seen close up. The broadly triangular leaves covered in downy 'velvet' are deciduous over the hot summer months. In its habitat it prefers dry, stony slopes and some overhead protection from rock ledges or bushes. The growing season is from mid-winter to early summer, just right for the water-wise Mediterranean garden. Propagation by cuttings is best done while the plants are in active growth, for though it is possible to take cuttings at any time the risk of rotting is greater when the plant is dormant. If dormant cuttings are kept on the dry side, however, they should form a callus at the cut end from which rootlets will develop when the growing season arrives. Like most succulents, and picking up on the clues to cultivation provided by the habitat information, it is sensible to give *Pelargonium echinatum* and other succulent geraniums a free-draining potting mix with extra grit, gravel and sand added.

While not at all common, except among a few devotees in succulent societies and geranium clubs, succulent geraniums have a fascination all their own and deserve to be grown more widely. They are easily raised from seed, as well as from cuttings – getting started might be the biggest obstacle to assembling a small collection. Be not daunted, the search is half the fun, so look out for *Pelargonium carnosum*, *P. crithmifolium*, *P. gibbosum*, *P. hirtum*, *P. lobatum*, *P. tetragonum* and *P. triste* as a beginning. From time to time others may be available from specialists' lists: *P. paniculatum*, *P. dasyphyllum*, *P. crassicaule*, *P. cotyledonis*, *P. laxum*, *P. multiradiatum* and several others quite rare in the wild and difficult in civilisation.

9 Perfect perennials

erennials are found in large numbers as natural components of Mediterranean climate landscapes. Not all of them are good garden plants, indeed some are so prolific and willing that they have great potential to be weeds when taken out of the habitat. In many countries imported perennials have become quite serious weeds – fennel for one is thoroughly established in Australia and California, along with scabious, endive, Italian lavender (*Lavandula stoechas*), giant fennel and various kinds of tuberous and bulbous plants. Even the lovely white form of *Iris germanica* has naturalised along creek beds and washaways in South Australia.

With careful selection, aided by the nursery industry and plant quarantine services, an increasing range of drought tolerant perennials is being

A mixed planting of drought-tolerant species grows and flowers during the rainy season and goes to rest through the annual summer drought experienced in Mediterranean climates. Even so, such a border can be a thing of easily maintained beauty and interest.

introduced that extends perennial gardening way beyond the traditional Anglo-American concept. There is now a much greater emphasis on mixed plantings of grasses, shrubs, climbers, bulbs and perennials, to which are being added succulents and many 'new' introductions from other Mediterranean climate areas. Plants considered tender in colder European climates often thrive without protection in Mediterranean climate gardens, while gems from Turkey, Morocco, California, Australia, California and elsewhere thrive. There is much good 'stuff' to be sorted from the never-ending stream of new plants imported and introduced every year, which is not to deny the usefulness of many plants with a much older pedigree, some of them included in this selection.

Geranium maderense

Geranium maderense, the giant of the Cranesbill family, is a plant with great structural qualities – large and domed in its habit, with rich green leaves of a distinctive shape and a magnificent head of flowers – marking it for distinction in any Mediterranean garden free of heavy frosts. Photo courtesy Clive Blazey.

Here is a plant, native to Madeira in the Canary Islands, that can be easily grown by Mediterranean gardeners in all but the frostiest of frost pockets. It is a giant in the genus, probably the largest of the perennial geraniums, and carries its large, much-divided 'palmate' leaves on long stems. A well-grown plant may be over 1 m (3 ft) across; a broad dome of foliage bearing on high a vast head of hundreds, well at least a hundred, bright musk pink flowers that resemble a smaller version of *Lavatera*, each with slightly darker veins and a dark wine-coloured boss of stamens and pistil.

Flowering lasts over an extended period with new flowers opening every day as the pollinated ones collapse, shrivel and fall. Flowering is usually initiated in spring and, in the case of mature plants, extends well into mid-summer.

In cooler, wetter climates *Geranium maderense* is often found to be almost biennial, growing in the first year and flowering the second, exhausting itself in a prodigious display and then collapsing from the stress of cold, wet and sunless weather. In Mediterranean climates it is perennial, elongating its woody stem year after year until it looks quite messy. Fortunately it self-seeds with relative freedom so it is permissible to take out the older plants before they get too ugly.

It seems to prefer tight crannies and crevices when it self-sows, and provided the volunteers are not in the way of passing traffic or liable to smother other plants they can be left in situ. However, they are also amenable to being transplanted, even at quite advanced stages of growth, and take perfectly happily to good loamy soils and traditional garden beds. Just give them room to grow.

Slightly smaller in all respects is *Geranium palmatum* (syn. *G. anemonifolium*), at about 80 cm (32 in) high and wide in open situations, a bit more in damper, sheltered spots. But it too is quite majestic and occupies quite a slab of space. For gardeners the main difference is that where *Geranium maderense* produces a massive head of blossoms on a single terminal head *G. palmatum* produces several heads on side-growths that are covered with magenta-purple hairs. The two appear to grow together without hybridising. An especially attractive way to deploy them effectively is under and between orchard trees or within tree plantations where there is 2–3 m (7–10 ft) clear space beneath the canopy.

Lower growing geranium species are numerous but many are unsuited to the Mediterranean climate regime. Among those that do well are *Geranium incanum* with finely dissected foliage and vivid magenta-purple flowers; *G. sanguineum*, Bloody Cranesbill – a vivid description of a vibrant magenta flower – and its numerous softer colour forms, and *G. psilostemon* – another strong magenta enlivened by a black 'eye' at the centre of each flower. Success may also be experienced with the different forms and hybrids of *Geranium macrorrhizum*, *G. dalmaticum*, *G. tuberosum* and *G. traversii*.

Agapanthus x 'Loch Hope' is one of the newer hybrids that combine the hardiness of older varieties with selected breeding lines designed to vary the colour range and height of the genus.

Agapanthus

'Not more aggies,' I hear my overwhelmed readers cry. Well, too bad, agapanthus are just too good not to witter on about again. I may not get another chance, so here goes.

As perennials go there can be few to best the agapanthus for adaptability and thrift in Mediterranean gardens. Seen everywhere, streamed alongside freeways, dumped unceremoniously in suburban car parks, plonked piteously on rocky embankments and clustered carelessly on roadside cuttings, they willingly answer the calls of landscape architects to solve all problems with a one-size-fits-all solution. And they do. But all too often the poor things aren't given much support for the difficult roles they are called on to fill – holding loose earthworks, binding rocky fill, stabilising unstable slopes, covering ugly scars, providing a sheet of green in some dusty unloved corner and generally being a botanical dogsbody.

In the hands of more supportive gardeners the humble agapanthus can rise above such unpromising circumstances and perform with grace, dignity and assurance. Although just about impossible to kill, agapanthus do respond to kinder treatment – a good mulch, a dose of fertiliser, a little water while they get established and an occasional lift, divide and separate and they will do sterling service without any further reward.

In the past many hybrids have been introduced from England and Holland, as well as the original species from South Africa, but now there are breeders active in Australia, New Zealand and California so that Mediterranean gardeners have the benefit of new varieties bred and selected in climatic areas very similar to their own.

See what is getting about in the nursery trade now, and keep eyes alert for the likes of *Agapanthus praecox* 'Storms River', a form selected in South Africa with white flowers bearing a very pale blue line down the centre of each petal – but be aware that seedlings are highly unlikely to replicate the colour pattern and insist on plants divided or tissue cultured from the clone itself; 'Purple Cloud', a New Zealand selection with tall stems, large flower heads and deep purple-blue colouration; 'Streamline', another New Zealand selection, this one a miniature, long blooming and upright where other dwarf forms tend to arching flower stems; the flowers are pale blue. 'Guilfoyle' is an Australian selection, evergreen, tall, with exceptional dark blue flowers in massive heads and upright foliage making for a plant that is tidier than most. 'Autumn Peace' is another Australian introduction from the nursery of David Glenn; it has the reputation of repeat blooming in the autumn, is dwarf and carries white flowers. 'Jahan' has been mentioned in other books as a terrific, vigorous and boldly marked variegated agapanthus. It too, is an Australian-bred plant. It has broad strong foliage and typical agapanthus-blue flowers in summer.

Polygonatum falcatum

To see the thick, succulent rhizomes of Jacob's Ladder, as *Polygonatum falcatum* is known in the Old Countries, is an explanation in itself of why this plant is included here. It has the storage capacity to survive quite well, at least in the slightly cooler and slightly damper areas at valley bottoms and in gullies. It prefers a shady area too, and soil that is loamy. From the strong rhizomes (swollen underground stems) that lie just below the surface of the soil, new growth arises rapidly in spring, using up the winter soil moisture and flowering as it goes. By early summer the stiff, slightly arching stems have finished their growth and flowering and the plant sets to work storing nutrients and water in the rhizomes, ready for the process to begin again the following spring, a pattern of growth that means the plants can go through summer with a bare minimum of irrigation.

Overall each arching stem reaches about 75 cm (30 in). Many stems arise from the mat of rhizomes that make up a colony and together these unbranched stems look quite good as they tend to arch in the same direction towards the light. Pairs of round apple-green leaves clothe each stem and from each leaf axil a pair of green-tipped creamy white bells hangs down on a short, wiry stalk. Quite attractive in a demure way and not to be looked down on for its willingness to colonise hard-to-fill, out-of-the-way corners. In wetter, cooler climates the leaves stay fresh until they turn gold and are shed in autumn but in Mediterranean regions are

Take a look at the finger-thick roots of *Trillium chloropetalum* and understand why it is capable of withstanding a long hot summer so long as its roots are not baked by direct sunshine. In a shady spot that is wet over winter it will grow quite well.

more likely to be decidedly ratty by summer's end. No matter, the rhizomes are strong and ready for next spring's performance. Pull away the dead and dying stems and tidy up; that's a pretty low level of maintenance by anyone's standards.

Slightly less vigorous is the variegated form which has broad creamy bands along the leaf margins. There are other species of polygonatum, but these all demand much more water for good growth than most Mediterranean gardeners would think worth the expense. If colonies of *Polygonatum falcatum* are successful it would be a worthwhile experiment to see how other similarly equipped plants fare. I have met with success in growing *Trillium chloropetalum, T. rivale, T. sessile* and *T. ovatum,* as well as Lily-of-the-

The small serrated leaves of this *Epimedium* are colourfully veined and sufficiently dense to create a weed-proof groundcover in lightly shaded areas. Thick semi-succulent roots store water to keep the plant alive over dry summer months.

valley (*Convallaria* spp.) and several kinds of *Asarina, Asarum* and *Arisaema* – all woodland plants that seem to tolerate dry shade once their active growing period is done with for the year. Like the Jacob's Ladder these plants have stout storage systems in their underground stems and so are well equipped to cope with Mediterranean summers, as long as they can be provided with summer conditions that are shady and not baked dry. Deep mulching in autumn can help create the woodsy conditions these plants prefer and they will happily push through the mat of rotting leaves when spring stirs them into growth.

Epimedium species

A number of epimediums have a surprisingly tough rootstock that equips them to handle shady, woodsy conditions in Mediterranean gardens. Not all are suited to our purposes; some are far too delicate to survive. Those alpine species from Japan and China are probably not a smart choice, no matter how beautiful their rose, lilac, purple and white flowers may be. They just don't have the constitutions to survive outside those parts that have summer rains, mists, fogs, cloud cover and all round dampness. Fortunately that leaves us with some that are still very attractive and useful.

Groundcovers by nature, the epimediums make dense mats of close-twined roots that rootle around just under the surface of the soil. From these arise wiry, delicate stems bearing three elliptical leaves – sometime toothed – and carrying short sprays of airy flowers. At first the leaves are pale yellow-green with bronze, pink and reddish tints and marked veining. As the season progresses the leaves lose these hues, taking on more sober green shades, and also develop a pronounced leathery quality that carries them safely, and attractively, through summer. As the days cool into autumn the leaves may develop bright red tones before finally collapsing in mid-winter. At this point the whole lot can be clipped off close to the ground and a mulch applied. Division and multiplication are easy. Simply plunge a sharp spade into an established clump and take out a wedge of the root mass. By squirting off the soil and teasing the roots apart any number of new plants can be made. These should be replanted immediately as the roots, though tough, are not large enough to withstand long exposure to dehydration.

Recommended varieties are *Epimedium* x *warleyense* (rusty orange), *E. perralderianum* (yellow, from Algeria) and *E.* x *versicolor* 'Sulphureum' (soft yellow).

William Stearn, *The Genus Epimedium,* The Botanical Magazine, Kew UK & Timber Press, Portand, Oregon, 2002. ISBN 0-88192-543-8

Iris Pacific Coast Hybrids

Standing just off the beach at Petaluma on the central California coast it is astonishing for spring travellers

The Pacific Coast Native Irises are a very varied bunch of wildlings that reach up and down the coast of California and northward. *Iris munzii* is one of the bluest and prettiest, but watch out for the colourful hybrids now available.

to see huge areas of low-growing blue iris flowering on the gentle slopes that lead inland to the famed wine region. The soil looks pretty uncompromising stuff; maybe it is the notorious black adobe that seems to be the bugbear of many a California gardener? But there the iris are, sturdy and flourishing in the teeth of a roaring wind off the Pacific Ocean, buffeted by spray-drift and exposed year round to everything the Mediterranean climate throws at them. My recollection is that these are colonies of *Iris douglasiana*, one of the Pacific Coast species, but I could be wrong. Fortunately that is not particularly worrying here because it is the hybrids that are by far most commonly found in gardens and nurseries.

While the dozen or so Pacific Coast species are all attractive enough to be included in gardens it is their numerous hybrids that really excite attention. These have been intensively bred in the USA, Australia and New Zealand for many years and their colour range, flower forms and sound constitutions make them very valuable additions to any garden. They do have a reputation for disliking alkaline soils but even this trait has been greatly reduced or bred out in some seed strains.

The plants are very tough and hardy with leathery foliage, or rich and glossy green, and the root system is vigorous. They are not necessarily long-lived and it is wise to renew plantings from strong-growing outside rhizomes every few years, especially if named varieties or special colours are to be kept going. The plants begin active root growth in autumn and are best transplanted at this time as the roots are renewed annually; if the timing is out the plants will sulk for months until the season for making new roots comes around once more. New roots are initiated at the base of the fan of leaves and can easily be seen; they are usually bright pink. When the root nodes first appear is the time to divide and replant. This treatment should not markedly disrupt the display of flowers in late winter and early spring.

The Pacific Coast irises readily hybridise among themselves and seed is freely set so seed-raised plants are no trouble to find. Frequently self-sown seedlings will appear in their hundreds in any garden where mature clumps are established. The seeds are also dispersed by ants and may spread to all sorts of unexpected places. Like many plants these irises enjoy the seedbed conditions provided by gravel paths and driveways.

Each country has specialist growers who seem to have released their own ranges of named plants. This makes recommending particular cultivars an exercise in frustration outside our own countries. My best advice is to select from potted plants in flower. Look out for glorious sandy and coffee-coloured flowers, broad-petalled and ruffled, or for the peacock-eyed strains with vivid dark thumbprints on each of the three main petals. Watch out too for deep wine-red-purples and flowers heavily netted with contrasting veins of colour laid over a solid ground of yellow, white, cream or golden orange.

Allium cernuum
Nodding Onion

As the name suggests, this is one of the numerous garlic tribe. And as might be expected in such a large family there are those that try the gardener's patience, such as *Allium giganteum*, some that are pests just waiting to become weeds, as *A. triquetrum* has in many parts of the world, and some that are well-mannered garden plants and useful pot herbs. *Allium cernuum* definitely fits into the latter category, at least in Mediterranean type climates. Elsewhere, in cooler, wetter places I suspect it might tend towards being too, too successful. This particular onion makes few offsets and self-sows modestly, so there are no pesky 'droppers' proliferating all over the patch, nor are there are masses of aerial bulbils just waiting to spread far and wide – all in all a most satisfying plant. The species is American and is very widespread, from east coast to west coast, north into Canada and south into Mexico. Covering such a wide geographic range suggests it must be pretty adaptable. Its bulbs are long and narrow and always in leaf. The soft purple-magenta flowers appear in early summer and are carried well above the foliage, the flowerhead characteristically nodding at the top of the stem.

There seem to be several selected strains getting about. My seed-raised bulbs from the Hardy Plant Society (international/UK based) are of a tall form. To me they seem just about the right height; any shorter and the plants would be lost in an average garden. Not being a great one for alpine gardening, with rockeries filled with minuscule plants of great fragility, tenderness and delicate constitution, such as are the objects of adoration of Alpine Gardeners, I would have to say the shorter forms find it difficult to win my favour. My colony is settled among clumps of Louisiana iris hybrids where they enjoy damp conditions until the whole area dries out in early summer. They cohabit with scrambling plants of *Clematis viorna* and *C. integrifolia*.

Neither the leaves nor the bulbs contain any garlicky or oniony odours so they are quite safe for those who have yet to develop an appreciation of Mediterranean smells as well as Mediterranean gardens; not that anyone would want to eat them anyway, the bulbs being too small as well as tasteless.

Domestic garlic, *Allium sativum*, is a denizen of most vegetable gardens throughout Mediterranean climate regions and beyond. There are numerous varieties selected and favoured by different ethnic groups over the centuries. Thus we have 'Giant Russian', 'White Chinese', 'Pink French' (harvested and sold 'green'), 'Purple Italian' – an altogether confused bunch, so much so that we could only guess at what kind of 'garlic' the ancient Egyptians fed the Israelites. Recorded in China from 2000 BC, garlic is believed to have originated from Central Asia from where it spread along trade routes east and west at a very early date.

Thymus herba-barona
Caraway-scented Thyme

This little native of Corsica and Sardinia is a low subshrub, barely more than a groundcover and with only very light twiggy 'wood'. It makes roots wherever its growths touch damp ground and can spread over quite a large area. It mingles happily with small bulbs and other low groundcovering plants or by itself makes a good mat of growth. It seems a most agreeable and adaptable plant. It is, and it has foliage strongly redolent of caraway – an extra bonus that makes up for its nondescript white flowers.

Of all the thymes I have tried to make a thyme bank with, this is the most reliable both for density and groundcovering capacity. It has moulded itself down a gentle slope of the most misnamed 'sandy loam', which in summer is baked hard like cement and in winter is saturated. The soil particles are so small that there is no air or drainage for the roots of any plant. Yet here *Thymus herba-barona* flourishes beneath *Pinus mugo* and *Carpentaria californica* (Tree Anemone). Various colchicums and autumn crocus assort with it comfortably and push through its mantle of growth to make their autumn displays. Quite effective, if I do say so myself.

It would be foolish to suggest that a thyme lawn would be a possibility under Mediterranean skies: it would need too much water for the climate and be too much work for the temperament! However, it is possible to achieve an effective blanket of thymes if you take a fairly liberal view of what constitutes a blanket. My own thyme blanket is made up from half a dozen plants of common culinary thyme interspersed with various others that have managed to stay the distance over at least two summers. There is Lemon Thyme, *Thymus* x *citriodora*, something called Pizza Thyme and a hairy grey one of unknown descent. The culinary thyme is the only one that needs renewing every now and then; it gets woody and begins to collapse into a mass of dead twigs. The rest regenerate themselves by making roots where the slender branches touch the ground.

The thymes are underplanted with the Mallorcan Peony, *Paeonia cambessedsii*, and seem to enjoy each other's company, the thyme giving just the right amount of cover to shelter the bases of the peony's stems, which would otherwise get scorched by the sun at mid-summer. There is also a growing patch of *Allium sphaerocephalum*. The narrow foliage of the allium spearing through the thyme blanket and the flowers above it bring no diminution of the vigour of the thymes. It is an arrangement that seems to work rather well for all concerned. It comes about as close to a piece of Provence as I am ever likely to achieve, and all for the cost of a few seedlings and a few packets of seed.

The thyme blanket is mulched with stones and pebbles that have been dug out as we have endeavoured to improve our rather wretched soil – subsoil really, the topsoil having been carried off years ago to enrich some city-dweller's garden with 'Hills loam' that (almost certainly) guaranteed blue hydrangeas.

Nicotiana sylvestris
Wild Tobacco

This plant almost escaped mention as a hardy perennial. Had it not drawn attention to itself by bursting into flower outside the window where I sit to write I should have completely ignored it. *Nicotiana sylvestris* grows in my garden in a piece of most unforgiving ground, if indeed it could be called 'ground', for it is actually a crumbling gravel, lime mortar and cement 'floor' left behind by a team of nineteenth-century mason-builders. In this unpromising stuff the wild tobacco thrives, self-sowing freely, and taking me by surprise by the way it manages to get through each summer with no assistance. Each autumn the ground-hugging rosettes of sticky green leaves send up towering spires of blooms that frequently reach almost 2 m (7 ft) high. Not a bad effort in such circumstances. The flowers give off a delicious perfume at night. I'm not so sure it would grow in more a propitious setting, no matter how much I might wish it. It seems to me very much a creature of its own will.

So what else might be tempted to offer a floral contribution to this latter-day archaeological site? Strangely there are a few, all of them volunteers. This summer past there have been the usual mats of *Geranium thunbergia*, a rather weedy thing but safe enough here and with pretty enough mats of small round leaves incised around the rim with shallow cuts – although the pale pink flowers are so small they make no contribution aside from ensuring a further supply of seedlings. A complete 'blow in' was a thorn apple, *Datura* sp. Once recognised I left it where it was to see what would happen. It grew into a low-branching and sprawling subshrub and on flowering threw out numerous long, twirled-up purple buds that unfolded into sweetly scented white trumpets. After the flowers faded a prickly round seed pod developed, not unlike a sparsely prickled chestnut. I decided that this vegetable stranger was most likely *Datura metel* and concluded that wherever it had come from I would welcome any further visitations. This particular datura is fairly common in European gardens and also in the USA, particularly in the South where it has a long history of cultivation and is known as Devil's Trumpet. The other willing volunteers are *Geranium palmatum* and *Verbascum olympicum*, described in detail elsewhere in this chapter. Of similar but even stronger willingness are the various colour forms of Kiss-me-quick (*Centranthus ruber*), a positive menace except when grown encased in cement. I try to convince myself I am better off without it despite admiring the white form whenever I see it growing safely in someone else's garden.

There are other kinds of *Nicotiana*, but none seem as hardy and free as *N. sylvestris*; many are complex garden hybrids or kinds with more tropical origins that don't take well to long, hot, dry summers. When I see them on offer as flowering pots o'colour in garden shops I pass them by; they need too much fuss and extra watering for my Mediterranean garden.

Verbascum olympicum

Here is another of those hardy perennials capable of giving a gardener a happy surprise by appearing where it's not expected, in all probability years after bought plants died. It seems the seeds of *Verbascum olympicum* are viable for some years, odd ones germinating when and where it suits them. By happenstance this usually means at the edge of some gravelled path where the broad white-felted leaves make a great show for months and months before a mighty candelabra soars up 2 m (7 ft) or more and shows off spires of bright clear yellow flowers. If by chance seedlings appear in settings other than at pathside, dig them up while they are small and move them to where they can best do their thing. Anywhere other than at the edge of a garden they are highly likely to swamp other plants with their dense flat rosettes of leaves. They are also liable to toppling over; this they can do quite gracefully at the edge of a path, and given such hard conditions it seems plausible that the roots would have a better grip on the soil and that growth would be tougher too.

It seems that there is a good deal of potential for confusion among the several kinds of verbascum. Are they a promiscuous lot? Interbreeding freely and carelessly and giving rise to generations of assorted bastards? There seems to be mixed success with getting hold of forms with solid silver-white leaves; once you do, be certain to ruthlessly weed out any lesser kinds. No greyish or yellowish kinds should be permitted to coexist with the better forms.

It should be borne in mind that *Verbascum olympicum* is strictly speaking a biennial; the species form is very reliable under Mediterranean conditions, unlike the fancy named cultivars such as 'Helen Johnson' and 'Cotswold Queen' that struggle to exist through drought and heat. Should you have had bad experiences trying to grow these lovely cultivars do not be put off until the species has been given a run. There are named seed strains available, usually branded with some showy moniker like 'Arctic Fox' or something equally vulpine. I am not convinced of their superiority.

Verbascums do tend to leave very large holes when they bow out, which is all very well if they are pathside and can be removed, the gravel raked and the whole lot made to look as though nothing is missing. Without doubt growing them at the edge of a garden is the way to go, but what else can go with them? Low things that spread seems a good answer, either that or have ready some well-advanced potted things that can be dropped into the gap(s). That would seem rather labour intensive in summer when Mediterranean gardeners are most likely seeking respite from over-exertion. Low plants such as the catmint 'Walker's Low' or *Sedum* x 'Bertram Anderson' might do the trick convincingly enough with a splash of extra water from time to time, or a hardy subshrub such as *Artemisia* x 'Poqurolle' could be an attractive option; if you are fairly laid back about floral continuity, as I am, there is always the option of a handsome terracotta pot, piled full of shells, pretty stones or pebbles or just left empty.

Clematis recta 'Purpurea'

One thing must be admitted about Mediterranean perennials and that is that many are on the quiet side alongside the traditional perennials such as delphiniums, hemerocallis, peonies and such-like flamboyant fellows. Consequently Mediterranean-hardy perennials need to earn their keep by means other than impressive floral power; form and foliage become of even greater importance than in cool climate gardens, as do the elements of scented leaves, colourful fruits, interesting seeds and perfumed flowers.

In the case of *Clematis recta* 'Purpurea' the telling factors are masses of starry white flowers – okay, so not really all that amazing – purple foliage and pleasing, fluffy, silver seedheads. That's hardly enough to knock dahlias off their perch as colour bombs but it is enough when the clematis is mixed with other plants that build a picture. I'd like to suggest that this rather blowzy perennial is set alongside misty bronze-leaved fennel, dark red-brown New Zealand flaxes and wands of purple-flowered *Verbena bonariensis*. This clematis is not one of the climbing sorts and needs some support to prevent it flopping about in an untidy mess. There may well be some selected strains with more compact growth but so far they haven't come to my attention.

Clematis recta 'Purpurea' is an easy-to-please plant. It prefers an open sunny position with a tad of protection from daylong exposure. Not particular about soil and with no pests more serious than the odd snail it is a model of amiability and thrift. It finishes its growth before summer heat is full-on. For the rest of its season it goes into a kind of green dormancy, in this case the purple leaves gradually losing their vinous colour and taking on grey-green hues. In favoured gardens this clematis, along with the bronze-leaved fennel, can be cut back hard and, given ample deep watering, will reshoot with a new crop of dark-hued foliage and eventually flower. That's not for me. I accept that we live where we do and must go with the flow of the environment and climate. So I look on my clumps of purple-leaved clematis as they change and admire them for what they have already provided and will willingly do again next year. There is no room, or reason, in a Mediterranean garden to be concerned about continuous floral display between spring and autumn. There is plenty else to look at and take pleasure in besides flowers, as I hope this book has demonstrated.

This clematis, unlike the large-flowered kinds commonly seen in cool climate gardens, is easily raised from seed sown in autumn and exposed to winter weather. New seedlings should begin to emerge with the arrival of warm weather in spring. Watch carefully for poorly coloured variants; these must be ruthlessly removed and destroyed. Seedlings will benefit from being pricked out and grown in pots for their first year after which time they will easily settle into their permanent positions in the garden.

10 Motley crew

Tail-enders but by no means least, the last ten plants in this personal survey represent some of my own, particular favourites. To meet the demands I make on plants these must be reliable and strong performers in a garden where we do not water in summer, though we do make use of grey water in some parts where soakage pits deal with the house water; nothing being wasted we don't call it 'waste' water. (We do make certain that no oils or fats go into the wash-up water, and we make sure we use soaps, cleansers and detergents that are not loaded up with phosphates and boron.)

The plants assembled here are genuine old-timers, cottage garden and heritage survivors. Some came to this garden from my grandmothers' gardens in the country north of here, both located in semi-arid Mediterranean climate regions with shallow alkaline soils over sheet limestone. Other plants have been scrounged from gardening friends who share my enthusiasm for collecting plants from our colonial era, and yet others are descendants of slips and seeds collected here and there from old gardens, churchyards and cemeteries. Like the members of Heritage Rose groups, the Rose Rustlers of Texas, the members of the National Council for the Conservation of Plants and Gardens and the various garden history societies, Mediterranean gardeners everywhere can learn much about good gardening for today by collecting and learning about the plants of yesterday.

Lepechina salviae

This shrubby plant was once far better known than it is today. Like the rather woofy smelling *Iboza ripara* and the doggy *Plectranthus canina* it had its day, and was bypassed in favour of subtler, sweeter things that did not make the noses of sensitive ladies and gents twinge, and their faces wince. Yes, the scent of the leaves is pungent, spicy and strong – but look at the flowers. Here is a bold bright colour, strong magenta-pink with hints of purple: a rich vinous colour that stands well among the arrowhead-shaped silver-grey leaves.

From the short semi-woody framework of *Lepechina salviae* a low subshrub rises to about 1 m (3 ft) in frost-free areas. Where frosts are common but not hard the plant may well be cut to the ground but new growth will come away from the rootstock once the weather improves. Even so it is worth taking the precaution of making some late summer cuttings and bringing them into some frost-free shelter for the winter. My feeling is the plants are not all that long-lived anyway and the older they are the greater the risk they will conk out from a frosting. Getting successful cuttings from the hollow-stemmed plants of the salvia family can be difficult. The best material is found low down on the stems where the growth points are very close together and the stem tends to be solid right through. Potted in a very sandy, free-draining mix, and helped along with a dash of fresh rooting hormone powder, there is a good chance of a reasonable strike rate. Young plants need nurturing and to be well established before they go out into the hard, cruel Mediterranean world.

Lepechina salviae is a new plant to many gardeners, and one that finds ready acceptance because of its hardiness, its colourful silver leaves and wine-purple flowers. Frost tender, it will come again from the rootstock but really does best where it gets no such setbacks.

Since *Lepechina* is a member of the salvia family its flower form can be brought to mind by recalling the typical lipped salvia flower which, in this case, comes at the end of a long tube. The flowers are held in a large head that appears at the apex of each main growing point in summer. A lesser crop of flowers usually appears on the smaller side-growths after the main flush, thus continuing the floral display over some months into autumn.

Utilising such a thrifty plant is easy. It assorts well with other silver-grey leaves and other richly hued flowers. The colour is positively Imperial toga stuff, deep, rich and magnificent. I cannot think of better companions than bold-leaved yuccas of the grey-silver-blue kinds and some of the purple-blue or wine-red salvias such as *Salvia leucantha, S. coccinea, S.*

chiapensis and *S. buchananii*. On a larger scale add *S. canariensis, S. clevelandii* and *S. semiatrata*. Come to think of it, the choice is much larger. Consult Betsy Clebsch, *The New Book of Salvias*, to see just how extensive the range is. Is it any wonder these simple, colourful plants are so popular? On their own they can tend toward a certain sameness and why would any gardener want to limit the choices available, so always look on them as suitable companions for a whole range of other plants. And that is where *Lepechina, Iboza* and even the canine *Plectranthus* come into their own.

Betsy Clebsch, *The New Book of Salvias*, Florilegium, Sydney, 2003. ISBN 1-876314-18-4

Lilium candidum
Madonna Lily, Annunciation Lily, Bourbon Lily

Here is the apogee of all cottage garden flowers. A familiar habitué of cottage gardens, seemingly so easy to grow, requiring no skill or any special measures, yet it confounds many a keen gardener. Could it be that they just try too hard? That they cannot leave it alone and let it get on with it? Not far from where I garden there is a thriving clump of *Lilium candidum* growing in an unkempt graveyard bang up against the trunk of a massive eucalypt. Half hidden by dead grasses, ribbons of bark and the stems of old Gallica roses, it flourishes on whatever nature provides. So how is it that many gardeners experience difficulties?

Take a lesson from this example. The climate is definitely Mediterranean; short, wet, cool winters, long, hot, dry summers; the lily comes into leaf with the first showers of autumn, grows and flowers in the rainy months and has formed and shed its seeds before the onset of summer – in other words, its growth habit follows the pattern of the seasons. It grows where the soil is undisturbed, its bulbs barely covered by earth, even though sheltered by a deep litter mulch.

Flowers of this lily have been identified among the floral tributes left in ancient Egyptian tombs, and it is thought they are depicted in the ancient Minoan wall paintings in the palace ruins at Knossos, Crete. Wild-growing forms still thrive from northern Palestine in

Lilium candidum, the Madonna Lily is a plant known since the days of the Pharoahs. A native of Greece and the Balkans it is very hardy and once established should never be messed with by digging or replanting. Unlike its namesake it has no need constantly to re-invent itself, such is the power of its enduring beauty and grace. Photo courtesy Clive Blazey.

an arc through Turkey into Macedonia. The bulbs have long been used to make medicinal ointments – at least since Medieval times and probably much longer.

Capricious is a word sometimes applied by lily fanciers to the Madonna Lily. Accustomed to fussing and fidgeting over the beauties they most admire, they just can't adjust their behaviour to address the simpler needs of *Lilium candidum*. The defenceless lily has also been blamed as a vector for viral diseases – as though the poor thing deliberately carries disease just to spite lily fanciers. In an ordinary garden setting where few other lilies are grown, Madonna Lilies showing tell-tale streaks of virus on the leaves can safely be left alone to do their thing. Seed-raised lilies do not carry viruses.

Lilium candidum is fairly simple to grow as long as it is understood that seed should be sown as fresh as possible. Within six months small plants with bulblets will be ready to transplant into the garden. Left to their own devices Madonna Lilies increase slowly by the bulbs growing larger and larger until they eventually 'split' and produce two or sometimes three growing points, the beginnings of new bulbs, even though they appear compressed into one large mass. While it is best to leave clumps alone as much as possible, the time will come when the whole lot needs to be dug up and separated into single bulbs. This should be done immediately after flowering, even when the stems are still green. The bulbs have a very brief period of dormancy, new roots being made soon after the stems die down, so things need to be done pretty smartly. Never leave the bulbs out of the soil for more than a few hours; they are not equipped with skins like daffodils or tulips, and should not be allowed to dry off, nor should the roots be cut off.

Lilium regale
Regal Lily

Unlike the Madonna Lily, the Regal Lily has a short history in Western gardens. It has been very popular since it was first introduced in 1903 from the semi-arid gullies of its homeland in the far west of China's Szechuan province. While the Chinese grow many lilies as food plants, the bulbs being the part cooked and eaten, *Lilium regale* seems not to have entered the cuisine; maybe they are not as palatable as some other species.

Fortunately for us, when English plant-hunter Henry Wilson saw the Regal Lily growing wild by the tens of thousands he didn't concern himself with whether or not it was edible. What took his interest was the tremendous quantity of blooms and their wonderful perfume. He understood instinctively that here was a plant of rare distinction and great garden value. Happily the Regal Lily has an easy constitution and apart from requiring good drainage, an open position and reasonable soil is accommodating and adaptable. While seed raising is possible it is a slow business, requiring a two-stage germination process that takes eighteen months to complete. The least bothersome method is to let the bulbs multiply by their own natural splitting habit. Otherwise the small bulbils that develop on the underground and lower parts of each stem can be plucked off and grown on until they reach the size of a golf ball, at which time they can be set out in their positions in the garden.

Lilium regale has become a feature of many small gardens since its introduction because it is so easy to grow. In the drier parts of the Mediterranean climate range it may need a little supplementary watering to finish its growing cycle but it is certainly worth that small concession. Like most lilies it enjoys growing where its roots and stems are shaded and sheltered by grasses, low perennials or small bushes, and where its flowers can be held up in full sun. Conditions such as these are not difficult to replicate in gardens where mixed planting is the preferred practice. Specific to Mediterranean gardens, plants like low-growing artemisias, cistus and lavenders make excellent companions for the Regal Lily. It grows equally well at the base of a Persian lilac but Heaven knows how I will ever be able to dig and replant them, the roots and bulbs of the two being so intimately intertwined.

Incidentally *Lilium regale* has two different root systems, one a semi-permanent system at the bottom of each bulb and the other renewed annually as part of each new flower stalk. Both kinds are important to the well-being of the plant. To allow for good stem-root development the key is to plant the bulbs at least 10–15 cm (4–6 in) deep.

Lilium regale, the Regal Lily is a hardy Chinese bulb from western China where it grows on steep rocky hill-sides exposed to cold winter weather and a baking summer sun. In the somewhat less extreme conditions found in most Mediterranean gardens it is a jewel, easy to establish and maintain, prolific, stately and beautifully perfumed. A not to be missed early summer sensation. Photo courtesy Bill Macaboy.

There are hybrids of *Lilium regale* but these are a regrettable instance of breeders trying to gild the lily; the wild form cannot be bettered by the meddling of Mendelists. The hybridisers generally focus on 'improving' minor differences that appear in the natural population, such things as increasing the intensity and coverage of the purple staining on the outside of each petal, or deepening the small tendency towards pinkness that appears in some flowers.

Ixia species

Ixia is another of the hardy bulb tribes so often overlooked by gardeners. Some less than lovely kinds, of muddled colours, are found as roadside weeds in places where there is some dampness after winter rains have slackened – washy mauve, pale pink, scruffy white, pallid turquoise, insipid pale blue – these are not worth the trouble of digging up and rescuing. Occasionally brighter, cleaner colours are found – golden yellow, soft yellow, lolly pink, soft magenta and a deep pink and white bicolour; these are worthy of a place in a garden. Even more rarely the teal blue form is found and should be rescued, especially if its most likely fate is death at the hands of a municipal worker wielding a spray-gun. Bulb merchants sometimes offer a restricted range of colours, most often with fancy names attached, such as 'Emperor of China' for the golden yellow form. This has some validity since there was a variety of that name recorded in nineteenth-century catalogues. Who can say if it is a genuine survivor from the past? And does it matter anyway? The colour is strong, clear, bold and fine.

All ixias make a typical broad, grassy fan of leaves that trail off into a few wispy threads at their tips. The leaves look much like those of a freesia, perhaps a little less wide, and smooth, without the pleating so familiar among babianas. The bulbs are small, round and covered in a fibrous tunic. They are tough and reliable plants. Ixias are particularly appealing because of the manner in which they carry their tulip-shaped flowers on tall, thin, wiry stems with each flower hanging down, the whole structure moving with every spring breeze.

They prefer an open sunny position such as might be imagined to be a grassy field or plain where the fields of flowers spread as far as the eye can see, as indeed they surely must in the habitat on the veldt. Most often associated with the hodge-podge of cottage gardens, ixias can be used very effectively *en masse* to create the effect of a wider, more open landscape. In an area of rough grass, such as might be found in a disused pony paddock or orchard, they can be tossed around in large numbers all of one colour, or a blend of colours that look well together. The English may have their meadow gardens with fritillaries, kingcups, cowslips, bee orchids and Lent lilies, but who is to say a successful veldt garden would not be equal to it? Ixias would form a component of such a planting matrix; either major or minor they could accompany the likes of freesia, babiana, sparaxis, maybe *Dierama* and *Dietes*.

Ixias increase at a modest rate that would satisfy most gardeners. Each mature bulb reproduces itself every year along with a few small bulbils that eventually grow to full size. Even in very favourable conditions they do not seem to go much faster. They are adaptable to many soil types but occur naturally on sandy soils that overlie a clay base, thus creating the damper conditions that they enjoy. They will do perfectly well in most ordinary garden situations as long as they get ample direct sunshine. The new foliage emerges after the first winter rains have fallen. The flowers follow in due course in mid to late spring. By early summer the whole kit and caboodle has dried off and a new bulb is waiting safe below ground for the next rainy season. The bulbs can safely be left where they are for many, many years. Indeed the only sensible reason for digging them up is to split up the clusters and replant them further apart to increase their coverage and in time the amount of bloom.

Pelargonium crispum
Lemon Geranium, Finger-bowl Geranium

Imagine yourself a hostess wishing to impress; how better to do it than by an elegant display of ultimate refinement? Would not a crystal finger-bowl set upon a lace doily and filled with warm water into which had been floated a few leaves of Lemon Geranium do the trick at any *conversazzione*, *musicale* or afternoon tea party? After a mouthful of sponge kisses, a nibble at an éclair, a taste of Battenberg or cucumber sandwich, what more could a hostess offer her guests than the opportunity to rinse their sticky fingers before they pulled on their gloves once more?

I cannot recall any of the senior women of my family ever bringing out the finger-bowls, even though among the mountains of Waterford and Stuart crystal I am certain there would have been small bowls that could have so served. But I do recall the tingle my nose got every time I passed by the bushes of Lemon Geranium in the gardens. I could not resist the urge to brush my hand through the crispy-edged leaves, feel their roughness and then sniff my lemony fingers. Who could? It is an urge that stays with us forever. Every time I go out into the garden I rub my fingers through the Lemon Geranium and then through the Rose Geranium, through the Peppermint Geranium and then the lemony leaves of 'Mabel Grey' and the Apple-scented, the Coconut-scented, the Lime-scented and the Nutmeg-scented kinds. All in all they make a fine way of edging a pathway to be followed around a garden. Perhaps you could even learn to do it blindfold?

Pelargonium crispum is a South African plant, one associated with the stony banks of summer-dry creek beds and the edges of gravelly washaways. It makes upright, compact growth with small rounded leaves, crimped around the edges, running up the stems almost in a double file. In early summer a small head of white flowers appears at the apex of each growing branch or shoot. Pretty enough, but the real reason for growing the plant is to relish its strong lemony fragrance.

This geranium, being accustomed to open spaces, quick-draining soils and periods of drought, is well equipped for life in Mediterranean gardens. It does require some pruning and renewal from time to time as the plants get older. Making cuttings of the short side-growths is an easy business: plenty of light so the young plants won't get drawn-out and careful watering until they are well established is the way to success. Use a free-draining potting mix and don't test for root formation by tugging at the cuttings. Wait. You will soon enough see white rootlets emerging from the drainage holes of the pot. Once rootlets appear it is safe to put the new plants into the garden where they are to grow permanently.

Rosa gallica
Rose of Provins

Most common by far of the old roses that are 'found' by present-day enthusiasts, the numerous kinds of *Rosa gallica* are among the hardiest of the hardy. Dense thickets are frequently found as the last survivor of a once-loved garden now standing derelict and ruinous alongside a roofless and tumbledown cottage. From California's Mother Lode country to the Golden Triangle of Victoria and the mining leases of New Zealand and South Africa, *Rosa gallica* is a common foundling. Whether it be the widespread 'Charles de Mills' (full double beetroot red) and 'Jenny Duval' (smoky lilac-rose) or the infrequently seen 'Tuscany' (deep dark red) and 'Cardinal de Richelieu' (dark slaty grey), the Provins rose is as tough as old boots, and far more beautiful. What helps this rose survive in Mediterranean gardens are its origins in southern and central France and its strong suckering habit which together enable it to establish wide-spreading colonies and to reshoot from the roots when top growth is eaten, burned or cut. This last asset is most likely why the rose can survive the depredations of churchyard wardens who occasionally sally forth armed with brush-cutters, slashers, flame-throwers and knapsacks of poison spray. After all the devastation and destruction the rose simply has the reserves to come back for more.

How then may the numerous kinds of *Rosa gallica* be utilised? Clearly their stout constitutions fit them well for survival, even under Mediterranean climate conditions. Indeed, so willing are they to grow and multiply that it is wisdom not to plant them where they get any special care or considerations such as additional water during the hottest months of the year. They do not need it. Given such luxurious treatment they will most likely go mad and grow so fast and so far that they completely take over a piece of garden. And then you have a real long-term problem in getting them back under control. A better plan for the enjoyment of these hardy beauties is to plant them where conditions will limit their growth and their tendency to sucker far and wide. Grown this way the plants will be far better mannered garden guests. Their growth will be tighter, more compact and less sprawling; they will still flower prolifically and they will give good ground cover in situations less than

propitious for other plants. Often found growing on road embankments and rail cuttings, and in gravelly and rock-filled soils, they exist quite happily in hard soils and dry conditions.

Most varieties are strongly perfumed and the dark red forms, particularly, are favourites with makers of potpourri and rosewater. Aside from the varieties already mentioned others worthy of consideration are 'Belle de Crecy' (parma violet colours), 'Camaieux' (magenta-violet-purple striped against a pale pink ground fading to white), 'Georges Vibert' (finely striped) and 'Versicolor' (syn. 'Rosa Mundi').

Grown on its own roots any Gallica rose will sucker far and wide within a few short years. This attribute has its uses in the wilder parts of a garden. Those supplied by nurseries as grafted plants will be better behaved and can be confidently planted in more orderly parts of a garden where they most often find a use as low hedges or as participants in a shrubbery.

Fuchsia magellanica

Fuchsia magellanica 'Tricolor' creates a screen of reddish grey foliage that sets off masses of small purple-red flowers from late winter into spring and summer. Tough and easy, it will spring up strongly from the base when old branches are cut down. I fancy that fuchsias are not among the first plants to come to mind when Mediterranean gardening is spoken of; indeed, they are most often thought of as rather fussy things needing water through summer and conditions more gentle and sheltered than can readily be supplied

Fuchsia magellanica 'Variegata' finds a place in gardens as a subtle background for many planting ideas. In winter and spring its numerous small flowers are a great attraction to honey-eating birds.

The rough leaves and sprawling growth of *Fuchsia splendens* can easily be hidden among the growth of surrounding plants. Grown this way, intermingled with other things, its cracker-like red and green flowers are a surprising sight.

in gardens of the Mediterranean persuasion. Yet there are a few that give every satisfaction under these conditions, *Fuchsia magellanica* and its derivatives being among the best. Also good are *Fuchsia glazioviana*, *F. coccinea*, *F. splendens*, *F. loxensis*, *F. sancta-rosa* and *F. microphylla*. Though less tolerant of a very dry atmosphere, *Fuchsia boliviana* and *F. arborescens* are also worth trying.

The Magellanic clan are graceful, tall, slender shrubs with small leaves and an air of delicacy that serves Mediterranean gardeners well for its telling relief to the solidity and angularity of many of the stalwarts on which we place reliance. Despite its appearance *Fuchsia magellanica* is reasonably hardy, bearing up through dry times and quickly springing into new growth and prolific with flowers within a few weeks of the first rains of the wet season. It responds best to deep friable soil and a deep mulch, for while the top growth is sun hardy the roots prefer coolth and shade. Grown among and under taller, tougher shrubs such as ceanothus and honeysuckles the fuchsia will revel in their company, giving colour and enjoyment for many months. Like most fuchsias these hardy South Americans are easily propagated from cuttings, and occasionally volunteer seedlings will be found under established bushes.

The basic species of the tribe, *Fuchsia magellanica*, is characterised by all the traits described above. Each small leaf is rimmed with a fine maroon-red line. The new sprigs are reddish too, adding to the appeal of

Fuchsia loxensis can be relied on for a good performance year round in sheltered Mediterranean gardens where some summer irrigation is possible. Its soft foliage and long trailing flower stems contrast with harder shapes and forms.

the plant. When the masses of flowers appear from the leaf axils along the new growth as it extends during the growing season, the colour is intensified at first by the slender wine-red buds, and then held in bold contrast when the flowers open by the deep purple-blue of the skirts of the inner petals (the corolla). At least three forms of this species are well worth growing as companions with their parent. These are 'Variegata', 'Tricolor' and 'Alba'. The variegated form is pleasantly and irregularly marked with creamy white; the flowers are the same as those of the parent. 'Tricolor' is much like the variegated form but the entire leaf surface is overlain with a reddish silver cast that renders the whole somewhat leaden but still colourful. 'Alba' has plain green foliage and overall pale pink flowers. Apart from 'Variegata', which grows to about 1.5 m (5 ft), these fuchsias grow into tall woody shrubs around 3 m (10 ft) or more. All are capable of making vigorous basal growth in response to accidental damage or hard pruning. Similar but more complex hybrids are found in 'Tom Thumb', a very compact form, and 'White Knight's Fairy', with larger but similar flowers to 'Alba'.

Iris unguicularis
Algerian iris

The Algerian Iris comes in several colour forms as well as several smaller allied species. Long renowned for its stay-ability and profusion of winter flowers, it should be in every Mediterranean garden. This unusual striped variety is *Iris unguicularis* 'Variegata'.

My first contact with this hardy iris came as a gardener's boy working for two ladies who seemed to grow almost everything. They had a pit greenhouse, half sunk in the ground, in which they grew ferns, chlorophytums, cane-stemmed begonias, one pot of slipper orchids and a few desultory cymbidiums, and struggled to master tuberous begonias. I was only allowed to work in those damp, cool conditions under direct supervision but outside I was pretty much my own master after I had received my orders for the day. Beside the top of the brick greenhouse walls, a few inches above the soil line, and in the rainshadow cast by the overhanging glass roof – whitewashed by me every year before Christmas – grew a long thick line of the Algerian iris. I was the only one light enough to go across the roof on a precarious ladder to apply the messy whitewash, and I was the only one lucky enough to get to give the iris a stern haircut every year before winter when their flowers would appear. This was some tough plant. The leaves were as of cast iron, slipping and sliding through my cheap secateurs, and the roots of the strongest nylon cord. By holding a sharp spade upright at 90 degrees among the clumps of leaves and jumping up and down, I could, after considerable exertion, manage to get through the tangled mass of roots and begin to separate the clump into new pieces. Reputed to enjoy a rubble-filled and alkaline soil, the plants thrived. The soil was naturally alkaline, as was the tap water we used so liberally in those days, and no doubt the whitewash runoff added to the high pH as well.

Coming as they do from Algeria it is reasonable to conclude this iris is pretty well indestructible, at least in Mediterranean climatic regions. The species has several distinct kinds and ranges into the eastern Mediterranean with allies in Crete and Turkey. Propagation is generally by division as seed seems to be set only rarely. The preferred time for dividing established clumps is in autumn when the entire plant can be taken up, the leaves cut back hard, the roots knocked or washed free of dirt and the clump attacked with spade and secateurs. Quite small pieces of root will establish as new plants, all that is needed is one small fan of leaves per division. Even leafless pieces will often shoot new growing points if replanted in some out-of-the-way spot. There will be few flowers in the first year after division but growth should be strong and the plants back in full stride in a year or two.

Should we plant the white forms, the striped forms, the pink form or the named varieties? The best answer is to plant whatever colour, form or name you like but to plant it in a decent swathe so it makes a good impression. A bold planting lined out along a drive or walk, large pools among well-spaced shrubs or clusters repeated at intervals are all good ways to use it. Generally the blue kinds are prolific and very easy; the white forms tend to produce fewer flowers and the pink needs careful placement to increase its impact. The dark blue forms 'Mia' and 'Cretensis' are lovely and just as hardy as their cousins, though the flowers are a little smaller and the plants a little smaller also.

Both's Hybrid Geranium is one of a large and colourful family known sometimes as Star Geraniums and sometimes as Staphisogroides Hybrids. All have starry petals and come in the full range of colours usually associated with geraniums. They are compact and hardy, just like the common geranium.

'Skies of Italy', one of the old multi-coloured Zonal geraniums (*Pelargonium* x *hortorum*), is a great stayer, colourful and equally adapted to modern gardening styles and old-fashioned cottage gardening. Always cheerful, its bright, clear colouration can easily pick up other colour notes in a design.

Pelargonium x *hortorum*
Pot Geranium

I must confess to a long period during which these fine plants were ignored by me. There were brief flirtations with miniature geraniums, with those with variegated and coloured leaves, and with those called Star geraniums, but otherwise my garden was not sullied by the likes of such commoners.

Quite by chance I renewed my acquaintance with these happy cottage-garden plants during the writing of this book. My conversion, if it may be called that, came about at a gardeners' market where I happened upon a splendid display of potted geraniums in full flower. What particularly struck me was the manner in which the clever trader had arranged her several hundred plants by colour. So it came about that I returned home with a selection of enchanting salmon-orange sorts, each variety in a pair so that I might play at arranging them effectively in pretty terracotta pots of antique French style. I resisted temptation and rejected the idea of displaying them in a wirework stand. That would be too twee, and contrary to the nature of these sturdy and much-loved commoners.

In contrast to the bold scarlet, magenta and crimson kinds favoured by my grandmothers these newer kinds, equally hardy, are more compact and more generous with their flowers – a fact that makes them extremely prolific. My salmon-orange selection included 'Deacon Suntan', 'Thornlands Embers', 'Cardross' and 'Moon Mist'. By themselves these names mean little; 'Deacons' are from a particular strain of breeding, 'Thornlands' is the name of a nursery business and the others are given at the fancy of those who introduce each variety. What is more important than the names is the manner of their selection based on colour and effectiveness as display plants. This simple act instantly overcomes the spotted dog impact all too often associated with cottage gardens. I quite surprised myself at my own sophistication: the idea of putting similar colours together had not previously occurred to me as far as lowly geraniums were concerned! But now the realisation has dawned it will not be held back for want of a wide range of colours to choose from. An interested gardener might easily select pale pinks, hot pinks, rose pinks, cheery reds along with many richer, deeper shades in order to fulfil their schemes and dreams. While the availability of particular varieties will vary from country to country it is almost certain that the colour range will be much the same everywhere.

Pot-grown plants are easily managed but suffer from the common assumption that they live forever without care; feeding, water and pest management seem to be overlooked in favour of letting them be.

Giving even a small amount of care, light feeding from time to time, regular watering and the removal of dead leaves and flowers, will significantly improve the performance of any geranium. Regular repotting in fresh potting mix enlivened with granules of slow-release fertiliser will see further improvements while starting afresh from cuttings every few years will ensure the plants remain in full vigour and carry the largest and freshest flowers.

Haemanthus coccineus
Blood Lily, Elephant's Tongue, Ox Tongue

In this, my final selection, we find a most satisfying plant. It satisfies our criterion that plants for Mediterranean climate gardens should grow and flower during the rainy season and rest when the weather is hot and dry. It also satisfies on any number of other criteria; it carries its own mystique and appeal as a noteworthy plant; the red paintbrush flowers are colourful and fascinating; the foliage that comes after the flowers have faded is bold, strong and remarkable. And the plant has cottage garden charm and a curious kind of sophistication arising from its unique appearance. There is no other plant like it.

Although bulbs of *Haemanthus coccineus* are on offer through bulb specialists it is the sort of plant that is just as easily obtained by keeping an alert eye for it in old gardens and scrounging for a few. Is this distasteful? It should not be. Most gardeners are only too pleased to share some green treasure from their gardens. The act of giving ensures the perpetuation of a special plant and in some ways creates the sense of a continuous link between gardeners long dead, those still living and those yet to acquire the gardener's art. And sometimes a sharp-eyed gardener can just strike it lucky. In my case I noticed one day an old garden being bulldozed to allow for the construction of new offices in an inner-city suburb. Something must have caught my eye because I stopped driving, got out of my car and walked into the wreckage of the garden. Lying in great piles ready for the tip-truck to take them to the dump were masses of agapanthus, ancient rose bushes, slabs of overgrown duranta hedging, long-dead rosemaries and sundry other scrawny shrubs. Tumbled in among all this dross was a considerable number of dormant bulbs. I recognised those of *Haemanthus* by the tell-tale manner in which each fleshy bulb scale ends as though it has been chopped off. There were others, slightly different and still carrying here and there the distinctive stems and seed pods of *Velthemia*, another Cape bulb valuable for its contribution to the range of winter-growing bulbs. Its dusky pink flowers are tubular and hang on tall stems in the manner of a giant *Lachenalia*. Thus it came about that my garden carries in it the survivors of another garden. I have become part of the chain that links gardeners across the centuries. You can too.

There are other kinds of *Haemanthus*, each interesting in their way but perhaps best regarded as curios for serious bulb collectors. Their scarcity and generally small scale make them poor candidates for inclusion in the wider landscape of a garden. They would all too easily get lost – physically and visually.

If *Haemanthus coccineus* is hard to come by in any quantity, a bulb can easily be induced to procreate by carefully cutting small wedges out of it at the point where the bulb scales join the root plate at the base. Left to dry thoroughly so there is no danger of rots developing in the cuts, the injured bulb will, on being replanted, generate numerous small bulbils around the cuts. To make the process easy plant the cut bulb at half depth in a pot of free-draining potting mix. The bulbils can be gently picked off and replanted to grow on to maturity. The process will take two or three years, depending on how the bulbs are nurtured during their infancy.

A few last words

As I have been writing, a strong debate has been raging in Australia about the use of irrigation to ameliorate the effects of climate on agriculture and horticulture. The discussion has centred on our self-conceived 'rights' to use water, as much as we want, for whatever purpose and at low cost; and on whether or not we have been experiencing a drought over the last seven years or so. The countering arguments are that we do not have the right to use water in whatever way we like, even if we can pay for it – to hose paving, to wash cars in a continuous stream from a hose, to run dishwashers and large air-conditioning systems, to grow crops of rice and cotton in desert regions and to nurture large areas of grass and water-dependent gardens. There are similar discussions concerning the nature of drought: 'Are we really in a drought?'; 'What is a drought in terms of the Australian climate?'; 'If extended dry conditions are a regular feature of our climatic pattern, are they a natural feature with which we have to learn to live, or are they unnatural?'

Needless to say the imposition of graduated water restrictions brings the discussion into sharp focus, as much for home gardeners – who ideally should be able to use water recycled through the sewerage system – as for commercial irrigators and businesses in general. There is a strong argument for learning to live, and garden, within the constraints of the natural range of weather patterns and this is the view taken in this book.

We can garden within the natural constraints of the weather patterns wherever we live, and have every confidence that we will meet with success, a great sense of satisfaction and considerable artistic achievement. Increasingly we are able to draw on the exemplars provided by gardeners who live in, garden in and understand the climatic conditions we experience in common. We are, in fact, developing a garden pantheon of our own; a literature of Mediterranean gardening, a compendium of Mediterranean climate garden design concepts, and a palette of plants perfectly adapted to these conditions. Every year this 'Mediterranean' ethos is compounded by the addition of more books, more websites, more journals and magazines, more nurseries supplying appropriate plant selections and more designers working within the scope of the climate type. Indeed, it could fairly be claimed that Mediterranean gardening and design has become a genre in its own right. And so it should be.

Let us celebrate this timely emergence; this happy happenstance; this most appropriate way of gardening in the places where we live. Never be concerned or daunted by the spectre of water restrictions; instead work with what the Mediterranean climate type provides and realise your potential to see, understand and express your own creative relationship with your own patch. That is, develop your own sense of place.

Recommended reading

Magazines and websites

Cactus Mall international portal
www.cactusmall.com

California Rare Fruit Society
www.crf.org

Coté Sud
175 Rue d'Aguesseau, 92643 Boulogne-Billancourt
Cedex, France
www.cotesud.fr

Pacific Horticulture
PO Box 680, Berkeley, California 94701, USA
www.pacifichorticulture.org

Mediterranean Garden Society Journal
PO Box 14, Paenia GR-19002, Greece

Mediterranean Garden Society
www.MediterraneanGardenSociety.org

Books not already listed

Some pleasant Mediterranean reading
Kinta Beevoir, *A Tuscan Childhood*, Viking, London, 1993. ISBN 0-670-84305-9
Dirk Bogarde, *A Short Walk from Harrods*, Penguin, London, 1993. ISBN 0-14-023130-7
Fulco Santostefano della Cerda, *The Happy Summer Days: A Sicilian Childhood*, Phoenix, London, 1976. ISBN 0-75381-057-3

Charles Dickens, *Pictures from Italy*, André Deutsch, London, 1973. ISBN 0-233-96383-9
Isabella Dusi, *Vanilla Beans and Brodo*, Simon & Schuster, London, 2001. ISBN 0-7432-0935-4
Henry James, *A Little Tour in France*, Houghton Mifflin, Boston, 1907 (no ISBN)
M.F.K. Fisher, *Long Ago In France: The Years in Dijon*, Prentice Hall, New York, 1991. ISBN 0-13- 929548-8
Fred Kaplan (ed.), *Travelling in Italy with Henry James*, Hodder & Stoughton, London, 1994. ISBN 0-340-51181-8
Iris Origo, *Images and Shadows: Part of a Life*, Harcourt Brace Jovanovich, New York, 1976. ISBN 0-15-144101-4
Mirabel Osler, *A Spoon with Every Course*, Pavilion, London, 1996. ISBN 1-85793-766-X
Mark Twain, *The Innocents Abroad*, Harper & Row, New York, 1911 (no ISBN)
Tony Perrottet, *Route 66 AD: On the Trail of Ancient Roman Tourists*, Random House, New York, 2002. ISBN 0-375-50432-X
Susana, Lady Walton, *La Mortella: An Italian Garden Paradise*, New Holland, London, 2002. ISBN 1-85974-916-X

More detailed books: ecology, history and science
Dorothy Burr Thompson et al, *The Garden Lore of Ancient Athens*, The American School of Classical Studies at Athens, Princeton University, New Jersey, 1969 (no ISBN)

Peter Dallman, *Plant Life in the World's Mediterranean Climates*, California Native Plant Society, University of California Press, Berkeley, 1998. ISBN 0-520-20809-9

Jean-Pierre Demoly, *Les Cèdres: An Exceptional Botanical Garden*, Franklin Picard Editions, Paris. ISBN 2-913863-03-5

Stephanie Donaldson, *Venzano: A Scented Garden in Tuscany*, New Holland (UK) 2001. ISBN 1-85974-590-3

Linda Farrar, *Ancient Roman Gardens*, Sutton Publications, Stroud UK, 1998. ISBN 0-7509-1725-3

A.T. Grove, Oliver Rackham, *The Nature of Mediterranean Europe: An Ecological History*, Yale University Press, New Haven, CT, 2001. ISBN 0-300-08443-9

Wilhelmina Jashemski, *The Gardens of Pompeii: Herculaneum and the Villas Destroyed by Vesuvius*, Caratzas Bros., New York, 1979. ISBN 0-89241-096-5

Predrag Matvejevic (trans. Michael Heim), *Mediterranean: A Cultural History*, University of California Press, Berkeley, 1993. ISBN 0-520-20738-6

Benedetta Origo, Morna Livingstone, Laurie Olin and John Dixon Hunt, *La Foce: A Garden and Landscape in Tuscany*, University of Pennsylvania, Philadelphia, 2001. ISBN 0-8122-3593-2

Iris Origo, *The Merchant of Prato*, The Folio Society, London, 1984 (no ISBN)

John Pemble, *The Mediterranean Passion: Victorians and Edwardians in the South*, Clarendon Press, Oxford, 1987. ISBN 0-19-820100-1

Charles Quest-Ritson, *The English Garden Abroad*, Viking, London, 1992. ISBN 0-670-83252-9

Jan Smithen, *Sun-Drenched Gardens: The Mediterranean Style*, Abrams, New York, 2002. ISBN 0-8109-3290-3

Lavinia Taverna, *La Compagnia di un Giardino* (privately published), Marchessa Livinia Taverna Gallaratti Scotti, Grossetto, Italy, 1997

Mary Jaqueline Tyrrwhit, *Making a Garden on a Greek Hillside*, Denise Harvey (pub.), Evia, Greece, 1998. ISBN 960-7120-13-2

William Weaver, *A Legacy of Excellence: The Story of Villa i Tatti*, Abrams, New York, 1997. ISBN 0-8109-3587-2

Chip Sullivan, *Gardens and Climate*, McGraw-Hill, New York, 2002. ISBN 0-07-027103-8

A useful source for books about the ancient world, Greece and Rome, and the Middle Ages is Oxbow Books: www.oxbowbooks.com, a business based in Oxford, UK.

Index